T0337375

Politics of Precarity

Politics of Precarity

Gendered Subjects and the Health Care Industry in Contemporary Kolkata

Panchali Ray

OXFORD
UNIVERSITY PRESS

OXFORD
UNIVERSITY PRESS

Oxford University Press is a department of the University of Oxford.
It furthers the University's objective of excellence in research, scholarship,
and education by publishing worldwide. Oxford is a registered trademark of
Oxford University Press in the UK and in certain other countries.

Published in India by
Oxford University Press
2/11 Ground Floor, Ansari Road, Daryaganj, New Delhi 110 002, India

© Oxford University Press 2019

The moral rights of the author have been asserted.

First Edition published in 2019

ISBN-13 (print edition): 978-0-19-948976-3
ISBN-10 (print edition): 0-19-948976-9

ISBN-13 (eBook): 978-0-19-909553-7
ISBN-10 (eBook): 0-19-909553-1

Typeset in Adobe Jenson Pro 10.7/13
by Tranistics Data Technologies, Kolkata 700 091
Printed in India by Replika Press Pvt. Ltd

Contents

Tables

Acknowledgements

Committing to paper one's indebtedness is hard but gratifying, and possibly the most difficult part of 'writing' a book. I owe too many people too much, who have helped in ways both big and small. I will try and make an attempt, however incomplete, in recording my gratitude. To begin with, I thank Professor Samita Sen whose critical insights and fine-tooth combing of my doctoral thesis sped me on the way to convert the dissertation into a full-fledged book. Her encouragement and support remained crucial in convincing me to embark on this rather daunting journey. I also take this moment to record my gratitude to Dr Subrata Guha Thakurta and (late) Dr Abani Roy Chowdhury who generously opened their contact book, introduced me to colleagues, and thus ensured the viability of this research project at a moment when all doors were tightly shut. I cannot thank enough the teaching faculty at the school and college of nursing, IPGMER-SSKM, and the nursing staff at BC Roy Hospital, who generously gave me their time and offered critical insights into the profession. I also take this opportunity to thank officials in Swasthya Bhawan, Health and Family Welfare Department,

Government of West Bengal, West Bengal Nursing Council, West Bengal State Archives, and the National Library. I specifically thank Subrota Sarkar (College of Nursing, SSKM), Anjana Sen (School of Nursing, Apollo Hospital), and Madhuchanda Gupta (BC Roy Hospital) who initiated me into the complexities faced by women who work as nurses.

In the various institutions that I have studied, researched, and taught at, I thank Sister Tina Farias, Tejaswini Adhikari, Anjali Dave, and Kingshuk Chatterjee for pushing me to challenge my limits. At Jadavpur University, I thank Mukul Mukherjee, (late) Jashodhara Bagchi, Shefali Moitra, and Malini Bhattacharya who shaped my engagements with feminist theory and politics. I also take this opportunity to thank my colleagues at the School of Women's Studies, JU, whose friendship and goodwill made this phase of book-writing an easier task; particularly Aishika Chakraborty, with whom I share a warm friendship. I thank Debamitra Talukdar, our librarian at JU, without whom this book would have never been complete; the staff—Anindita Bhaduri, Jolly Bose, Abhimanna Sarkar, and Dipankar Haldar for our shared joys, laughter, and light-hearted banter that made the unbearable heaviness of academic life so much lighter.

I take this moment to acknowledge my intellectual debt to those who shaped my thoughts, heard me out, and gave critical feedback that made me rethink my positions—Mohan Rao, Indrani Majumdar, Janaki Nair, Geraldine Forbes, Mary John, Anuja Agrawal, (late) Sharmila Rege, J. Devika, Maitrayee Chaudhuri, Nirmala Banerjee, Gita Sen, Anuradha Roy, Ratnaboli Chatterjee, Moinak Biswas, R. Radhakrishnan, Mohamed Mehdi, and Anuradha Talwar. I wish to thank my friends (in no particular order), whose sustained moral/intellectual/emotional support has seen me through various phases of my life and sustained me through the isolating and solitary life of a researcher: Sunit Talukdar, Parvati Chandra, Meenu Pandey, Ram Menon, Tanu Chabra, Ekta Hattangady, Souvik Chakraborty, Anirban Roy Chowdhury, Devraj Paul, Shadab Bano, Syndhya John Sammeul, Kaushik Ghosh, and Brin Daz. There are friends who directly influenced my research and I am lucky to count among them—Mithilesh Kumar, Biswajit Prasad, and Saran Dutta. I thank my students at the School of Women's Studies, who have sustained me with their intellectual rigour, questions, and debates, particularly, Sayan Bhattacharya,

Silpi Dasgupta, Rajashi Mothey Sengupta, Shankar Mukherjee, Kathakali Biswas, Madhuparna Karmakar, Tapas Soren, Amrita Dasgupta, Sampriti Mukherjee, Ahana Ganguly, and Srijan Uzir. Much of this work has been conceived and thought through in discussions, disputes, and readings with Rajlaxmi Ghosh. She influences my thinking and being, reading and writing, in ways that far exceed any attempts at recognition.

This book is richer for the critical feedback of the two anonymous reviewers and I cannot thank them enough for the close reading of the manuscript. I also thank the editorial team at Oxford University Press, India, whose efficient intervention and editorial skills saw the manuscript through. It is customary to thanks one's family. In my case, this is more than just custom—Krishna, Bejoy, Gautam, Ishani, Sugata, and Atreyee whose love and affection, encouragement, and solidarity has not just seen me through my days of research but life as well; particularly, Sugata, with whom I share a creative and intellectual kinship. I also take this moment to thank Meera and Sarawati, whose invisible labour is central to freeing me from household responsibilities which allows me to engage in a world of research and learning. Finally, I cannot thank enough those women who participated in the research project, and despite long and tedious shift hours, welcomed me with open arms. They found the time to share their lives with me, inspired me with their optimism and hope, and taught me the value of laughter, even in the face of serious concerns.

For Krishna, my mother, a single parent, a feminist-without-knowing-it, who brought us up to question everything, and often bore the consequences of it—this book, with all its faults, is dedicated to her.

1 Introduction

(Re)productive Work, Affective Labour, and Health Care Services

et against a city in transition, *Pratidwandi* (The Adversary), 1970, the first of Satyajit Ray's 'Calcutta trilogy' is as much a commentary on modernity as it is about changing gender relations and the moral collapse they precipitate. Focusing on Calcutta, a city struggling with partition, unprecedented scales of migration, economic stagnation, loss of land, dispossession, high levels of unemployment, de-industrialization, and a raging militant Left politics, the film narrows down on changing gender relations, in this case, the tension between beleaguered masculinity and an increasingly assertive, transgressive femininity. The protagonist, Siddhartha, desolate from his inability to find employment, is cajoled by his friend to accompany him to a decrepit building for an 'adventure', and comes face to face with a woman who works as a nurse and offers paid sexual service. As the 'prostitute-nurse', performed by Ms Shefali, a 'prostitute-bar dancer', undresses down to her petticoat and brassiere in front of two men, and brazenly asks the obviously tense Siddhartha to light her cigarette, the film turns briefly to negative image, accompanied by pulsating music in the background.[1] This sudden and rather bizarre dramatization of a moment that embodies a head-on conflict between two worlds can be interpreted as the film-maker's inability to respond to the changing political economy of urbanizing Calcutta. However, unwittingly, it also reflects societal perception of women's employment/ occupations as much as it represents failing patriarchal ideologies. The representation of the nurse indulging in prostitution as a part-time occupation struck a chord. A nurses' delegation met Satyajit Ray to protest and he was forced to edit the film, removing the scene showing the badges and lapel pins that indicated she was a trained nurse in a government hospital.[2] However, more than the representation, what remains striking is the language of resistance. Instead of demanding a censuring of the entire episode, the delegation insisted that the nurse depicted as the prostitute cannot be shown as a trained one. It was less a defence of the profession and more a politics of distancing and differentiation.

It is this politics of distancing and differentiation that informs the core of my research on a deeply stratified workforce, within the heavily gendered health care industry. Contrary to a common understanding, nursing is not a homogenous sector, but is composed of women with different levels of training, skills, and qualifications. That this stratification is reflected and constituted by material realities, such as wages, terms of employment, levels of skills, and possession of qualifications is nothing new. However, I am concerned with the cultural processes that deploy structural inequalities, socially and historically produced, to secure marginal gains for some sections of the workforce at the expense of the others. Nursing care is indispensable to healing processes; yet, it is plagued with innumerable problems, least of all stigma, abjection, and precarity. In Kolkata, the sector

[1] There is considerable debate on the use of negative image. Many who had seen earlier versions of the film do not remember the negative print. It was possibly used as a device later to contain the supposed 'outrageousness' of the image. I am thankful to Moinak Biswas for alerting me to this possibility.
[2] The principal of West Bengal Government College of Nursing, SSKM Hospital, one of the oldest nursing colleges in Kolkata, narrated this in a personal interview on 19 July 2009. This protest is also mentioned in Robinson (1989: 212).

comprises both registered and unregistered nurses, nursing aides (known as 'private sisters'), and attendants who give nursing care. Given the diversity of skills, training, recognition, and social identity of the workers in a predominantly feminine workforce, it makes for an interesting case study to examine how the service economy within the health care industry deploys social and cultural identities to consistently discriminate against and exploit women who seek employment. This research is thus about labour that has, over time, increasingly moved from the familial space to the public domain and the ramifications and the politics embedded in the processes of institutionalization. Given the gradual withdrawal of the government from crucial social sectors along with privatization and processes of informalization, the health care industry is witnessing a reconfiguration, particularly in the predominantly feminine workforce offering various kinds of nursing care. The employment of women with varied education, training, and skills in different ranks contributes to a culture of alienation and exploitation, as nursing care is cleaved along lines of 'prestigious' and 'dirty' work. And those employed to perform differently ranked labour are rewarded differently, in both economic and non-economic terms. Needless to say, those employed at the bottom of the heap fit the classic typology of the new global precariat—whose employment is organized around flexible and informal jobs and is marked by insecurity, instability, and high levels of exploitation. This book, apart from examining precarious working conditions and degrading work that some women are compelled to engage in, also examines how members of the workforce participate in politics that reinforce precarity for some and fortify secure working conditions for others. The book raises a number of questions about working-class politics: How is precarity maintained and reinforced? What does the precariat workforce struggle for and against? How are cultural meanings that legitimize a stratified labour market and a differentiated workforce produced?

While influential theorists have defined the precariat as an 'underclass' that is yet to wield any significant collective power, or even as the 'new dangerous class' at loggerheads with itself,[3] I argue that the precariat is equally constituted and divided by caste, gender, and sexuality that pre-empts any solidarity based on strategic location

---

[3] Standing (2011).

within the economic system/production process. Scholars have argued that worldwide, the decline of worker's structural power, associations of collective bargaining, and fragmented labour markets have contributed to the growing precarity of the working class.[4] However, women who are already marginalized within the existing political economy and/or formal associations of collective bargaining are rarely included in this analysis. Looking beyond the relation and/or conflict between the employer–employee, the book examines the politics of precarity, defined as a symbolic struggle between differently located members of the workforce to maintain and secure their rights and privileges vis-à-vis the other. An already feminized occupation, which falls back on historically produced and socially secured identities to legitimize inequalities as well as further vulnerabilities, nursing provides fertile grounds to examine how workers' social identities intersect with occupational hierarchies.

Interestingly, the health service sector, particularly nursing, has not been given the same emphasis and importance by scholars and activists, as say other commodified reproductive/affective labour, such as domestic work, surrogacy, and sex work. The plausible reason being that while the other three are in the informal sector that is now seeing an engagement with law and policies, albeit with completely different outcomes, nursing service has always been located in the cusp of both formal and informal economy. Nursing is a curious case of commodified reproductive labour. Unlike other forms of women's work, nursing has been cleaved into trained and untrained labour, with specific sets of skills, which corroborate with occupational positions. Therefore, while certain sections have witnessed formalization, modernization, and professionalization, others have not. And like most modern professions, trained nurses, with a monopoly on skills and educational qualifications, aimed for occupational closure, leaving out vast sections of women with various degrees of training to provide health care as informally employed, badly paid workers. Scholars have linked such 'professional projects' with gendered class formation, where a restructuring of the labour market has set the terms for middle-class women to enter and participate in the professional sphere.[5] In contemporary

---

[4]   Silver (2003); Wacquant (2008).
[5]   Witz (1992).

India, this strategic aspiration of nurses has witnessed limited success, though nursing has seen a degree of professionalization and stratification, largely emerging from the discourse on skills. Overall, it continues to remain a stigmatized and devalued occupation. Given the location of the profession within a caste-dominated patriarchal society, it provides fertile grounds to study the ideological and political reconfigurations when mostly unpaid feminine labour transits from the family to the market.

The Politics of Re/productive Labour: Reviewing the Debates

The Greek philosophers of antiquity, we are told, held labour in great contempt, more so the labour of the *oikos* (household) that produced and sustained life. It was, of course, necessary labour—not for its own sake but to sustain and (re)produce life—and such labour, it was argued, was best relegated to women and slaves. A cursory reading of the history of Western philosophy reveals that the constitution of the political was almost always premised on the exclusion of the feminine, yet this exclusion was never absolute. The philosophy of ancient Greece, which viewed women as sexual and social reproducers, continues to influence Western political thought, right to the contemporary. This is perhaps best exemplified by Aristotle (384–322 BCE), who powerfully articulated this denied dependency in the *The Politics* where he argued that the oikos was the basic social unit of the *polis* (Greek city state) and the citizen is one who is freed from all (reproductive) labour that sustained the oikos. Hannah Arendt's publication of *The Human Condition* (1958) saw a detailed discussion of the differences between labour, work, and action, the latter two crucial for a contemplative life or *vita contemplative*. The relegation of labour to the private sphere to be performed by women and slaves, who by their 'virtue' or inherent nature were excluded from citizenship, formed the basis of the polis.[6] Thus the contempt for harsh, monotonous, and repetitive labour relegated to women and slaves is not only an incidental ranking of labour but constitutive of citizenship in the Greek city states.

Hannah Arendt stopped short of critiquing the explicit connections between patriarchy, re/productive labour, and production of the public

---

[6] Arendt (1958).

realm and it was left to feminists—particularly in the decades of the 1970s and 1980s—to make a powerful case against patriarchal devaluation of women's reproductive labour.[7] Betty Friedan's classic text, *The Feminine Mystique* (1963), argued that domestic work dehumanized women, with its monotonous nature and was an impediment to women's rightful place in the public domain. Friedan's mandate that women's participation in the public world would help them realize their individuality and give them a sense of personhood did not ask who will now take on the everyday chores of reproducing life.[8] bell hooks' trenchant critique of Friedan's brand of white liberal feminism was based on the argument that it was class and race, rather than gender, that kept white middle-class women out of the labour force. College-educated, white American women refused to take on low-paying, low-status jobs available to most women in the workforce.[9] Stigmatized, dehumanized, ill-paid, repetitive, back-breaking, monotonous work—washing dishes, doing laundry, cooking, sweeping, cleaning, dusting, rearing children, nursing the sick—remained the lot of black and poor white women.

Pat Mainardi in her essay 'The Politics of Housework' (1970) wrote, 'Liberated women—very different from Women's Liberation!' She argued that the 'liberated woman', a product of liberal feminism, was the new commodity within capitalist patriarchal economy who occupied (limited) space in institutions otherwise over-represented by men—universities, professions, and the likes—but did not demand radical shifts in the way gendered societies were organized. On the contrary, 'women's liberation' demanded that men participate equally in what has historically and traditionally been perceived as women's work.[10] So while the former propagates inclusion of women in the public sphere without questioning the private, the latter insists that the private be opened up to ideological and political questioning that would finally lead to its democratization. In less than a decade, a post-colonial text, Mahasweta Devi's 'Stanadayini' (1979), calls into question liberal feminists' preoccupation with this commodity—liberated

---

[7]   Barrett (1980); Delphy (1984); Eisenstein (1979).
[8]   Friedan (1963).
[9]   hooks (2000).
[10] Mainardi (1970).

woman.[11] The representation of the subaltern as a gendered subject in 'Stanadayini' and her struggle against the joint forces of indigenous patriarchal institutions and capitalist formations, brings to the fore how class (as well as caste) was crucial to the emancipation of the 'new' woman. 'Stanadayini' is the story of Jashodha, a 'mother by profession', 'universal mother', 'mother of the world', who suckles babies of the local landlord family for wages, food, and clothes, ensuring her livelihood by uninterrupted gestation and lactation. Her capacity to biologically produce children allows for the commodification of her sex-specific labour as a wet nurse, which informs and constitutes the 'emancipation' of the young wives/daughters-in-law of the Halder family. Thus, the trained, educated, and professional woman is aided by the labour of subaltern women.[12]

Circumventing the linear argument of men exploiting women's bodies and harnessing their (un)paid labour for social reproduction, 'Stanadayini' draws connections between women of privileged classes and their collusion in power structures that is buttressed by the labour of women unprivileged by caste and class. The argument that women be seen as a 'sex class', who as a group are exploited for their 'sex/affective labour' that meets human needs across economic divide[13] was shot down by some feminists. They argued that middle-class women are complicit in ensuring low wages are paid to those who they hire to take care of their 'second shift'.[14] Patricia Hill Collins linked exploitation with ideology to argue that the cultural production of black women as the 'mammy' was crucial to the segmented labour force that placed coloured women in low-paid industrial and clerical work or as domestic workers in white homes.[15]

Over the years, there emerged a remarkable and significant scholarship on women workers crowded in segregated labour markets, particularly domestic labour, which addressed ethnic and racial politics between the employer and employee that further compounded existing

---

[11] Devi (1979).
[12] Spivak (1997).
[13] Ferguson (1979).
[14] Brenner (2000).
[15] Collins (1990).

class inequalities.[16] The subsequent research and theorizing has led to many fallouts; one that is important for us is the recognition that women's labour, despite its entry into the public sphere, continues to rank much lower than men's work. It is now a well-established fact that low wages, harsh working conditions, rampant exploitation, and no opportunities for growth continue to plague women's work. The second important contribution over the last few decades is the recognition and acknowledgement that occupations which commodify women's reproductive labour are crucial grounds for analysing power structures emerging from the interstices of gender, caste, class, race, and ethnicity.[17] Not all women experience work similarly; for some, it is more exploitative than for others even if they belong to similar segments of the labour market.

Women's reproductive labour and its commodification make for an interesting segment to study intersecting inequalities. Who are the women who enter this devalued service sector? How different is the low-paying service work from the equally ill-paid, menial factory/mill/mine work? How does working as nurses, attendants, wet nurses, governesses, and domestic workers produce feminine subjects for whom the transition from the private to the public is filled with ambiguities and contradictions, given the nature of the workplace? How do women struggle to expand, explain, and give meaning to their labour, their workplaces, their relation with their employers and their wards, given that these affective ties are filled with contradictions that include disparate emotions of loyalty, affection, as well as hatred, humiliation, and subjugation? How does the specificity of paid reproductive labour constitute women's identity, first as gendered subjects and secondly, as workers, wage earners, and breadwinners?

Service Sector in Capitalist Economies: Emotional, Affective, and Care Labour

It is now widely accepted that women are disproportionately represented in service sectors such as domestic work, nursing, childcare, sex work, waitressing, social work, entertainment, and so on. Of course,

---

[16] Chin (1998); Cock (1989); Davis (1981).
[17] Glenn (1992).

sexually segregated markets are not new to feminist theorizations; however, renaming certain activities within this female-intensive service sector as 'emotional labour', 'care work', 'caring labour', and 'nurturant care' that begs a reconsidering of the conceptualization of both productive and reproductive labour has taken on an urgent spin in recent years.[18] The expansion of the 'old' debate on reproductive labour to formulate what has been loosely termed as the 'care sector' has animated much feminist theorization on women's work. The renewed interest in women's un/paid labour was initially spurred by research focusing on the complex relations between globalization, poverty, and women's empowerment with adaption of Structural Adjustment Programmes (SAP) in the 1990s in the Global South. The new political and theoretical insights within the framework of Gender and Development (GAD) attempted to tackle the gendered impact of restructured labour markets, collapse of employment, intensification and ghettoization of women's labour, increasing informalization, and precarious working conditions, particularly in the Global South.[19] Feminist economists have argued that the impact of the restructuring of the labour market with debt crisis and aid dependence has led to families/communities coming up with innovative means to negotiate survival with disastrous consequences for women, minorities, and the working class.[20] The withdrawal of the government from important social sectors put the onus of survival on households, resulting in intensification of women's labour, particularly the task of caring, crucial for the survival of daily life.[21] Feminists demand that unpaid 'care' activities associated with social reproduction, hitherto subsumed under women's reproductive labour, be acknowledged, made visible, and integrated into analysis that influences policies on women's employment.[22]

Apart from research emerging within the framework of GAD, the intersection of migration and labour studies have contributed to transnational research on this loosely defined service sector. The

---

[18] Duffy (2011); England and Folbre (1999); Hochschild (1983); Smith (1992).

[19] Tinker (1990); Young (1989); Young, Wolkowitz, and McCullagh (1981).

[20] Beneria and Feldman (1992).

[21] Beneria (1992).

[22] For an excellent discussion, see Razavi (2007).

emergence of analytic and political categories such as 'international division of reproductive labour',[23] 'global care chain',[24] and 'crisis of care'[25] has brought on board inequalities of race, gender, and ethnicity in understanding the (re)configuration of commodified reproductive labour across countries and its myriad ramifications. The racialization of the questions of class and gender by Third-World feminists along with cross-cutting temporal-spatial analysis initiated by diaspora and migration studies have highlighted how transnational migration has led to the concentration of women from impoverished countries such as Thailand, Philippines, and India into service sector of the Global North.[26]

The turn to affective labour was inaugurated by Hochschild's *The Managed Heart: Commercialization of Human Feeling* (1983), which brought the discussion of steady marketization of affect to the fore. Kathi Weeks critiques Hochschild on the grounds that *The Managed Heart* takes as given a separation of private and public spheres as well as a core self prior to estrangement.[27] This theorization of affective labour was further taken up by Michael Hardt and Antonio Negri, who conceptualized it as central to the entire reorganization of bio-political economy. They argue that the current postmodernist global order is witnessing newer kinds of labouring practices: communicative labour, interactive labour, and affective labour, which are central to production of life in 'controlling societies'.[28] Hardt, for instance, argues that affective labour is central to producing subjectivities, sociality, and finally society itself. His argument is that though affective labour was never located outside capitalist production, the current paradigm shifts in contemporary political economy have made it directly productive of capital. And since they do not produce durable goods, he calls it 'immaterial labour': labour that produces knowledge, communication, and services. This 'informational economy' is dependent on affective labour (a component of immaterial labour), given its capacity to create, manipulate affect, and

23   Parrenas (2000).
24   Hochschild (2000).
25   Benería (2008).
26   Ehrenreich and Hochschild (2002); Parrenas (2000).
27   Weeks (2007).
28   Hardt and Negri (2000).

produce subjects.[29] Hardt and Negri argue that the division between productive and reproductive labour has never been rigid and proposes a new theory of value where economic production and social reproduction are indistinguishable.[30] Hardt is quite clear that the theorization of affective labour is not new; feminist challenges to Marxist theory of value was based on the theorization of reproductive labour as productive, but what is new is the gradual location of affective labour as central to the economy.[31] The similarity between post-Marxist theorization of affective labour and feminist theorization of emotional labour/care work is striking as both link it to bio-political production of life. While Hardt and Negri take the crucial step in arguing for the centrality of the service economy in current capitalist regimes, they stop short of gendering affective labour and linking it with occupational segregation and patriarchy.

Feminist concerns about affective labour or the service economy stem from a sociological, anthropological, and philosophical concern about the material ramifications of both feminization and of labour, occupational segregation, and gender wage gap, given the predominance of women from minority groups in the sector. It also follows from concerns that the feminization of labour in post-Fordist economies suggests that affective and emotional labour has eroded all distinctions between work/leisure public/private as increasingly one's personality and affective life is set to work, in service of one's job.[32] However, the adaption of 'care' as a lens to understand paid reproductive labour including affective and emotional labour and its low economic and social worth could do with some probing. More so, given that the experience of 'caring' is constituted and inflected by women's social identities. Given the skewed nature of care providing, particularly care embedded in globalized circuits of migration, reproduction, and gender relations, and its implications for poverty and exploitation, one could ask how women experience the 'care' component of such labour.

The conceptualization of caring labour is not very clear. How does one distinguish between reproductive labour, affective labour, and

---

[29] Hardt (1999).
[30] Hardt and Negri (2000).
[31] Hardt (1999); Hardt and Negri (2004).
[32] Power (2009).

caring labour? While certain reproductive labour is more amenable to commodification, other forms of labour such as childcare, care for the elderly, and creating and sustaining affective spaces that are central to social reproduction are not so hospitable to commodification.[33] Given the increasing racialization and devaluation of paid reproductive labour, can we say 'care' is a normative rather than a purely descriptive or analytic category? In India, the question of women's work is almost always embedded in social identities and the stigma embodied in such labour. The challenges posed by intersectionality and the instability of the category 'woman' precipitates the feminist rethinking of what counts as women's work. For instance, in India, domestic work has had a constitutive role in the formation of both caste and class identity. The homogeneity of the category 'women's work' is fractured by caste- and class-based division of labour, which ensures that different women perform different kinds of labour, even within narrow sub-sectors. So, while Dalit women worked both in the public and private domain, upper-caste and middle-class women were relatively restricted in their economic activities due to lack of mobility. However, scholars have pointed out that historically upper-caste and middle-class women never performed manual or menial labour even in the private realm. On the contrary, status mobility required hiring domestic workers to perform menial labour within the household. In fact, in Bengal, the very construction of the *bhadramahila* (respectable woman) meant a distancing and a disassociation from any labour that is manual and menial, even within the household.[34] This did not mean middle-class women were free from household tasks, rather, a division of labour emerged where non-manual, non-corporeal unpaid supervisory roles were performed by female kin and manual, corporeal tasks were assigned to women who sold their labour power in the market. In a context where 'taking care', 'caring for' dependent members of the family—primarily stigmatized corporeal labour—was allocated to Dalit men and women, or the penurious but upper-caste woman, one can question the extent of emotional support between the care-giver and the care-receiver. When affective labour is commodified and brought to the market as exchange-value labour, what implications does it have for the emotional–affective dimensions of

[33] Barker (2005).
[34] Banerjee (2004).

that labour? Kumkum Sangari has argued that the commodification of domestic work raises questions about the impossibility of reproducing ideologies of love and sacrifice associated with reproductive labour.[35] Where historically, 'caring' labour—nurturing and nursing—is closely associated with lower-caste, working-class feminine labour (even within the home) and therefore stigmatized as menial and manual labour,[36] does commodification dispel the humiliation and degradation embedded in it? And can such kinds of labour be (re)valorized, given social and economic worth by emphasizing on its emotional and affective component?

It is this complex relation between power, subjectivity, and affect that informs perceptions of women's labour as 'caring work'. The uneasy and complicated relation that certain labour shares with certain kinds of emotions governs and produces the affective economy. If social fields are not passive, contained spaces but actively constitute subjectivities, one wonders how women entrusted with caring, altruistic roles fare in labour processes that devalue such emotions. The strict division of labour within health services produces an oligarchy of labour, which restricts itself to clean and prestigious tasks, and delegates the everyday menial, corporeal, and somatic labour to women located symbolically, culturally, and materially right at the bottom.[37] It is in this context that one must place the different meanings given to nursing labour by those located differently in the hierarchy and raise the question of (re)producing and sustaining ideologies of love, care, sacrifice, and nurture, traditionally associated within kinship within the labour market.

Is Nursing Labour 'Caring' Labour? The Question of Nursing Ethics

The urgency to label nursing labour as 'care labour' could also arise from nursing ethics, which has a history of accommodating care ethics in its methodology. Nursing overlaps strongly with domestic work. The distinctions between affective labour that calls for 'taking care', 'responding to needs' of the recipient of care and menial/manual labour oriented towards cleaning rather than caring is at best fuzzy.

[35] Sangari (1993).
[36] Sen (2009); Somjee (1991).
[37] Ray (2016a).

The domestic worker, nurse, or governess fulfils a role that is crucial in reproducing life in its most crude and biological form. What exactly comes under nursing care, and what under other domestic services? The difficulty in disentangling nursing from other kinds of domestic labour often leads to a conflation between the two, thus extending the stigma associated with the former to the latter. In fact, the struggles of the nursing profession have been to disassociate itself from domestic work and establish itself as skilled, trained labour, often leading to compartmentalization. While nursing within the domestic sphere overlaps with other kinds of reproductive labour, it is assumed that the professionalization of nursing would have countered such trends.[38] Nursing labour is essential for reproduction of life—cleaning the sick body, tending to bed sores, feeding, aiding in daily ablution, fanning and sponging, uttering soothing words to calm patients enough to administer medicine or take temperature, keeping the environment clean, making the bed, disinfecting and sterilizing instruments, watching over patients for symptoms that help in diagnosis—a range of activities that include menial, manual, and affective labour which requires varied skills. For example, changing soiled sheets without making the sick person get up from bed requires not just skill but also strength and dexterity. It goes without saying that diagnosis and administering medicine is one component of healing; regular care, cleaning, and vigilance over the sick body and the environment forms the backbone of the healing process. Not just reproduction of life, nursing, like domestic work in middle-class households, is also status-producing work; it is bound with reproduction of lifestyles. Nurses have the responsibility of ensuring that both the sick person and his/her environment are not dirty, infected, and contaminating. They are the keepers of the boundaries between sickness and health, ill-being and well-being, contamination and purity. Thus a nurse is not just responsible for ensuring that there are no open festering wounds, infected equipment, dirty and soiled bandages/clothes, but also for maintaining a clean, sanitized, and cheerful sick room essential for reproducing social order. The classification of nursing labour thus poses a problem given the multiple tasks that fall under its ambit,

[38] Duffy (2011).

which range from purportedly unskilled domestic work to highly specialized medical tasks.

The increasing commodification of women's reproductive labour raises newer questions on ethics. The tension between acknowledging the relational and the emotional component of feminine affective labour and the difficulty in measuring and adapting it to market values informs most of the debates on paid care work.[39] The demand for valorizing reproductive labour as skilled work so as to be able to ascribe a market value to emotional/affective labour is in direct tension with understanding 'care' as a distinct feminine quality that escapes masculine market transactions. It would be fruitful to look at the intersection of feminist debates on care ethics with newer concerns of renaming paid reproductive labour as care work, particularly in the context of nursing. Carol Gilligan's *In a Different Voice* (1982) sparked the debate on care ethics, where she argued that feminine morality and conception of the self as relational, interdependent, and located in a complex web of social relations gave rise to an 'ethics of care' as against the masculine 'ethics of morality'.[40] This context-bound character of care ethics informed much of later theorization on work ethics, particularly for health service providers; nursing ethics, for instance, is far more hospitable to care ethics than others. Feminists have critiqued the traditional Western health care system that presumes that doctors are the sole repositories of specialized knowledge, and patients are constructed as passive recipients and beneficiaries. The questioning of such traditional views of knowledge has highlighted the role of patients and other health care providers as equal participants in knowledge production.[41] This challenge to traditional ways of knowing has opened up debates on nursing ethics that perceive nurses as equal participants in the healing process but distinguishes them from that of a physician.[42] Nursing ethics highlights the 'caring' role of nurses as relational and context-specific interventions that stress on affective bonds as against medical approaches. However, traditional nursing ethics are hardly feminist; deploying gender-oppressive norms and stereotypes, it promotes nursing as secondary to other forms of medical

---

[39] Tronto (1987).
[40] Gilligan (1982).
[41] Beauchamp and Childress (1994); Lebbacqz (1985).
[42] Pence and Cantrall (1990).

interventions.[43] The association of women's work with care implied that historically doctors distanced themselves from such roles, carving out a professional function that had no linkages with affective/emotional labour. In later periods, when nursing education was modified to incorporate scientific and medical components, it occasioned debates regarding the suitable role of a nurse.[44] This sexual division of labour within health care services reflects wider hierarchical binaries of objective/subjective, reason/emotion, masculine/feminine whereby male doctors practiced medicine and female nurses healed through affective labour, both inhabiting normative gender roles.[45]

With intensification of technology and emphasis on documentation, nursing personnel are more and more involved with computerized patient records, logbook maintenance, keeping account of linen and laundry, drugs, and other supervisory administrative roles.[46] However, the expansion of the nurse's role and functions to include managerial work has not questioned the deeply entrenched hierarchies in the health industry. It did not, for instance, democratize medical roles with more doctors participating in caring processes; instead, it has reproduced power equations deploying race, class, and caste identities. In the Nightingale model, every nurse was to give bedside care; now the staff nurses leave it to nursing auxiliaries and concentrate on cleaner and more prestigious administrative tasks.[47] Florence Nightingale's initiation of reforms included training, which was divided into theoretical and on duty/ward training. This learning or knowledge dissemination is usually seen as the inception of the power struggle between doctors and nurses. Such medical training was meant to ensure an informed, ancillary labour force that doctors could rely on, which in turn would allow him/her to function as a skilled consultant. The medical component in nursing training, however, became the ground for new claims on scientific knowledge by nurses, which challenged the doctor's stated monopoly in diagnosis and treatment.[48] Nurses also demonstrated a

---

[43] Oakley (1993).
[44] Jecker and Self (1991).
[45] I have discussed this hierarchical binary in detail in Ray (2016b).
[46] World Health Organization (1957).
[47] Glaser (1966).
[48] Gamarnikow (1991).

preference for technical work rather than affective work, which made the division of labour and hierarchy in the medical profession and within nursing self-evident.[49] In America for instance, from the mid-twentieth century, the medical workforce was no longer divided into doctors and nurses (corresponding to gendered cure/care binaries), but a new rank of workers emerged, and were increasingly formalized as aides, ancillary workers, and orderlies who gave hands-on nursing care. Registered nurses were careful to draw boundaries that distinguished them from unregistered semi-trained nursing ancillaries. Both categories remain overwhelmingly feminine, however, over the years, the latter was predominantly composed of black and immigrant women.[50]

Though the increasing focus on techno-curative model of providing health services has challenged the gendered binary of cure/care, it has not necessarily been a cause of cheer for feminists. Conceptually, the nurse is the caregiver, the healer, and the nurturer of the sick, ailing body; however, in reality, the overlapping and contradictory tasks of doctors, nurses, nursing aides, and attendants challenge the form and content of caregiving. In fact, the struggle in the organizational strategies of contemporary health service is to ensure that optimal care can be delivered by a curious mix of cure and care. Needless to say, this juggling is amongst nurses and ancillary nursing staff, with the former moving closer to cure and the latter staying locked in traditional caring activities. Doctors, on the dint of possessing scientific knowledge, have always been excluded from such organizational strategies. It is in this context that one must locate the relational self as the feminist subject. The notion of the Enlightenment subject as atomic and rational disassociated from the social has been crucial in delegitimizing women's nurturing roles within the family. Gilligan's care ethics is a point of departure from such conception of the subject, as she argues for a subject constituted and sustained by the social, thus bringing women's caring roles, the relational self, into the heart of discourses on morality. Nurses based on their traditional gender roles are perceived to offer care within the modern, mechanical medical system and, therefore, feminize otherwise masculine modes of curing. It is assumed that breaking the gendered coding of the nurse would lead to relationships based on reciprocal and

[49] Smith (1992).
[50] Duffy (2011).

mutual care, thus breaking down hierarchies between doctors, patients, and nurses and democratizing both knowledge production and lopsided power relations. Nelson, for instance argues, that, for nursing ethics to be feminist, it must borrow from care ethics without essentializing and valorizing traditional and oppressive norms; instead, it must focus on politicizing care, which promotes a social ideal of interdependency and non-hierarchy.[51]

However, feminists have questioned the prescriptive and universal nature of care ethics; for instance, McLaren in critiquing care ethics draws heavily from Foucault's *The Care of the Self* to argue that while Gilligan sees social relations as mutually sustaining and nourishing, Foucault perceives the relationship between self and the social as antagonistic and power-laden. While both reject the disembodied self, they also disagree on the nature of relation of the self with the social. McLaren concludes by pointing out that the universal nature of care ethics tends to ignore asymmetric relations of power and the manner in which it constitutes subjectivities.[52] The dissolution of the category 'woman' in feminist theories of subjectivities further points to the inadequacies in prescribing caring roles for women in labour markets, given that race, ethnicity, and caste mark women and their labour. In the Indian context, such caring roles—stigmatized as servile, sexual, and caste-based labour—prevents any explicit connection between subjectivity and moral agency. The recognition of asymmetrical power relations, the role of power in constituting subjects, and the historical and social specificity of women's location in labour markets point to the inadequacy in adapting 'care' as a lens to understand women's paid reproductive/affective labour.

Nursing in India: Laying Out the Field

In the context of colonial India, there have been mostly two strands within the scholarship on 'women and medicine': first, historiography that questioned the colonial medical discourse which posited the *dai* as a symptom of India's primitiveness;[53] and secondly, the emergence of

---

[51] Nelson (1992).
[52] McLaren (2002).
[53] Forbes (2005); Guha (2006).

Indian women as 'lady doctors' in the colonial medical apparatus.[54] The question of the nurse has been seen in context of either replacing the dai or as an assistant to the female doctor who was trying to make inroads into the field of gynaecology and obstetrics. The nurse has been posited differently by different scholars: those examining the hegemonic aspirations of the colonial state via medicine locate nurses as instrumental in reaching the heart of the zenana which was outside the pale of imperial domination,[55] as a signifier of European modernity,[56] or as instrumental figure in the discourse on the 'white woman's burden'.[57] More recently, studies on nursing in colonial India have focused on the complex relation between the profession and social identities.[58] Scholars have focused on both racial discrimination and indifference of the colonial state to a largely feminine profession, which dissuaded respectable women from taking up nursing as a career.[59]

Scholarship on nursing in contemporary India can largely be grouped around two issues: professionalization[60] and migration of women trained in nursing.[61] The first study on nursing in independent India was published in 1978, which was a comparative study of levels of professionalization achieved by medical workers where doctors were considered 'full-fledged professionals' and nurses were labelled as 'semi-professionals'.[62] Molly Chattopadhyay, in her in-depth research on the nursing profession explores how adverse nurse-patient ratio, lack of proper medical equipment, and non-cooperation from Grade IV staff are the three main organizational constraints in effective occupational role-performance of the nurse. Chattopadhyay argues that the low status, stigma, as well as low pay and arduous working conditions worked as a barrier for middle-class women to train as nurses.[63] With international migration,

---

54 Burton (1996); Dali (1888); Forbes and Raychaudhuri (2000).
55 Sehrawat (2005).
56 Nestel (1998).
57 Burton (1996); Forbes (1994); Lal (1996).
58 Nair and Healey (2006).
59 Healey (2010).
60 Eswara (1989); Healey (2013); Oommen (1978).
61 Nair (2012); Percot (2006).
62 Oommen (1978).
63 Chattopadhyay (1993).

nursing is gradually turning into a more acceptable profession, however, it continues to be devalued.[64] In India, historically, doctors came from learned castes, however, nurses have no such antecedents, thus making it easier to for nursing be identified as a feminine caste-based occupation. The migration of Third-World women, which has been termed as the 'international division of care labour' or the 'new service economy', has had as its focus unskilled care workers like 'nannies, maids and sex workers',[65] however, recently there has also been an increasing focus on nurse migration from poorer to richer countries. The 'global care chain'[66] has been explored to include, at one end of its continuum, skilled care work such as nursing in institutional settings.[67] This focus has largely been the result of a growing alarm amongst policymakers, nursing administrators, and health officials at the large flow of nurses from Third-World countries to the First World, impacting health services in the former.[68] This increasing demand and mobility of Indian nurses to the West has seen a large number of women train in nursing, especially in the southern states. While some scholars have pointed out the empowering potential of international migration for nurses in terms of social mobility, status, autonomy, and economic stability,[69] others have highlighted the stigma associated with such migrations.[70]

Moreover, the supply crunch of nurses in the local market has not increased their bargaining power; on the contrary, salaries continue to remain low with high unemployment. Despite a large number of nurses completing training every year, vacancies remain in government hospitals. Registered nurses work in private establishments for dismal salaries while they wait for public-sector postings or for opportunities to migrate abroad. Studies done on nurses show the immense dissatisfaction they feel regarding low wages, poor working and living conditions, lack of job prospects, and low status of the

---

[64] Somjee (1991).
[65] Ehrenreich and Hochschild (2002).
[66] Hochschild (2000).
[67] Yeats (2009).
[68] Buchan (2007).
[69] Percot (2006); Nair (2012).
[70] Damodaran and Menon (2007); George (2000); Nair and Percot (2007).

profession, particularly in the private sector.[71] This large-scale movement of nurses to the West leading to a vacuum in the labour market has been offset by the employment of unregistered nurses. If nurses are marginalized, semi-professional personnel within the health care industry, unregistered nurses are doubly marginalized—first by the registered nurse who is peeved by the saturation of the market and perceives them as detrimental to the image of a nurse in an ever-expanding global knowledge-driven economy; and second, by the larger medical establishment, which treats her as cheap, dispensable labour.

This brings us to the third concern regarding nurses, private sisters, and attendants—the question of (in)formalization and registration. While in America, nursing aides have been given certain recognition, in India, it is more ambiguous. Most feminine service workers (domestic workers, sex workers, nurses, ayahs, and the like), at least in India, have never been a part of the formal economy: however, in the case of nurses, we have seen attempts at formalization, albeit only a small section of elite, trained nurses. Concurrently, formalization, and therefore, professionalization also meant a reconfiguration of the work of a nurse. The registered nurse takes on the more managerial-administrative-medical aspects of nursing service: she is now an expert-consultant, whereas the menial hands-on, day-to-day care of the patient is left to unregistered private sisters and attendants, largely labelled as nursing aides, who are usually located at the informal end of the labour market. The politics of informalization, by which employer-establishments increasingly employ unregistered nurses—deploying existing inequalities based on social identities and the discourse on skills—have played a crucial role in institutionalizing discriminatory and exploitative labour practices.[72]

Given that the masculinization of the Indian labour force and informalization of the economy played a decisive role in the devaluation of women's labour, it might be useful to spend a moment in understanding the macro labour processes over the last ten decades. Feminist economists have pointed out that Bengal Presidency was way ahead of the rest of the country in women's labour force participation, however, with modernization and mechanization, women workers in Bengal lost out to

---

[71] Thomas (2006).
[72] Ray (2016a).

men in the three major industries: jute, tea plantation, and collieries. And they were equally displaced in traditional labour-intensive non-agricultural occupations, thus crowding into the only sector that offered them employment, resulting in feminization of domestic services.[73] Scholars have also pointed out that Partition and consequent demographic changes, de-industrialization and increasing informalization, agrarian crisis and ensuing distress migration swelled the city's poor leading to a vulnerable workforce ready to work for almost nothing. The coming to power of the Left Front government, and the consequent land reforms had limited effect, and could not stave off the agrarian crisis. Women's marginalization in industry and agriculture meant that they had no option but to take to domestic service, for very low wages, or nothing at all, thus uprooting migrant men and feminizing paid domestic work.[74] All over the country, we witness similar trends as women's labour force participation gradually declined. The 1970s and 1980s saw a slight jump in women's employment both in the rural non-agricultural sector and export-oriented industries, however, it has largely been at the informal end of these sectors.[75] After the 1990s, there has been a sharp decline in women's employment and the gains of the 1980s were lost in the following decades.[76] Scholars have argued that most women's employment has happened at the lowest end of the informal economy—home-based piece-rate work and industrial outsourcing, among others;[77] however, despite being a minority in the informal workforce, the bulk of women workers (96.33 per cent) are in the informal sector.[78] Scholars insist that globalization and ensuring economic reforms in liberalizing India, instead of narrowing the gap, have intensified existing inequalities based on social identities within the labour market.[79]

[73] Banerjee (1989).

[74] For an excellent overview of the changing political economy of Bengal from Independence to contemporary times, see Chakravarty and Chakravarty (2016).

[75] Banerjee (1991a).

[76] Ghosh (1994); Mazumdar and Neetha (2011).

[77] Unni (2001).

[78] Patrick (2001).

[79] Kannan (2014).

The earliest ideas of the informal sector, informed by dualism, have been challenged by scholars who see the formal and the informal sector as two ends of a continuum.[80] Informalization was always linked to feminization. The dualistic framework suggested that the formal economy is modern, capitalist, and is also masculine whereas the informal economy, characterized by 'under development' or a 'lack', is feminine. However, this association of informalization and feminization has not been empirically grounded. While Guy Standing's thesis based on the international division of labour claimed a feminization of the labour force,[81] the reverse is true for the Indian economy.[82] In nursing, formalization has been restricted to the topmost layer of the profession where there has not been any significant masculinization. Nursing continues to remain a female-intensive profession; instead, a rise in informalization and casualization from the 1990s led to an increasing induction of unregistered nursing staff as against formally employed registered nurses. The nursing profession strongly contests the dualistic understandings of the formal and informal sector. Formally employed registered nurses coexist with informally employed, unregistered nurses and attendants in the government; whereas, in the private sector, casual and informal employment of nurses (both registered and unregistered) is the norm. Seen in the context of earlier debates of the formal/informal sector as two separate distinct spheres, the nursing profession appears to be a contradiction. However, seen in the context of recent shifts in the definition of the informal sector, which focus on informal employment as a defining feature,[83] the nursing service is not an anomaly. The global pressures of informalization and international demand for skilled nurses have played against each other to ensure that nursing services employ an increasingly differentiated workforce—differences based on identities, skills, and knowledge—which invariably reflect socially and historically produce inequalities.

The central concern of this book is the restructuring of the service economy within the health care industry, namely the nursing sector,

---

[80] For an excellent review of the debates, see Chen, Vanek, and Heintz (2006).

[81] Standing (1989).

[82] Ghosh (1994).

[83] Chen, Vanek, and Heintz (2006).

where certain segments have witnessed professionalization while others continue to struggle with non-recognition of skills and stigmatization of labour. Trained nurses are located on the cusp of scientific and affective labour and have laid claim to professionalization on the basis of a specific sets of skills in a knowledge-driven economy. It is the 'behind-the-scenes' unregistered nurse, nursing aide, and the attendant who offers devalued 'dirty work' who continue to struggle. Of course, one cannot place the trained nurse and the wide gamut of un/semi-trained nursing aides in easy binaries; there are various overlaps, in tasks allocated, in levels of skills as well as social identities of the women belonging to the various categories. And these overlaps, continuities as well as attempts at homogenization have led to politics of differentiations and distinction, which is the subject of my research. Nurses struggle to establish themselves as medical workers, rather than health care service providers, to distance themselves from caring/affective/reproductive labour, leaving it to lesser trained women, thereby delegitimizing traditional nursing labour on grounds of gender, caste and class. Thus, the research examines how, not just employer-establishments, but also women workers participate in divisive strategies and politics that produce a differentiated workforce. The study is as much about labouring lives, as it is about labour. The various contestations around gender, caste, class, sexualities, among and between ranks of workers emerge from everyday politics that deploy modernity, morality, and social norms as strategies to exclude social groups, based on existing inequalities. Thus, I argue that workers participate equally and with full gusto in politics that produce a differentiated workforce. Some of the central questions I ask in this volume are: How did the trained nurse come into being? What are the dualistic practices within the labour market that discursively produce workers by deploying social identities as well as socially produced notions of skills, education, and knowledge? What are the conditions/constraints that facilitate women's entry into the labour market? How do levels of consciousness and practices as gendered subjects constitute desires, yearnings, and aspirations of women, both at home and the workplace? The cleaving of labour into managerial-medical-supervisory roles and manual-menial-affective labour requires distinct workers, who are recruited from disparate social groups. How do women working in different ranks of a similar segment of labour force participate in politics that normalizes social relations of domination/subordination as well as inequalities? Studying this segment of health care service providers enables me to address the complexities embedded in quotidian relationships that reproduce hierarchies based on intersecting identities through daily practices and rituals.

In this research, I have not only examined the stratified labour market of health service providers, but also taken the opportunity to explore subjectivities and agencies of women historically posited as antagonistic social groups—the bhadramahila and the *chotolok* woman (respectable and non-respectable women).[84] The bhadramahila has been subjected to various discourses and attempts of definitions; however, she has no counterpart. The plebeian woman, masculinized by her sexuality, coarseness, and participation in the workforce is subsumed under the category 'chotolok'. My research uses this binary of bhadramahila and chotolok woman to understand how antagonistic social groups are brought together in mutual need, as well as distinction and separation. This division of workers based on social categories of the *bhadralok* (respectable, middle class) and the 'chotolok' draws as much from cultural practices as well as perceived entitlements stemming from possession of education that places different women in different ranks of the labour market. The fact that all nursing personnel, irrespective of their social identities, locations, and education are employed in the same segment of the labour market complicates and contests boundaries that set apart the bhadramahila from the chotolok woman; it also intensifies and gives urgency to the politics of distancing and differentiation. The subjectivities of both groups of women constitute one another, framed by quotidian relations of subordination, domination, humiliation as well as practices of resistances. It is these everyday practices that constitute subjectivities, contest fields, and produce workers that is the subject of my research. I submit that women located in privileged groups need the subaltern woman to maintain and preserve their identity, while for the latter, the experience is one of exploitation and subordination.

Methodology, Methods, and Field Notes

My interest in nurses and nursing labour arose from both an intellectual curiosity as well as a practical impediment, given that I was confronted

---

[84] For a detailed discussion on the two relational but antagonistic categories, see Chakraborty (1993); Chatterjee (1993).

with the absence of women in the manufacturing sector in my attempts to frame a 'research topic' for my doctoral dissertation. My required readings on questions of 'women and work' pointed out that women's workforce participation has been rapidly dropping and the only feminization has been in the heterogeneous service sector, which gave employment to 35.9 per cent (National Sample Survey, 2006) of urban women.[85] Not convinced, I visited factories in the industrial belt of Howrah and Kolkata, bordering either sides of the river Hooghly, seeking to interview women working in jute and leather industries, only to be greeted by their absence in manufacturing units. All the three jute and leather factories I visited employed male workers with a handful of women employed as cleaners, sweepers, and in other low-end manual services. Around 40 to 50 per cent of the tasks were subcontracted to agents, including cutting and stitching, while it was only men who were employed in assembly line production units. My interviews with managers and owners of factories as well as representatives of the Indian Jute Manufacturing Association and government officials of industrial restructuring revealed that representation of women in assembly line production units had reduced to about 5 to 7 per cent. I was told that women did not/could not work in factories as they were not suited to the discipline, routine and standards of professionalism required of modern offices and factories. The rapid retrenchment of workers, from assembly line production units, and farming out of jobs, as well as increasing masculinization of the factory space, augmented the crowding of women into the feminine service sector.

Faced with locating women workers in the new economy, I naturally turned to the service sector. Given that in the Indian context, emerging research projects were looking into commodified reproductive labour, such as domestic work, sex work, and surrogacy,[86] nursing in institutional settings seemed a relatively unexplored field. My interest in professional nurses and attendants working in medical establishments, rather than households, where the overlap with domestic work is more obvious, stemmed from an interest in politics emerging from the interstices of processes of informalization, organizational strategies, social

---

[85] Ghosh (2009); Mazumdar (2007).
[86] Kotiswaran (2011); Pande (2009); Qayum and Ray (2003).

identities, and an increasingly differentiated workforce. Research on the new economy and the service sector has demonstrated that despite an increase in women entering health services, nursing has shown a decline in absolute numbers from 2000 to 2004; and it is possible that the increase has either been at the level of ancillary nursing staff or women doctors. Given that 91 per cent of women workers—whether it is agriculture, industry, or services—are employed in the menial end of the poor-income sub-sectors,[87] I decided to explore the nursing profession with its different ranks and hierarchies, which are equally constituted by social identities, as much as commonsensical perceptions of skill, knowledge, and dispositions.

For this research project, I used a mix of archival reading and ethnography to understand the specificity of the nursing profession, as against other service work. The turn to archival material was motivated by conversations with nurses and teachers in nursing schools and colleges, who continuously harked back to the colonial roots of nursing to explain the current predicament of the profession. Particularly, the figure of the dai loomed large. To understand the evolution of a caste-based occupation into a modern profession, withstanding pressures of masculinization, demanded a historical analysis; thus, I approached the state archives with the intention of 'extracting' information that would support my contemporary research. The initial explorations of the archive proved to be disheartening, with most colonial records focusing either on the hereditary dai as an obstacle to progress or the emerging Indian 'lady doctor' trained in colonial medicine as the harbinger of modernity. The turn from an 'extractive enterprise' to viewing the archive as a process, as a subject, emerged from my surprise at the lack of colonial records on nurses. As Stoler argues, archives are read as sources to validate 'colonial invention of traditional practices or to underscore cultural claims'. She urges researchers to view the archive not as a 'site of knowledge retrieval' but as 'sites of knowledge production'.[88] What are the social and political contexts that produced documents that tell the 'truth' about 'women in medicine' in the late eighteenth- and nineteenth-century India? Which were the stories worth telling and which were not? Ranajit Guha, for instance, argues for 'the small voices of history' that challenge dominant

[87] Mazumdar (2007).
[88] Stoler (2002: 90).

narratives of Indian history located within frameworks of colonialism and elite nationalism.[89] And Foucault reminds us that archives are not just an institution that preserves history, but a key component of knowledge production, that sculpted a set of discursive rules.[90] The erasure of subjectivities in favour of classification of objects of colonial discipline makes for most of the records; hence the excess of records, statements, reports around the traditional dai and the 'lady doctor'. The absence of the nurse (and not the wet nurse) in commission reports and studies point to the underrating of their role in technologies of biopolitics that linked mortality, morbidity, and child care with the state and its apparatuses. The absence of records and reports on the pre/colonial nurse and attendant in the hospital economy or their marginal presence as footnotes or bylines in documents that were dedicated to understanding and recording the difficulties of establishing colonial medicine in a country, proving reticent to imperial discourse of scientific progress and modernity, along with memoirs of British women working as doctors and nurses, manuals on child birth, medical guides, missionary reports, hospital reports, and transcriptions of conferences of fledgling associations of medical women became my point of departure in trying to understand the invisibility of the un/trained nurse in the colonial medical economy. Such non-statist records may/may not be 'authentic sources' that tell us the 'truth' about the nurse or the ayah but they do provide us with glimpses into the lives of women labouring in invisibilized occupations peripheral to colonial statecraft.

The bulk of my research is an ethnographic study of nurses, private sisters, and attendants in the contemporary city of Kolkata. However, I find it difficult to compartmentalize my research according to methods as both archival readings and ethnography have facilitated each other. There are as many feminist methodologies as there are feminisms: multiple perspectives like feminist empiricism, standpoint theories, postmodernist, post-structuralist, and post-colonialist feminisms have influenced, informed, and constituted projects of knowing, of critiquing, and of transforming epistemological and methodological significance of knowledge production. Equally, there are many methods of knowing, as there are methodologies: survey and experimental methods,

---

[89]   Guha (1987).
[90]   Foucault (1972: 79–134).

interview research, inductive fieldwork, Marxist and ethno-methodological approaches, action/participatory research, oral history narratives, and so on.[91]

Feminist research is a transformative project which attempts to break down hegemonic social and political hierarchies, mostly left untouched by positivistic methodologies. Feminism is not centred on a single issue of gender oppression, but complex and overlapping hierarchies, based on multiple social identities.[92] My choice of using feminist ethnography to research women's experiences that constitute their choices emerges from a response to the dominant trends of representing Third-World women as hapless victims of both patriarchy and capitalism. Third-World women do not constitute a universal category but are equally constituted and differentiated by class, caste, community, and sexualities. Chandra Talpade Mohanty, for instance, argues that methodologies that produce this monolithic subject, a universal Third-World woman, deploy generalization, de-contextualization, and an assertion on the basis of numerical strength.[93] The failure to understand contradictory and varied experience of women located in the Third World often emerges from a refusal to engage with local, context-specific norms and practices.

It is in this context that one can argue that standpoint feminism is a position popular among feminists, given that it is rooted in research concerning the everyday existence of women. It takes social stratification on board and multiple axes of inequalities as constitutive of knowledge production.[94] However, standpoint theory has also faced a number of critiques, including privileging one standpoint over others, 'strong objectivity', levels of oppression among the oppressed, the 'authenticity' of experience, and the question of relativism spurred by postmodernism.[95] For some contemporary feminists, postmodernism, however, seems more promising to the feminist task of addressing the question of the 'other' in social research.[96] As stated in the beginning, there is no one

---

[91] For a full discussion, see De Vault (1999).

[92] Tharu and Niranjana (1994).

[93] Talpade (1991).

[94] Collins (1986); Harding (2004).

[95] Hekman (1997).

[96] Hesse-Biber, Leavy, and Yaiser (2004).

feminist methodology, but multiple ways of knowing and researching and I have borrowed liberally from different schools of feminist methodologies, particularly standpoint, post-colonial, post-structuralist, and postmodernist feminist theories.

I used feminist ethnography to understand women's experiences of labouring as nurses, private sisters, and attendants in hospitals and nursing homes. Feminist ethnography documents women's lives; it focuses on those aspects that are considered trivial by mainstream research. It tries to understand women in their cultural specificity, the context that constitutes women and their choices. My goal in using ethnography to understand different women's experience of labouring in a stigmatized occupation stemmed from the recognition and acknowledgement that all women do not experience the world similarly. Likewise, the experiences of nursing have not been homogenous for all the women who participated in the research processes. Seen within the larger context of informalization and casualization, women marked by class and caste have experienced work differently.

Women's experiences have often been excluded from mainstream research citing irrationality and ambiguity coming in the way of rational, objective theory.[97] In my research project, the goal has been to record women's experiences, despite knowing the pitfalls of 'experience' as a category of analysis.[98] Ethnography demands that the researcher 'be there' in the field, which initially posed a problem for me. I was unable to get permission from hospitals and nursing homes to 'be there' outside visiting hours, to interview their workers, to sit around and observe. I had the option of contacting nurses in their residences and ask them to grant me an interview and then introduce me to a colleague and so on and so forth. However, the need to observe women's work, working conditions, moments of conflicts and crisis; to engage in conversations and 'chit chats' outside official interviews (with a tape recorder); and build rapport with my respondents made me reject this interview-based method as the only method.

I chose two private medical establishments to conduct my research, on the basis of obtaining permission. Refused by owners and administrators from a few hospitals and nursing homes, I was forced to look

[97] Foss and Foss (1994).
[98] Scott (1992).

within my own social group for help and was introduced to owners of two private establishments. The reason I selected the government hospital where I conducted part of my research is because it is one of the oldest, and most prestigious hospitals in Kolkata; second, it has both a college and school of nursing attached to it; third, it is also one of the first government hospitals where nursing aides, more popularly known as private sisters, are recruited on a daily-wage basis. I chose my interviewees using the snow-ball technique; after each interview, I would ask my interviewee to introduce me to a colleague. Sometimes, nursing staff would volunteer to give interviews of their own accord. I also faced disruptions from ward boys, who would walk into the room in the middle of an interview and start asking questions or cracking jokes. These interruptions stemmed more from curiosity than humour. This happened mostly in the government hospital and I dealt with it with a firm hand, asking them to leave, as the interviews were confidential.

My intention to write a book as a feminist ethnography posed a dilemma: both feminism and ethnography poses a challenge: the relation between the self and the other. The binary mode of knowledge production that splits the knower and the known also posed an ethical problem for me. How was I to breach the gap, between the 'researcher' and the 'researched'? One of the core components of feminist ethnography is reflexivity, an acknowledgment of power and hierarchies embedded in the research process. I was particularly struck by methodological questions raised by Kamala Visweswaran, as she raises critical issues regarding the practice of feminist ethnography. She discusses in detail concerns regarding the politics of naming, of speaking, of silence as well as of identities. She writes that classical ethnography foregrounds men's relationship to one another, or even women's relationship to men. Feminist ethnography, she urges, could focus instead on women's relationship with other women and the power differentials embedded in such interconnections.[99]

One of the political aims of feminist ethnography is to breach the unequal and hierarchical divide between the researcher and the researched. How was I to negotiate my upper-caste, middle-class, educated, urban identity? When I interviewed nursing administrators and faculty members, certain solidarities based on class and caste were

[99] Visweswaran (1994).

assumed, reflecting in conversations which started with 'women like us ...' or 'our kind of family ...' that repulsed me. Again, working-class and/or lower-caste attendants made me stop and think when they asked why they would divulge information about their life to me so I could advance my career. This led me to rethink feminist concerns with differences and the impossibility of solidarities based on gender. I insisted that I just wanted to hear and learn from their experiences as workers, and as women; and, while I explained that my task to take what I hear to platforms, where grievances will be redressed, is limited and impossible, these moments were disconcerting.

Not just hierarchies embedded in education, class, and caste, our perspectives of the world differed greatly. While I went to the field thinking of nursing as caring labour, women reminded me of the harshness of the work they do, their alienation, and the stigma they face in their everyday lives. Gopal Guru, writing on Dalit women, for whom labour is a painful experience rather than one of joy, given that most of them do exhausting and drudging work, argues that Dalit women acquire a distinct subjectivity which is an intellectual response to their contexts.[100] My task as a researcher was to acknowledge and recognize the subjectivities of women living and labouring very differently from me. This reflexivity of acknowledging differences and understanding how it constitutes each of us, the choices we make, became a way, even nominally, of appreciating the impossibility of the category 'woman.'

Over a period of three years (2009–12), I was able to conduct in-depth interviews with 100 women from different categories of the workforce. Apart from these, I interviewed eighteen male Group D staff (six from each establishment) and six male nurses, nine women supervisors (ward-in-charge), and matrons of all three establishments. I also held eight focus group discussions with students from different years of schools and colleges of nursing, both in the private and government hospitals as well as three departmental heads, principals, and three faculty members. I was also able to interview the owners, managing directors, and medical supervisors of the hospitals and nursing homes, sometimes more than once. While the interviews with the representatives of the management were semi-structured with both open-ended and closed questions, the

[100] Guru (2015).

interviews with women workers had no planned structure; it took on the life history method, also called unstructured qualitative interviews. While some would talk about themselves from their childhood, others would start from their marriage, and yet others who would start from the present and reminiscence back to their childhoods. All the interviews were recorded, transcribed, and translated by me and I have changed all the names of the respondents to keep confidentiality and anonymity of my respondents.

In some moments, in some places, I met with resistance. For instance, in the government hospital, private sisters of a whole ward refused to talk to me, because the sister-in-charge directed them (rather rudely) to grant me interviews. It escalated to a point where the matron 'ordered' the private sisters to talk to me. I realized that I was witnessing a power contest between permanently employed nursing staff and casually employed private sisters. Their refusal to engage with me also brought the subject/object divide between the researcher/researched to the forefront; their refusal to be 'objectified' by the researcher, to be the source of 'knowing', challenged the traditional hierarchy embedded in such lopsided power equations. Their resistance to hierarchical knowledge production brought home the fact that those I was 'researching' were subjects, with critical perspectives on their lives and the world around them, and not just women who provide me with 'data' to write a book.

In the beginning, I went to the hospitals and nursing home during the day but met with little success. Interviews were interrupted because the nurses and attendants were needed back in the wards; women were not too forthcoming and would keep glancing at the door expecting some-one to come in; supervisors and ward managers and those located at the top of the hierarchy would challenge my presence or, at least, look at me with suspicion and attempt to eavesdrop on/interrupt conversations. When I shared my frustration with a woman working as an attendant in the private nursing home, she suggested that I come during night shift, when the wards were less busy, quieter, and the surveillance minimal. This brought a remarkable change as conversations became longer and more intense. Surprisingly, no one objected to my use of a tape recorder after being promised complete anonymity. In fact, many women were happy to speak of their lives, experiences, hopes, and disappointments and were surprised that their voices mattered. While almost all women, especially the older ones, had a lot of questions for me regarding my education, marriage plans, and family background, it was the fact that I could move freely in the middle of the night that intrigued them the most. Answering their queries of how I escaped patriarchal control at home, which allowed me so much mobility, also required me to share details of my family structure and the way patriarchy functions within my home. These conversations did displace, I hope, some notions within mainstream ethnography of the relationship between researcher and the researched and helped me move towards a more egalitarian process of knowledge production.

Going to the hospitals during night shifts brought a remarkable change in my research process. The freedom to be there and the lack of surveillance made it easier for me to establish rapport with my respondents. Particularly after the doctors had finished their rounds, patients were fed, and records updated, the nights were long and still. It was then that I realized something: As much as constant demands on one's labour and bodily activity, which is physically and morally tormenting, reduces one to fatigue and exhaustion, the boredom of staying awake throughout the night while staring at walls and machines and waiting for signs of life, interrupted by snores, grunts, and moans of pain, reduced one to equal weariness and an impassionate state of ennui. Keeping vigil at night was as debilitating as the laborious daily chores that occupied most of their working days. Given the boredom of the night shift, women working in different ranks of the workforce found in me a pleasant distraction. Along with giving me interviews and asking me questions about my family, work, and intimate relationships, they took me around the hospitals showing me places where they eat, change clothes, and sit around in idle time, escaping the keen eyes of the ward managers, nursing supervisors, and security guards. These tours were accompanied by anecdotes on how collectivities were formed, surveillances cheated, disciplinary processes subverted, and the affective economy that was built around such resistances. These conversations, along with the interviews, gave me an insight into the spectrum of resistances as well as constructions of hegemonic caste and class practices. Ethnography demands field notes—'thick descriptions' of the field—interpretation of culture and not just a recording of facts. While I did take field notes, noting down impressions, I was aware of the hidden power dimensions embedded in such an ethnographic technique.[101] Instead, I chose to ask my respondents what certain actions meant, why some people behaved the way they did, and what were the meanings they accrued to such actions and words, allowing their interpretations to inform most of my analysis and arguments.

The Three Medical Establishments: A Government Hospital, A Corporate Hospital, and A Private Nursing Home

The government hospital is one of the most prestigious tertiary referral hospitals and national research institutes in Kolkata. It is the first hospital in eastern India to house postgraduate medical studies dating from 1957. It is also the first hospital where training of nurses started (1926) and by 1955 the School of Nursing was established. Currently it houses both a school and college of nursing. Located near the race course ground it is well connected with the metro, railway, buses, and auto-rickshaws. The 1770-bed hospital has seventeen operation theatres and departments like Medicine, Surgery, Ophthalmology, Cardiology, Nephrology, Endocrinology, among others, as well as specialized facilities like a dialysis unit, a 30-bedded intensive cardiac care unit (ICCU), a neonatal intensive care unit (NICU), an intensive care unit (ICU), burns unit, and so on. It has both indoor and outdoor departments and state-of-the-art equipment. It has more than 100 per cent occupancy, and due to paucity of beds in the surgical, maternity, and medicine wards, cots and mattresses are laid on the floor for patients. Though I was unable to get any official record of how many people worked in the hospital, I was able to piece together bits and pieces of information, gained from interviews, to get an idea of the workforce. Among the 1087 nursing posts that have been sanctioned, only 739 posts have been filled. Over and above that, only 653 posts are fully functional, that is those who were reporting to duty. Other than that, there are 270 nursing students from both the college and the school of nursing who conduct their practical

---

[101] This notion of 'thick description' has been criticized as an example of the hidden authority of the ethnographer. For a more detailed discussion, see Crapanzano (2011).

exercises in the wards. There are about 500 private sisters (who work in the cabins) and more than 2000 attendants, ward boys, and sweepers.

The hospital was built in the early twentieth century, and over the years, newer constructions have come up. Spread over a sprawling campus, it is built in a circular manner with a pond, and large open grounds in the centre. Though touted as one of the premium medical institutes of eastern India, it is not exactly well maintained, similar to other government establishments. Portions of it have seen recent work, new buildings, haphazardly added wings, and some maintenance work where the walls were almost collapsing. The hospital at any given point of day seems to be bursting at its seams, there is always a sense of too many patients, too little resources. There are people cramped everywhere, the lobbies, the outpatient department (OPD), the emergency department, and even the grounds outside. Corridors are filled with sick people waiting for treatment with stray cats and dogs for company. Wards are overflowing with patients and their families who have set up camp to take care of sick relatives. Though there are security guards posted at every ward entrance, they do not pay much attention to the traffic of people. During the entire length of my fieldwork, I was not stopped or questioned even once, from entering the wards or the nurse's hostel, though I rarely went during visiting hours. It is only in the intensive care units and the VIP wings that there seems to be a semblance of peace and order.

Each ward has a nurse's changing room, with a bed and toilet, to allow them to rest and change. In the government hospital, nurses wear white saris and white caps, with name badges and different lapels that signify designations. Private sisters wear brown saris with name badges, but no cap or lapel pins. Attendants wear beige-coloured saris. Earlier, private sisters in the hospital would also wear white sari and caps. A prolonged agitation by registered nurses for their removal from nursing services did not lead to their expulsion, but led to them being 'stripped' of their uniform. They could not wear the white uniform anymore and were not to be addressed as nurses; they were given a different name and officially became unregistered nursing aides. Before starting my fieldwork, I had already gone through government reports on the working conditions of nurses, where special mention had been made on their inadequate living conditions, but nothing prepared me for reality. The nurse's hostel is a tall building with large corridors and steep, wide staircases. However, the sense of spaciousness ends there. The interior of the building is damp and dilapidated, and each room has been further divided into smaller rooms by false partitions. The rooms can barely hold two to three beds and cupboards, maybe a rickety chair, and a small gas oven where nurses cook their meals. There are two to three bathrooms for each floor commonly shared by 30 nurses. The student nurse's hostel is even worse: the building is a new construction and no sunlight comes inside and even during the day, electric lamps have to be lit. The staff nurse's hostel has no security, however, the nursing student's hostel has a warden, who is usually never around. This is not unique to the government sector alone, even private establishments have similar living conditions.

The private hospital is located in the fringes of the city of Kolkata. It is a subsidiary of a public limited company, which was founded by a group of NRI doctors and is funded by an NRI businessman who runs a chain of hotels and pubs in Sweden. Currently, the company has seven directors. Located just outside the metropolis of Kolkata, it draws clients from both the suburbs of the city as well as from the districts. It is a 150-bed hospital, sixteen wards with four operating theatres, and all major medicine and surgery departments and state-of-the-art equipment. It has a nursing strength of 172 nurses (both registered and unregistered) and approximately 170 women attendants and ward boys. It has about 120 private sisters on duty at any given point of time. Though I was refused any information on financial matters including annual turnover, breakup of costs, and so on, the managing director did tell me that workers' salaries constituted 18 per cent of their expenses. The hospital is like any other private hospital, with large, glass-panelled swinging doors, squeaky clean floor, and a large lobby with a reception desk which is buzzing with activity at any given moment of the day. The campus of the private hospital cannot be more than one-tenth of the government hospital: its growth is more vertical. There is one main building with all the wards, operation theatres, and doctor's chambers and a car park at the back; adjacent to the car park is another block which houses the administrative and managerial staff. The administrative block is under strict security, where even workers from the hospital cannot enter without prior appointment or permission. However, unlike a government hospital, there are no overflowing wards or families camping on hospital premises. Heavily guarded with security at every conceivable turn, one cannot enter a ward or floor at will. Visits to patients can only be made during visiting hours and that too with proper passes. Having secured permission to conduct my fieldwork at the hospital, I was given a special pass which allowed me to come and go at will. At first, I was stopped and there was curiosity as to who I was and then I became a part of the routine and no one raised an eyebrow when I went around wards. Each floor has a main lobby with a ward manager and a nurse's table. Each floor is unique in terms of spatial arrangement. Some floors house only wards. All the intensive units are on one floor and another floor is divided into private cabins. The nurses wear loose trousers and shirts and no caps, lapels, or badges. Different coloured uniforms signify different levels of training; navy blue for unregistered nurses, sky blue for registered nurses, full green for those working in intensive care units (could include registered and unregistered nurses), green and white for the sister-in-charge who are usually registered nurses. Private sisters wear white saris without any caps and attendants wear brown saris. Though there are different uniforms for differently skilled staff, it is not obvious to either hospital clients or outsiders. These different levels of hierarchies can only be interpreted by those who work in the hospital and are familiar with the colour coding. Hierarchies are simultaneously established as well as not made obvious to those who pay for it.

The private nursing home is located in north-central Kolkata, on the main road that connects the city to the airport. Owned by a doctor-couple, it is a private limited company established in the year 2001, and by 2008–09, it was recording an annual turnover of 400 lakh rupees. It is a 60-bed nursing home, with 2 operating theatres, and some of the major medicine and surgery departments. It has a nursing staff of 46 personnel with 3 registered nurses and 43 unregistered nurses. There are about 75 attendants and approximately 20 private sisters at any given point of time. Its main expenditure is on medicine purchase (60 per cent) and worker's salary constitutes about 9 per cent of its expenses. The nursing home is one building, cramped between a bar and a large furniture shop. There is no parking lot and its one ambulance is usually parked outside the main gate. The ground floor houses the reception, the doctor's chambers, the pharmacy, and the laboratory. The next three floors are the wards, operation theatres, and the like. The topmost floor is the administrative block, the canteen, the nurse's changing room, and so on. The floors that consist of the wards and cabins have a nurse's table, located at a point where either the whole ward or the entrance of all the cabins can be centrally monitored. Though there is strict security, I was not given a pass. Instead, I was introduced to the head of the security forces who, in turn, informed the guards, and I could come and go at ease. All the nurses wear green trousers and shirts, and no caps or badges. The attendants wear brown saris and the private sisters a white one. There was no way to distinguish between a registered and unregistered nurse. During the day, I was not able to take any interviews as there was no private space or an empty room available. The nursing home usually has 100 per cent occupancy. It was only when I started visiting during night shift that I could sit in the matron's office, and take interviews behind closed doors, join the nurses at their table, or sit around the wards observing and engaging in conversations.

The Plan of the Book: Chapter Divisions

In the second chapter, 'Disciplining "*Seba*": The "Trained" Nurse in Colonial Bengal', I explore the emergence of the modern nurse in colonial India, as it developed from a curious mix of traditions of 'indigenous' women healers and Western-trained professional medical women. Existing scholarship suggests that the hereditary dai was seen as an impediment to the expansion of colonial medicines; however, her influence over the 'native' population made it impossible to eliminate her. In this chapter, I argue that the intention was never to eradicate her but co-opt her as a domesticated 'other' within the modern nursing profession. Nursing, whether in the metropole or the colonies, was struggling to establish itself as a modern profession for educated women. The enactment of occupational closure was therefore aimed at eliminating women from working-class backgrounds, who were predominant in the service. In India, the logic of purity/pollution implied that a stratified workforce deploying hierarchies based on social identities was necessary for caste-based labour that made up nursing care. This differentiated workforce was pivotal to the construction of the nurse as a skilled professional worker of the modern health care system. However, despite the division of labour, middle-class, upper-caste women refused to enter the profession, or did so nominally. I explore the discourses around *seba* (service) to argue that the need to establish professional nursing as a spiritual service and thus a component of feminine respectability, emerged from two contradictory trends: first, the indifference exhibited by the state towards the profession reflecting in low allocation of public funds; and secondly, the need to establish nursing as a profession for middle-class women. However, professionalization without state support was next to impossible, and nursing as a profession continued to struggle with its internal contradictions, even in independent India.

The third chapter, 'The Nursing Labour Market in Contemporary Kolkata', traces the evolution of the nursing profession from 1947 to the contemporary, to argue that the gendered nature of the labour (along with caste and class markings) significantly arrested the growth of the profession. Constructed as an ancillary service, peripheral to medical care, it was neglected and ranked low in budgets and policies. The consequent fall-out was that the nursing sector could not provide dignified employment to middle-class women preparing to enter the labour market. Those who did opt for nursing education took to the international labour market, which continues to draw women from the service economy. The local establishments, instead of improving service conditions that would attract registered nurses, preferred hiring women with unrecognized training to fill the gap. In this chapter, I discuss in detail the differentiated workforce and the structuring of the labour market, which takes on a pyramidal shape with each layer corresponding to political notions of skilled, semi-skilled, and unskilled workers. I describe the wages, the working conditions, and terms of employment to draw a picture of what it means to be a nurse, private sister, or an attendant in the contemporary city of Kolkata.

In the fourth chapter, 'The Matrix of the Family and the Market: (Hetero)normative Economies', I argue that the linkages between the oppositional binaries of public/private, market/home are neither linear nor causal. To make such an argument, I examine why women choose to work in a devalued segment of the labour market. While it makes perfect sense for employers to hire women with minimum and unrecognized training as unregistered nurses, private sisters, and attendants who learn on the job, thus keeping wages low and refusing entitlements, I ask whether it is just poverty that deprives women of adequate training, education, and skills that precipitate their crowding in the menial end of the service sector. There have been many studies that examine how women's entry into the labour market has done little to challenge patriarchal norms at home. However, there is not much empirical research on women's aspirations, desires, and yearnings when it comes to labour market decisions. In this chapter, I open up the family as an institution to examine how a gendered subject is produced who enters the labour market as an extension of her feminine duties and obligations. I further inquire how hetero-patriarchal norms produce women as subjects who see themselves as secondary and ancillary to men, whether in the family or at the workplace. I also examine how such (hetero)normative social structures continue to influence women's decisions within the labour market as well as how they circumscribe any potential change in gender relations. In this manner, I hope to challenge economically determined arguments of 'rational choice' guiding women's decisions in both her family and workspace, to argue for a nuanced understanding of women's subjectivities produced by social and cultural norms.

In Chapter five, '(Re) producing the 'Other': Spatializing (Un)touchability, Dirty Work, and Inequalities', I explore the divisive politics that a section of women workers engages in to secure marginal gains at the cost of others, in an otherwise devalued profession. While a large corpus of literature has examined how, historically, men have collided with capitalists and union leaders to discriminate against women, my research looks into a predominantly feminine workforce to argue that caste, class, and sexualities often become sites of marginalization and modes of discrimination amongst and between women. Given that women of different castes work in a similar segment (nursing) but in different ranks (nurses, private sisters, and attendants), it is the practices of tactility and being that constitutes the everyday politics of labour. Historically, nursing is a caste-based occupation that engaged women from marginal communities. With modernization, there have been some changes in the composition of the workforce, yet, it has not lost its caste and class characterizations. An increasingly complicated division of labour performed by an increasingly differentiated workforce has meant that women from different communities have to labour side by side. The anxieties of purity and pollution generated by the imminent threat of a breakdown of the dominant caste order have spurred politics and practices that focus on maintaining social order. The affective economy built around lived experiences of work and livelihood, exploitation and struggle, along with material processes of labour produce subjects who are docile, embarrassed, and wounded. I argue that space plays a central role in this subject-effect. A space is not just a vessel, an empty place that is to be occupied, rather space is constitutive of social relations.

This chapter looks at the role of spaces, practices of (un)touchability, and the notion of dirty work in producing the 'other'.

In Chapter six, '(Re) Producing the "Other": Stigmatized Lives, Unruly Dispositions, Sexual Transgressions', I ask how subjects come into being. I focus on the processes of class formation to argue that not just economic but non-class factors such as attitudes, behaviour, gestures, and sexual practices play a distinct role in class processes. I argue that class must be seen in context and not as a disembodied experience, and within this framework, I examine how women labouring in stigmatized occupations live and express class. A comparative study of women working in different ranks allows me to examine class as relational, embodied, and context-specific. The oppression, marginalization, and exclusion of a certain section of worker, located at the lower end of the hierarchy, is justified by their everyday apparent inferiority. Apart from their purported lack of skills and education, their behaviour and morality, in sum, their culture, is represented as inferior and deviant. The tendency of women located at the top of the labour market to express class disposition, that is, to behave as a class in relation to groups of people located at the bottom are structured as meaningful responses to the circumstances of the workplace. Given that the contemporary nursing profession is staffed by differently ranked women, identities such as class becomes pivotal in perpetuating, sustaining, and reproducing boundaries. These processes are, however, greatly dependent on the 'otherization' of the working poor. The central concern in the chapter lies in the construction of 'respectable' worker—which draws heavily from the construction of the bhadramahila and the chotolok woman—as against the stigmatized worker. I ask, how are differences created, sustained, and reproduced that legitimize exploitation and precarity? How are meanings assigned and how does the subject come into being?

In the last chapter, 'Narratives of Resistance: Whither Politics?', I explore questions of agency and resistance in everyday politics of labour, to argue that women as workers are not passive, inert objects, rather subjects who resist discourses, culture, and norms that produce them as inferior women as well as unskilled workers. I argue that the quotidian is a critical site in understanding how subjects are constituted, as well as how such constructions are resisted. I explore the everyday politics of labour to understand women's agency as I argue that women often subvert dominant ways of knowing and being to make meanings of their lives. These resistances rarely take on the form of a violent, visible, and organized movement that threatens to overturn the existing social order; instead they are often dispersed, scattered, and spread out, taking different forms, whether it is an evasion of norms or the failure to reflect ruling standards of consciousness. I argue that similar to power, resistance is ubiquitous, local, relational, and disparate, often showing up where it is least expected. In this chapter, I submit that the recognition of embeddedness of the subject in the social is an important starting point in understanding the relational nature of both power as well as resistance.

2 Disciplining 'Seba'

The 'Trained' Nurse in Colonial Bengal

D
r Hilda Lazarus, the first Indian woman appointed to the Women's Medical Service (1917), gave an impassioned speech at the All India Women's Conference regarding the status of nurses in colonial India. Her appeal was that without nurses, successful medical care was unobtainable, as the intimate, everyday care that was essential for the recovery of a patient was not delivered by surgeons and physicians but by the nurse. In her speech, Dr Lazarus argued that without 'good quality' nurses, healing was not possible. It was an 'art' that could only be done by 'cultured', 'cultivated' women from 'good families'. Nursing could not be left in the hands of working-class women.[1] This speech spoke to the heart of the 'nurse problem': devalued and stigmatized as menial, sexual, and servile labour, nursing was perceived as an

[1] Lazarus (1945).

occupation over-represented by women from lower-caste and/or working-class communities. The imperative of the colonial medical apparatus, which tried to graft a completely different medical system onto a political economy that was very differently organized, saw the emergence of big colonial hospitals. However, in a society stratified by gender, class, and caste, the accessibility and popularity of these medical institutions depended on the social identity of the service provider. This meant that the Indian elite would only enter hospitals if both service provider and consumer came from similar social strata. When it came to doctors, this did not pose a problem, but nurses were, for very obvious reasons, women from 'inferior' communities. The imperative to modernize nursing, thus, stemmed from the need to establish it as a profession for respectable women, which could only be possible if its associations with lower caste, working class norms could be severed. Central to this construction of the 'new' nurse was the notion of seba. At the turn of the twentieth century, nationalism, along with Hindu revivalism, saw the emergence of various discourses that sought to produce the 'new' Indian woman. One of them, as propagated by Swami Vivekananda and Sister Nivedita, was the notion of seba as the feminine duty of serving the poor and dispossessed, and thus the race and the nation. The notion of seba, deeply rooted in spirituality and self-sacrificing femininity, was a useful trope for medical, nursing, and bureaucratic reformers who were trying to reformulate nursing labour as a spiritual task, rather than an occupation, for outcaste and distressed women. In this chapter, I argue that the struggle of the trained nurse was informed and inflected partly by ideologies of bourgeois femininity and partly by the real and material endeavor of becoming a professional nurse. Finding a foothold in a sector that was either the occupation of the lower-caste hereditary Indian dai (midwife)[2] or the trained European nurse who enjoyed both power and prestige accruing from racial superiority, was not easy.[3]

It is generally accepted that in colonial India trained nurses slowly and gradually replaced the dai.[4] However, in this chapter, I explore the

---

[2] In the face of lack of records on nursing in pre-colonial India, specifically in the field of gynaecology and obstetrics, it is generally agreed that the female birth attendant was the dai.

[3] Healey (2010).

[4] Singh (2005).

cultural and social constructs of the 'trained' nurse to argue that the she did not, in fact, *could not* replace the dai: the former's functions and locations were of a different nature, as were her aspirations. Instead, we witness the emergence of a labour market within the modern health care services that called for a differentiated workforce, which included the doctor, the trained nurse, and a category called the 'ancillary nursing staff'; the latter included a gamut of retrained dais, untrained/partially trained nurses, nursing aides, and attendants. In this chapter, I trace both the processes of exclusions as well as the institutionalization of hierarchies within the nursing labour market. I argue that the discourse on skills, along with hegemonic markings of gender, class, and caste, had structured health care services in a manner that contested the dualistic framework of cure/care, reason/emotion, doctor/nurse that has been put forward by Western scholarship on sociology of medicine.[5] The hands-on nursing care with its manual-menial component, was perceived as caste-based labour, and allocated to women who took on bedside care. The trained nurse performed myriad tasks that were partly medical, partly administrative, and mostly supervisory, distinctly separate and marked out from the stigmatized hands-on nursing care that hereditary dais/untrained nurses/attendants offered. In this chapter, I trace the origins of the modern nursing profession as it developed from a curious mix of traditions of 'indigenous' women healers and trained professional medical women.

Appropriating the Dai: Imperial Encounters, Global Politics, and Local Contexts

Medicine, as it has been argued, was one of the strategies central to the consolidation of modern power, or rather an era of 'bio-power' in which 'there was an enormous explosion of numerous and diverse techniques for achieving the subjugation of bodies and the control of populations'.[6] Colonial medicine in India was one among the many sites on which the history of domination and hegemony has been written. Indeed, there exists a large body of literature debating whether medicine, along with education, represented as the quintessential 'white man's burden', was a

---

[5] For a detailed discussion, see Smith (1992).
[6] Foucault (1990: 140).

tool of hegemonic control by colonial powers.[7] However, this discourse of colonial medicine treated women's bodies with cold impassivity; it was only from the 1870s that there was a gradual inclusion of reproductive health of Indian women in colonial medical discourses.[8] While there are several arguments explaining this inclusion, most scholars agree that there are three groups of actors whose interventions, not necessarily in agreement, brought the female body into focus: (a) the colonial administration, (b) the British missionary and/or medical women, and (c) the nationalist reformers.

The hegemonic aspirations of a colonial state meant that women had to be included in the ruler-ruled dyad, thus it was imperative that they come under the net of public services.[9] Also, the predominant imagination of the zenana as a feminine, uncolonized space brewing political intrigue meant that it needed to be brought under the colonial gaze, either through education or medicine.[10] Scholars also contend that medicine was linked to the modernizing mission—to 'civilize savages'.[11] However, before women's health became part of the colonial statecraft, it had already emerged as a nodal issue for missionary societies and/or medical women in Britain and America in the nineteenth century. The 'white woman's burden' constituted saving 'our little brown sisters' who were supposedly dying due to lack of medical attention.[12] British women pursuing medical education found in India a prolific ground to sow their ambitions. Unable to break through the strict hierarchies and gender coding of English society, the newly educated woman doctor turned her gaze to the colonies. The figure of the suffering Indian woman legitimized and spurred the migration of women doctors and activists, who claimed that 'respectable' Indian women did not have access to male doctors, due to class and gender norms. Missionary zeal, maternal imperialism, and professional aspirations of newly graduated women doctors, constructed the Indian woman as a figure, who needed to be helped and/or saved by the civilized, emancipated, white, Christian women, whether in the

[7] Arnold (1993); Bala (1991).
[8] Arnold (1993).
[9] Arnold (1993).
[10] Nair (1990).
[11] Bashford (2004).
[12] Lal (1996: 57).

name of Christ or for the sake of science.[13] The 'indigenous' responses to Western medical science and colonial practices were not passive. The social reform movement had already kindled nationalist debates on modernity and tradition, and women's bodies had become the grounds of 'contentious traditions'.[14] Nationalists resisted the attempts of the colonial state, missionaries, and medical women to alter, modify, and radically change childbirth practices in the country. The history of childbirth practices in the nineteenth century meant different things to different people. On the one hand, it was decried as an aping of the West; and on the other hand, it was closely tied to the modernizing project, that is, the reformer's self-modernization through embracing Western medicine, science, and education.[15]

During the nineteenth century, the transference of European biomedical knowledge to the colonies had seen the emergence of large hospitals funded by the colonial administration and philanthropic organizations. While there were some attempts to introduce the colonial nurse within the newly emerging hospital system, this move also led to an increasing endeavour to replace the dai with the former, at least within the field of maternal and child health. In India, traditional medicines like *Ayurvedic* and *Unnani* were already codified as masculine and were often in competition with one another. There was a strict hierarchy between traditional medicine whose practitioners were mostly men and the largely feminine folk medicines.[16] We have no records of women's large-scale participation in medicine; instead, accounts left to us point to dais who were part of folk healing—marginalized and at the bottom of the hierarchy. We do have a handful of names of women in traditional medicine, such as Jadur Maa and Rajur Maa: two women doctors from early-nineteenth-century Calcutta, who were hailed as legendary practitioners. In fact, they were often celebrated for their knowledge and skill as surgeons and posited as symbols of the East's resistance to the West, particularly in the field of science, medicine, and technology. The fact that they were women further served to demonstrate the superiority of Indian medical knowledge-practices, where even women with their ordinary barber's

---

[13] Forbes (1994); Lal (1996); Ramusack (2006).
[14] Mani (1998).
[15] Forbes (1994); Van Hollen (2003).
[16] Bashford (2004).

blade could defeat the Englishman's scalpel, successfully demolishing Europe's claim to superiority based on scientific knowledge.[17]

However, the general rivalry was between colonial and traditional medicines, where women's participation was few and far in between. Folk medicine, on the dint of its marginal status, was generally excluded from such contests. The *Caraka Samhita* and the *Sushruta Samhita* (two foundational texts on Ayurvedic medicine, dated about sixth century BC) mention child birthing processes, but they are mostly related to the preparation of the labour room. Given its polluting status, child birthing was left in the hands of the dai.[18] The dai was consulted by women for various female-related illness, including reproductive diseases, abortion, infertility, childbirth, and post-partum care. Ranajit Guha, in his essay, 'Chandra's Death' (1987), posits the possibility of writing Indian history outside the dominant frameworks of colonialism and elite nationalism. Reading depositions submitted to a court of law by relatives of a woman, who died from a botched attempt of self-induced abortion, along with the depositions of the person who had prescribed the medicine, he gives a sensitive detailing of the social and cultural milieu and the patriarchal norms that govern sexuality, kinship, and family. He succinctly argued that natal care has always been marked out as women's domain in most societies and could be seen as their resistance to the patriarchal order, particularly abortion, which was closely linked to the politics of sexual morality of a given society. Thus, Guha posits 'another solidarity' that functioned among women and served to subvert the authority of the patriarchal kinship structure and the dai was a key player in the way this alternative solidarity expressed itself.[19] This 'solidarity' and 'empathy' amongst women, to protect one of their own from patriarchal disciplining and punishment in a phallogocentric social order, required the dai's knowledge and skills. The dai was not just a female birth attendant but also a part of the social fabric of the village society. Mostly from the barber caste, they were closely linked to the families they served and were indispensable in their everyday lives. Acting as mediators of marriage alliances, they were integral to rituals of birth, marriage, and death.[20]

[17] Ray (2014).
[18] Jeffery (1988).
[19] Guha (1987).
[20] Kelman (1923).

This close-knit women's community, where knowledge and skills were shared and passed on intergenerationally, was distinctively different from the Western medical system. It is in this context that one must place the representations of the trained nurse and the dai, who were locked within hierarchical binaries of West/East, modern/primitive, scientific/superstitious, clean/dirty, and civilized/barbaric. In Europe, modernization and medicalization of childbirth had paved the path for masculinization of the profession. Unlike nursing and medicine, which was mostly women's unpaid labour within the domestic sphere or part of community service, midwifery in Europe was a remunerated service. It was not just a profession but also an *exclusively* female one.[21] Medical men, the state, and the church, came together to professionalize medicine and to create conditions that excluded women healers and midwives, who were branded as witches, persecuted, tortured, and burnt on the stake. On the basis of claims to technical superiority (invention of forceps), as well as discourse that labelled midwives as 'superstitious' and 'primitive', women were eliminated, thus successfully masculinizing a traditionally feminine profession.[22] This masculinization of gynaecology and obstetrics was not just taking over a profession from women; it also meant shunning women's knowledge of their own bodies, pathologizing and medicalizing childbirth, and hegemonizing medical knowledge-practices. In India, the attempt to appropriate childbirth in colonial medicine did not witness a masculinization, but rather a co-option of traditional midwives and their knowledge-practices. Colonial medicine never made a clean sweep; it had to compete with local, 'indigenous' traditions, that were deeply rooted in the social and cultural ethos of the country. This was not just specific to women's health; even Ayurveda and Unnani were able to hold forte against Western allopathic medicine. Supriya Guha argues that the distinction between traditional and Western medicine was never sharp, and both borrowed liberally from each other.[23] A Western medical science that stood in a hierarchical opposition to 'indigenous', 'primitive' medical practices, in complete conflict, was more conceptual rather than a reality. Scholars have highlighted how both Indian medical systems coexisted along with Western

---

[21] Clark (1919).
[22] Ehrenreich and English (2010).
[23] Guha (1996).

medical practices, particularly in childbirth.[24] Colonial records point out that the dai was often consulted regarding childbirth by male medical practitioners trained in Western medicine. One of the reports stated that the presiding gynaecologist of Calcutta Medical Hospital would often call in a dai to help him in the labour room.[25] In fact, the head dai at the Imambara hospital in the district of Hooghly in Bengal was a dai named Champa, who was known for her expertise in both natural and difficult childbirth.[26] Thus, the epistemological struggle between feminized, 'indigenous' folk healing and masculine, colonial, techno-curative methods saw not an eradication but an appropriation of the former into the latter. In fact, it seemed that the indigenous population had more faith in their traditional medicine and preferred it to Western medical knowledge-practices.[27] Emma Wilson, a nurse with the Lady Minto's Association, records in her memoir that despite being called to look up patients, both the doctor and nurse were kept under strict surveillance, and every drug administered was examined by the ladies of the house. *Vaid*s and *hakim*s were simultaneously consulted and often given preference over European medical knowledge-practices.[28] All over the country, middle-class Indian women preferred the dai to the re-trained midwife, trained nurse, or even a lady doctor. Observers noted that 'there are still to be found in India, women [...] who maintain that the introduction of European ideas with regard to the care of mothers and infants are unnecessary and superfluous.'[29] Reports of families calling the dai as well as the trained nurse, during childbirth, point to how the Indian populace did not view the two medical systems as disparate, but part of a continuum, to be accessed according to convenience and suitability.[30] Pitted against the dai, both the colonial female doctor and the nurse were unable to hold their ground, as the former not only offered medical aid during childbirth but stayed with the mother for post-partum care; a service not offered by the doctor or the nurse. In fact, households

[24] Arnold (1993).
[25] West Bengal State Archives (henceforth WBSA) (1922c).
[26] Guha (1996).
[27] Rao (1939).
[28] Wilson (1974).
[29] Kelman (1923).
[30] Wilson (1974).

engaged dais to come and reside with the mother and infant for a certain period of time while some families even had the service of family dais. The relationship between the mother and the dai did not end with childbirth.[31] Apart from the local populace's resistance, the endeavour to eradicate the dai was also an expensive affair, as it would necessitate training and employing more doctors and nurses. Wilson further notes in her memoir that trained nurses from Britain were called in on house cases mostly by British residents, particularly for childbirth.[32] Indian families were never really the client-patron of the newly trained nurse.

Due to the paucity of doctors, it was mostly the nurse who attended to childbirth, which meant that she was no longer the doctor's aide but a medical actor—her functions increased from just bedside care to diagnosis, child delivery, consultant follow up/home visits, and so on. Even among European families, during childbirth, the nurse substituted for the colonial doctor. Wilson writes, 'Sometimes a doctor would be called in an emergency. Often no doctor was available and a worried nurse supported by the husband shared responsibility.'[33] This also meant that she came face to face with the traditional dai or the Indian ayah, who was employed for post-partum care. Wilson records this phenomenon, where the nurse, in the absence of the doctor, performed medical tasks but was reluctant to stay back to offer care. Medical science was integral and critical to the official perceptions of a statecraft that reflected the 'white man's burden', yet the trained nurse received no special attention in colonial medical discourses; neglected, marginalized, and substituted, she struggled to make a niche for herself in the vast colony. Perceiving her role as closer to medical duties rather than the affective and emotional labour of nursing the mother and child, Wilson wrote, 'After the nurse leaves, ayahs take over—ayahs are "coolie class women".'[34] Working as an ayah or a wet nurse to the Britishers was considered polluting work, as the foreigners were considered outcaste—mleccha. It was only the lowest castes, such as women from the sweeper castes, who were willing to work in British residences.[35]

---

[31] Guha (1996).
[32] Wilson (1974).
[33] Wilson (1974: 24).
[34] Wilson (1974: 24).
[35] Sen (2009).

The rituals of childbirth in India demanded certain commitments from the dai that were not part of Western medical knowledge-practices, such as burying the placenta, washing clothes, and extended post-partum care. As trained nurses refused to perform such tasks, the dai had to be domesticated, appropriated, re-trained, and brought under the colonial fold but as a menial and inferior worker. While the dai's knowledge-practices was surreptitiously incorporated within Western medical systems, the figure of the dai was relegated to the margins. She was the 'other' who gave coherence and meaning to caste- and gender-based division of labour within health care services. A domesticated 'other'—un/ semi-skilled, partially/retrained, ill-paid, dispensable worker—who performed all the menial, servile, and affective labour that a trained nurse refused. Thus, newer hierarchies were created, which while retaining the feminine nature of midwifery, produced a differentiated workforce. Given the absence of doctors and the reluctance of nurses, post-partum care was offered by women unrecognized by the colonial medical institutions. The question remains whether the attack on the dai was a colonial strategy to delegitimize indigenous medical knowledge-practices; or was her inclusion within the colonial medical apparatus, as a domesticated but inferior 'other', a strategy of negotiating gender- and caste-based division of labour that came in the way of the expansion of colonial medicine?

Supriya Guha has argued that even midwifery, already a caste-based occupation, was further divided along sub-castes, corresponding to birth-based purity, and perceived levels of skills, and rewards and payments were meted out accordingly.[36] Thus, even within a segmented market of gynecology and obstetrics, there was considerable fragmentation. However, increasing employment of the dai in lying-in hospitals, to act as nurses, meant a homogenization of the category. The differences within the occupation were collapsed. All dais were projected as unskilled, low-caste women who performed affective labour during childbirth, a caste-based labour that professional nurses refused to perform. Instead of invisibilizing and/or eradicating her, the Western colonial medical apparatus brought her within its fold as the domesticated 'other', institutionalized as an inferior worker—a paramedical nursing staff. In fact, there started to emerge categories of nursing staff that blurred the

[36] Guha (1996).

boundaries between the dai and the nurse. The Canning Nursing Institute in Kolkata, Bengal, meant for training and providing nurses to hospitals and private homes (that could afford to pay the salary and give suitable accommodation), sent re-trained dais instead.[37] A category called the nurse-dai came up, which was that of the re-trained dai working in hospitals.[38] This phenomenon was prevalent in Bengal, where even medical practitioners employed re-trained dais as general nurses.[39] It was argued that a dearth of trained nurses led to the employment of the dai, especially for maternity cases, and they would be replaced as soon as qualified nurses were available.[40] The trained nurse could never take over all nursing duties; it was neither possible nor desirable. The lines between the nurse, the dai, and the ayah were constantly blurred and all three were employed in hospitals and residences in different capacities. This was so widely practiced that at the time of Independence, trained dais were employed as ancillary nursing staff, while some even carried out duties that could be defined as nursing.[41] However, this blurring of the categories of nurse and the dai did not go down well with medico-missionaries, health administrators, and nursing leaders. If the colonial nurse continued to be identified with the indigenous dai, it would mean that nursing would be perceived as a caste-based occupation—a stigma that would prevent 'respectable' women from joining the profession. Secondly, it would mean a defeat for the colonial medical apparatus, as epistemologically, gynaecology and obstetrics would continue to be identified with indigenous medical knowledge-practices. Thirdly, if nurses could not represent Christian values that medico-missionaries trained them in, it would defeat the purpose of the 'white woman's burden'. The nursing profession found itself in a double bind: on the one hand, the trained nurse refused to perform affective, intimate, and menial labour tied to caste identities, and on the other hand, the continuing presence of the dai (even if retrained) in nursing services meant a continuing identification of nursing with hereditary midwifery. Either way, the

---

[37]　WBSA (1913).
[38]　WBSA (1922c).
[39]　The Countess of Dufferin's Fund (1935).
[40]　The Countess of Dufferin's Fund (1936).
[41]　Jeffery (1988).

nursing profession found it impossible to work its way out of the markers of caste, class, and gender that constituted women in medicines. The imperative then was to mark the dai's body clearly as a necessary but separate category of worker, the inferior but domesticated 'other'.

Professional Projects: Exclusions, Contradictions, and Struggles in Nursing

Anne Witz, in her excellent study on professions, argues that labour market strategies are deployed to maintain and reinforce occupational monopoly over skills, competence, and training. Referring to the medical profession, she argues that occupational closure, that was deeply gendered, created a class of women who were ineligible, thus securing for men privileged access to rewards and opportunities in the labour market.[42] However, in the case of nursing, historically a female-intensive profession, the call for professionalization was not an attempt to change the gender composition of the occupation, as men were not interested in the ill-paid, feminine, menial, and affective labour that constituted nursing care. Rather it was a labour market strategy to eliminate working-class women from the profession. Thus, the call for professionalization was what Witz refers to as 'inclusionary usurpation', that is, certain women seeking to be included within the medical profession, by meeting all the criteria that has been set up to exclude them.[43] In the context of nursing, middle-class nurses set up criteria that would necessarily exclude the working-class woman, and thus, occupational closure would allow the nursing profession to be elevated to a prestigious and respectable profession, if not at par, at least a close second to doctoring.

The push for professionalization in colonial India had a similar logic; nursing had to be transformed from a caste-based feminine occupation to a prestigious medical service performed by educated, skilled bourgeois women. Historically, the first records of nursing training in India, albeit informal and sporadic, can be traced to the Anglo-American medical missionaries stationed in India. The missionaries recruited nurses

---

[42] Witz (1990).
[43] Witz (1990).

from their traditional constituency of Anglo-Indians, and later Indian Christian converts.[44] The zenana was their main target as Christian evangelism in India was primarily aimed at conversion of upper-caste, middle-class *purdanashin* (women who maintain seclusion) women, and medical workers, specifically nurses, were able to reach them faster than lady doctors. Accounts left by missionary-medical practitioners point to the twin task of healing the body as well as the soul, medical and affective labour that was allocated to nurses, rather than women doctors, who were trained as both evangelists and as medical aides.[45] Apart from women missionaries migrating from Anglo-American countries, Indian women were also recruited and trained in nursing, so that they could be bearers of both medical and spiritual healing.[46] Women missionaries outnumbered their male counterparts and in the nineteenth and early twentieth century, India drew more women medical missionaries than China or Africa.[47]

Apart from medico-missionaries, the British Army stationed in India demanded professional nurses, and the first contingent of British nurses arrived in 1879 to staff the military hospitals.[48] Around this time, nurses were actually non-existent; it was male attendants who nursed the sick.[49] Facing hostility from medical men in the army, newly recruited nurses struggled to establish their presence.[50] The establishment of 'The National Association for Supplying Female Medical Aid to Women in India', popularly known as the Lady Dufferin Fund (1885), was the first concrete step towards encouraging 'women in medicine'. The fund's stated objectives were to provide medical tuition (training and teaching) to women doctors, hospital assistants, nurses, and midwives and provide medical relief through construction of dispensaries, hospitals, female wards, and appoint trained female medical personnel. The popular story about the inception of the fund reflects the need of the colonial power to

[44]   Balfour and Young (1929); Jeffery (1988); Wilkinson (1958).
[45]   Bleakley (1940).
[46]   Foster (1911).
[47]   Arles (2008).
[48]   Stewart and Austin (1962).
[49]   Wilkinson (1958).
[50]   Wilkinson (1958).

establish itself as a maternal state concerned with the welfare of its Indian subjects, specifically women.[51]

Within the first three years of its foundation, the fund was associated with twelve female hospitals and fifteen dispensaries;[52] however, by 1905, the fund had only forty-two lady doctors of the first grade (those who are qualified to practice in England), eighty-seven assistant-surgeons or practitioners of the second grade (those who have Indian qualifications), and 274 hospital assistants or practitioners of the third grade. At that time, ninety-nine women were undergoing training as assistant-surgeons, 115 as hospital assistants, and 323 as nurses, retrained dais, and compounders.[53] Between the years 1921 and 1926, the number of nurses enrolled for training had risen dismally from 178 to 208.[54] Very few Indian women wanted to train in nursing. Scholars have argued that nursing was never considered an important and integral part of health services. Considered as unskilled/menial labour, nursing was not given adequate attention, in terms of allocation of funds and infrastructural investments.[55] This, coupled with social perceptions of nursing as caste-based labour, ensured that it was not an immediate choice of profession for the emerging ranks of respectable women seeking employment.[56] It continued as a sector that offered opportunities for distressed women who were socially shunned and lived in the margins of society.

Take for instance, Rokeya Sakhawat Hossain's (1880–1932) famous short story, 'Nurse Nelli', which was first published in *Sawgat* magazine (1919), and later reprinted in *Motichur* (1922). In making an argument for the importance of education for women, failing which they would

[51] The story follows that Elizabeth Bielby, a medical missionary, took care of the Maharani of Pune, who after recovering wanted that the conditions and sufferings of Indian women be known to Queen Victoria and requested Miss Bielby to personally meet the Queen and pass on the message. On her return, Bielby had an audience with the Queen, who reportedly said that, 'We had no idea it was as bad as this. Something must be done for the poor creatures. We wish it generally be known that we sympathize with every effort made to relieve the sufferings of the women of India'. Balfour and Young (1929: 20–1).

[52] The Countess of Dufferin's Fund (1906).

[53] Tooley (1906).

[54] Balfour and Young (1929).

[55] Healey (2010).

[56] Nair and Healey (2006).

fall prey to Christian evangelism, Rokeya writes of Nayeema, a middle-class Muslim woman. In her quest for education, Nayeema abandons Islam, and converts to Christianity, and subsequently labours as a nurse in one of the missionary hospitals. Observing Nayeema (now called Nelli) in her daily menial chores and learning of her background, Rokeya expresses her horror, 'Christian Nelli ... Methrani Nelli ... the same hands that touches the bucket of despicable blood and fluids touches the holy Quran'.[57] The perception that trained nurses would never do the same job as the lower-caste woman led Rokeya to wonder whether Nelli was a sweeper or a methrani (caste-name) but was called a 'nurse' by the sister-in-charge.[58] The need to separate the trained nurse from the methrani/sweeper meant a closing of ranks; only women with training, education, and social and cultural capital, could find their way into the nursing profession. The social identity of the nurse was crucial to her acceptance in health services. European nurses were hard to find and expensive to bring over and there were even reports that some of them were refusing to offer bedside care. Facing rigid caste-based division of labour prevalent in India, European nurses responded by refusing tasks that would identify them with the 'char woman' or the 'pankha-coolie' woman.[59] Florence Nightingale was of the opinion that in India, nursing labour must be split into two distinct parts: supervisory and medical work done by trained European nurses and bedside care by 'casteless coolie women'. She writes, 'Because if the women (trained European nurse) would do the bedside care, they will be looked down upon. The Mehter-sweeper-casteless is the bedside nurse'.[60]

Despite having men and women of lower-caste communities performing the undesirable and polluting labour that constituted nursing care, trained nurses could not escape the stigma associated with menial labour. In India, the trained nurse and the traditional dai were dangerously close to each other. The name of the nurse was tied intimately to that of a dai. The logic was circular: the stigma associated with nursing ensured that only marginalized women entered its ranks as a distress

[57]   Translation mine. Nahar (2001: 182).

[58]   Nahar (2001: 182).

[59]   The Association of Nursing Superintendents in India (1905: 16–17).

[60]   Notes from interviews with Medical Doctors, ADD, Mss 45675, f108. 1867 in Vallee (2006: 782).

sale of labour; the continuing presence of 'disrespectable' women in the profession signified the work as stigmatized labour and contributed to its marginalization. Thus, it remained locked as cheap and substitutable labour not requiring professionalization that would ensure better working conditions and pay. This effectively prevented respectable women from entering in its ranks.

The anxieties faced by nursing leaders in the colonies were nothing new; even in England, nurses were suspect. Professional nurses usually came from the lowest rungs of society and were often paid lesser than a 'competent servant'.[61] Highly unorganized, nursing was seen as a dispensable part of the healing process, with nurses having no major responsibilities. They were not offered proper accommodation or decent and liveable wages and were dismissed at a moment's notice. As historians argue, nurses were worse off than menial cleaners in hospitals and mostly came from the rank of 'prostitutes'.[62] Facing such stigma and disrepute, nurses were hardly in any position to organize and establish themselves in the colonies as skilled, respectable professionals. The struggle of nurses in colonial India was an extension of their struggle in the metropole. The newly migrated English nurse wanted to rehaul the medical system in the colonies whereby they could carve out medical-supervisory-administrative roles for themselves, second to doctors, while the rank and file were to be filled by Indian nurses with training in Western medicine. And the position of the 'charring' woman was offered to the partially trained/untrained dai and a host of women with different levels of skills, who were clearly marked out as the abject but necessary other. Thus, the process of professionalization followed in the Anglo-American world to establish monopoly over nursing skill and competence was replicated in colonial India. The need for inducting Indian women into nursing reached the legislative council, where the question was raised more than once. It was stated that if Indian women would take nursing training, it would secure greater economy in hospital management, as they would be a cheaper alternative to European nurses and could fill up the middle ranks.[63] The need to eliminate the lower-caste woman and the outcaste Eurasian woman from medical

---

[61] Clark (1919).
[62] Brian (1961).
[63] WBSA (1922b).

services was essential if nursing was to attract high-caste women, whose inclusion would change social perceptions of the profession. A resolution was called for in the conference of the Association of the Nursing Superintendents in 1905, that 'only those women should come into nursing, who will adorn the profession and not bring it disrepute'.[64]

Consequently, there were attempts to regulate the profession, including governing and setting up criteria for entry, a code of ethics, standardized training and examinations, and so on. Training and registration was one of the ways of creating a differentiated workforce, where the dai, the untrained nurse, and the ayah would continue to work as nursing aides taking care of the polluting tasks that 'respectable' women refused. Either because of the paucity of trained nurses or the expenses involved in hiring them, the untrained nurse or the ayah has always been an easy substitute. However, the call for registration was to make nursing labour scarce so that the status and pay of the trained nurse would get enhanced, as well as clearly mark out the trained nurse from the untrained menial. By 1920, a proposal was passed which standardized training and examination of nurses and midwives in the province of Bengal as well as maintained registration so that the medical faculty could regulate, restrict, and supervise their practice.[65] Within two years, the State Medical Faculty of Bengal inaugurated a standardized course of training and qualifying examination with both a senior and a junior certificate of nursing.[66]

Systematic, organized education and training for nurses meant that the tasks of a nurse were clearly laid out; unlike the dai, nurses were not expected to offer pre- and post-partum care and/or affective labour for the new mother. All bodily service was left to the unnamed and unrecognized nursing aides. It was hoped that this refashioning of what constituted nursing labour would give it the status of a profession. In Anglo-American countries, the professionalization project was meant to redefine nursing and demolish the 'old' (working-class, money-grabbing, dirty) for the 'new' (middle-class, professional, pure, clean) nurse.[67] The process of reforming nursing in the West was replicated

---

[64] The Association of Nursing Superintendents in India (1905: 17).
[65] WBSA (1922a).
[66] WBSA (1922b).
[67] Fitzgerald (2006).

in colonial India, however, here the 'old' nurse was the dai. The practices of childbirth—which included the long residency of the dai with the family, as the primary caregiver, staying with the expecting mother before and post birth, giving bodily service, cleaning the room, burying the placenta—was now dealt with a differentiated workforce. The trained and therefore superior category of nurse assisted in childbirth and the re-trained/partially trained dai or the lower-caste sweeper woman gave post-partum care. It was hoped that this reformulation of nursing would bring in women from bourgeois families to enter medical work as nurses.

Disciplining the 'Native' Nurse: Essentialism, Identities, and Hegemonic Ideals

> Instead of respectable middle-class women, the nursing profession is predominantly composed of lowly, out-caste, immoral and disrespectable women. What kind of nursing care can be expected from these women?
> —Amiya Jibon Mukhopadhyay[68]

Around the turn of the twentieth century, the nationalist discourse had as one of its focal points the body of the bhadramahila as representative of an incipient national community. Hegemonic femininity demanded that women as wives/mothers perform emotive labour and inhabit affective spaces that included a reworking of the ideologies of the bourgeois family: serving the family/nation became intrinsic to the construction of gendered relations that set apart and established the superiority of the bhadramahila, as against the Western woman or the lower-caste and/or working-class Indian woman. The emergence of nationalist discourses, along with the social reform movement, which operated on the cusp of colonial humiliation and a rising Hindu militant politics, tried to negotiate the challenges posed by a 'rational', 'scientific' modernism (as propagated by colonial powers) as well as defend and/or rework institutions, and practices of traditional societies, steeped in social and religious mores. Sumit Sarkar argues that resistance to the racist and arrogant claims to modernism of the colonial powers often saw a reworking of traditional

---

[68] Mukhopadhyay (1943: 42).

religious and social practices that were deeply gendered. Saints, such as Ramakrishna Paramahansa (1836–1886), who enjoyed great influence over the middle class, saw the root of evil in lazy and corrupt bourgeois wives, whose greed for gold and luxury items pushed their husbands in to the bondages of clerical office jobs (*chakri*) in the colonial admin-istration: the shamelessness of women and the loss of male authority within households were symptomatic of *kaliyug*.[69] Ramakrishna did not care much for social reform, anti-colonial struggles, the upliftment of women, the poor, outcastes, and the downtrodden; his contribution lay in making *bhakti* (devotion) synonymous with worship. The model was the mother goddess and her childlike devotee who abandons all rationality in his unquestioning surrender. However, his disciple, Swami Vivekananda/Narendranath Datta (1863–1902), broke faith with his master's teachings by dislodging Bhakti as central to the Hindu man's quest to *Vedantic jnana* (knowledge), and instead made *karma* (redefined now as social service rather than ritual) as the ultimate act of worship.[70] Therefore, in Bankim Chandra Chattopadhyay's *Anandamath* (1882), we find militant young men in service of the mother/nation, symbolic of a militant revivalist Hinduism,[71] while Vivekananda along with his band of young educated *sanyasis* went out to serve the low-caste and the downtrodden and often nursed victims of plague, as a way of serving the nation.[72]

In the works of Vivekananda and his disciple Sister Nivedita (1867–1911), we witness a recodification of *desh bhakti* (devotion to the nation)/*desh seba* (service to the nation), as a breaking away from religious and personal salvation, to a notion of care and service for the welfare of the community/nation. This was a break from traditional Hinduism, where karma was no longer predestined caste-based rituals and obligations but civic and social responsibilities. Vivekananda was scathing in his criticism of prevalent Hinduism and its degradation of women by depriving them of education; he believed that Indian women could be restored to their former glory by exercising spirituality, sacrifice,

---

[69] Sumit Sarkar (1992) describes Kaliyug as 'the last and worst of the four-fold succession of eras in the traditional Hindu conception of cyclical time'.

[70] Sarkar (1992: 1543–66).

[71] Sarkar (2001).

[72] Swami Vivekananda (1971).

and self-control and pledging their lives to seva-dhamma.[73] It was this notion of seba as dhamma that Nivedita took as a corner stone in constructing the ideal Hindu woman, in the ideal Hindu nation, set apart from her emancipated Western counterpart. She writes, 'The purifying of the heart connoted the burning out of selfishness. Worship is the antithesis of use. But service or giving is also its anti-thesis.'[74] Thus for Nivedita, seba was infused with bhakti; they were not distinctly different, but the former was a recodification of the latter that looked at individual salvation in renunciation and worship of the divine. Now worship meant service—to the nation, to the race and in serving lay not just personal *mukti* (salvation) but the salvation of the land.

Sister Nivedita argued that the West, with its focus on individualism and rationality, could never comprehend, let alone compete, with Indians, who were culturally different. In this context, sexual difference played a defining role, where mukti and sattitva (less chastity and more purity) lay in service and welfare of others. Nivedita wrote, describing the Hindu woman, 'She is more deeply self-effacing and more effectively altruistic than any Western. The duty of tending the sick is so much a matter of course to her that she does not dream of it as a special function.'[75] The marking of Indian civilization as equal but culturally different drew from gendered nationalist discourses surrounding the spirituality of Oriental homes and their women. The Hindu woman remained the mother, but a mother not to be worshiped as divine, and in later appropriations, as the motherland, but an active agent who would serve, nurture, and care for the sick, the poor, and the outcaste. This motherhood was not bound and limited by the family and the kin, but in service to the nation and the race. Nivedita thus urged, 'Let us be indiscriminating in our services. Such is the Indian woman's conception of a perfect life.'[76] The religion of the Hindu woman remained no more worship and submission but a desire to serve, investing her with civic, social, and political agency.

[73] Swami Vivekananda (1971). Dhamma cannot be easily translated but can mean duties, conduct, and/or virtue. Thus I understand Vivekananda's *seva-dhamma* as service/charity as a way of living or conducting oneself.

[74] Sister Nivedita (1967: 51).

[75] Sister Nivedita (1967: 68–9).

[76] Sister Nivedita (1967: 458).

Women's education, for Nivedita, was a training of this affective temperament that they were naturally endowed with, to be modified, disciplined, and channelized for the welfare of the nation and the race. Drawing from racialized, essentialist assumptions about the Hindu woman, she believed that with training, education, and leadership, women will be able to grasp the urgency and relevance of nationalism, thus wholeheartedly participating in the nation-making project. Thus, seba was pivotal to the construction of the 'new woman', which held on to the older Brahminical values of chastity, self-sacrifice, and devotion while negotiating the Victorian ideal of the 'enlightened companion'. Education of women was central to the disciplining of the affective qualities of the Hindu woman. However, this practice was fraught with tension, as conservatives needed the reassurance of women upholding traditional, cultural practices that preserved the family and did not question existing gender relations. With education, women's aspirations to enter professional ranks started gaining grounds; employment, however, proved to cause more anxiety than education. In a sex-segregated society, it was only logical that more and more women become teachers, doctors, and nurses (as a response to more and more women entering schools and accessing colonial medicine), yet women who sought white-collared employment faced extreme hostility. The bhadralok encouraged women to educate themselves to be better mothers/wives and not workers.[77] Thus, investing education and employment with a good dose of seba meant women would now perceive and harness their 'empowerment' in service of the home/community/nation.

Women entering medical services in the nineteenth century had to negotiate rough terrains, and for those who entered mostly stigmatized occupations such as nursing, it was even harder. The necessity of establishing nursing as a `noble' profession, and re-signifying nursing labour as respectable work, implied that nursing care had to invested with the affective charge of seba, which in turn was tied down to ideologies of home/community/nation. The debates around nursing were restricted and had a limited audience—nurses and reformers, medical bureaucracy, and missionary men and women. However, the little literature that is available points to the disciplining of the body of the nurse and her temperament that would be judged by reason, affective appropriateness, and

[77] Bhattacharya (2002).

morality. One could argue in the context of nursing that the disciplining of the native nurse never took on the urgency of a panoptic imperial state but were sporadic efforts that mostly failed. The ideological charge of converting nursing from a caste-based occupation to a spiritual exercise of healing humanity was bound up by contradictions inherent within the profession.

The various discourses surrounding nursing care foregrounded the affective and spiritual charge that nursing labour embodied; it was not to be a professional service but a spiritual journey that was marked and constituted by the normative ideals of class, caste, gender, and sexualities. The terrain of seba was deeply contested—domesticity, hygiene, and disciplining of women's affective labour was the focal point of various contradictory and contesting discourses that drew connections between the family, community, and the nation. Professional nursing care was never really part of this discourse: nursing was and continued to be a marginalized, menial job performed by outcaste women. Nursing occupied the luminal space between cleanliness/dirt, order/chaos, health/sickness, metropole/colony, and policed the threshold of the empire and its subjects. The Western trained nurse was the agent of purification and embodied the values of imperial femininity. Thus, she had to uphold high moral values, chastity, and purity and maintain strict discipline and display total obedience to the hierarchies and norms of the colonial medical apparatus. Disciplined, coerced, and compelled into docile obedient bodies, celebrated as ideal subjects of feminine care, compassion, and virtue, nurses found themselves in a profession with limited growth, no respect, overburdened, and ill paid.[78] Given that professional nursing was a caste-based labour, who was the nineteenth-century nurse? The European nurse, the missionary nurse, the locally trained 'native' nurse (low-caste/Christian convert), the retrained/partially trained dai, the untrained sweeper/methrani/coolie woman, and so on were mostly mleccha, low-caste, and women failed by patriarchal ideologies, residing in the margins of society. The discourses on nationalism and hegemonic femininity were not concerned with such bodies; it was the bhadramahila who was to be disciplined into the ideal Hindu woman. Women were marginalized from the formal labour market and were concentrated in the lowest end of the informal economy.

[78] Prasad (2015).

At the turn of the twentieth century, the increasing hiring of 'servants' as a marker of status by middle-class Bengali families coincided with the marginalization of women from traditional caste-based occupations,[79] as well as distress migration related to partition, deindustrialization, and the agrarian crisis.[80] Given the rapidly changing political economy, the feminized nursing profession offered employment to women both from its traditional constituency as well as to those who desperately needed an independent income.[81] Increasingly, the 'other' was not restricted to the outcaste and working-class woman, but all those who took to paid work. The political economy, along with failing patriarchal ideologies, meant that more and more women were seeking employment, thus blurring the boundaries between the low-caste public women and the high-born but destitute woman.[82] Women who took to public nursing were not spared. Amongst the entire feminized service sector, nursing was a step up from domestic work but below teaching, in terms of status and respect. If women of respectable classes were compelled to take up nursing, they were also given the responsibility to protect, uphold, and preserve the honour of their class.[83]

Amiya Jibon Mukhopadhyay's *Nurse o Nursing* (1943) cites examples of how middle-class women entering the profession had to fight the stigma associated with public labour—servile, menial, and sexual. Mukhopadhyay believed that nursing had to be reformed and nursing labour had to be (re)codified to make it an acceptable and suitable profession for women of respectable classes, who were naturally best suited to the task of care and nurture. Holding up the missionary nurse as an example, he believed that nursing could *never* be an occupation, but an act of seba anchored in devotion towards humanity. He writes, 'European women see it as a religion—as spirituality and Bengali women see it as livelihood. They pray before they go to terminally ill patients, but Bengali nurses, they curse when they see such patients.... If Bengali women want to be respected as nurses, they have to internalize it as a spiritual act; as a religion ... for them it is only a

---

[79] Banerjee (1989); Banerjee (2004).

[80] Chakravarty and Chakravarty (2016).

[81] Ray (forthcoming-a).

[82] Sangari (1993).

[83] Ray (forthcoming-a).

livelihood and that too a dishonourable one.'[84] The spiritual charge of nursing implied that women from respectable backgrounds should become nurses as a service to the nation/humanity and not as a means of livelihood. He further writes, 'Good women must come to nursing not for the sake of the medical system but for the sake of humanity, for the quality of care that is being offered.'[85] Clearly, there were two separate but interlinked trends that were operative: first, as more and more women started entering the profession, the need to establish nursing labour as both skilled as well as a spiritual task that only virtuous woman could perform was essential to drain it of its menial and servile component. Secondly, given that the working bhadramahila blurred the lines between the disrespectable *bazaar* woman and the virtuous house-wife, the *sebika* (care-giver) had to be disciplined to discipline herself. Outside the familial gaze, she would have to police herself and locate her employment and its monetary rewards (though negligible) within the matrix of seba and dhamma.

Mukhopadhyay was clear that the quality of care offered depended on the character of the women; women from disrespectable back-grounds could never care in the manner that educated, refined, sophisticated women could. He put the onus of the dismal state of the profession on the nurses themselves, insisting that Indian nurses were opportunists, who had come to the profession out of greed, and supplemented their earnings by seducing respectable men and engag-ing in 'prostitution'. He describes the nurse's hostels as 'dens of vice' and 'pros quarters'.[86] As I have argued elsewhere, these hostels and boarding houses offered accommodation to working women, who migrated in search of work from the districts to the city. The relative freedom from male control that these hostels offered is debatable, but what is remark-able is the sexual paranoia associated with these women-only spaces.[87] The charge of prostitution is not new; in fact, women labouring in industries, plantations, mills, and mines too faced similar allegations. Historians have argued that apart from sexual codes that had class and caste embedded in them, which automatically signified women in the

84 Mukhopadhyay (1943: 11–15).
85 Mukhopadhyay (1943: 25).
86 Mukhopadhyay (1943: 48–9).
87 Ray (forthcoming-a).

public domain as available, working-class women were crowded in badly paid, low-end, menial jobs. Apart from gender segregation, the gender wage gap meant that more and more women had to resort to sex-work to supplement their meagre earnings.[88] It would not be surprising if nurses, particularly at the lower end of the hierarchy, did take to sex-work to offset their negligible earnings in hospitals and residences.

Mukhopadhyay, along with other reformers in the medical profession, did believe that Indian women would make good nurses, if they were trained, both in skill as well as in their capacities as sebikas. Instead of focusing on low wages and exploitative working conditions, the emphasis was to draw women from middle-class communities who would take to nursing as an extension of social or religious services. The argument was that Indian women were naturally disposed to caring and nurturing but lacked a worldview that encompassed serving humanity at large. This lack of evangelist zeal, celebrated in missionary nurses, was the reason why Indian nurses could never become the paragon of compassion, care, and virtue. She was a caregiver/nurturer but essentially a domestic woman who could only excel in her familial role. Due to her inherent lack of exposure, sophistication, and endowed with a narrow world view, she was unable to provide and bestow the same care and affection outside the family. In conferences, where the dearth of good Indian nurses was discussed, it was reported that, 'The average Hindu woman will make a capable nurse, deft with fingers, clever and full of resources ... we see Hindu mothers and wives as most devoted and self-sacrificing nurses at sick bed of their parents, husbands and children: but ask them to bestow a little of this wealth of affection on outsiders and they will generally be unresponsive.'[89] Brought outside the familial setting, she did not have the capability to be a good worker: 'to be reliable and punctual in every matter comes not naturally to them; everything is done in a casual way'.[90] Thus existing stereotypes of the Hindu woman as a nurturer par excellence, a superior homemaker, was punched with practices of Western capitalist disciplining that required a trained, efficient, and productive body suited to the rhythms of professional life. The bhadramahila's potential outside

[88] Chandavarkar (1994).
[89] The Association of Nursing Superintendents in India (1908).
[90] The Association of Nursing Superintendents in India (1908).

the familial setting needed to be examined and her services had to be brought outside the domestic sphere into the colonial market, where she would then excel, because of her inherent caring nature , subsequently honed by superior European training. It was argued that 'the Hindu woman can learn much from her European sisters ... patient training at home and at school, and thorough instructions in private classes, above all by good and practical example, the Hindu woman will find one of her chief vocations in the sick room, in the nursery, orphanage or other charitable institutions'.[91] This, however, also had other implications: the discourse on femininity and domesticity which were actively deployed to encourage Indian women to become nurses, resulted in nursing increasingly getting constituted as a feminine, domestic labour, which in the subsequent years came in the way of professionalization.

Upper-caste, middle-class Indian women did not take to nursing services despite it being given the contours of a profession. Apart from caste, class, and sexual connotations that constituted nursing as a menial and immoral profession, the prospects of an Indian nurse in colonial India were not promising. Colonial administrators and European nursing leaders either laid the blame on the deeply feudal and caste-stratified nature of Indian society, which was not accustomed to seeing the bhadramahila in paid employment, or on the primitive, child-like nature of Indian women who were not capable of entering a modern profession. It was argued that 'things need to be repeated over and over again, even to senior girls and to graduates. They are like children and need to be guided'.[92] Mukhopadhyay, in his book, lists the capabilities of a European nurse that made her a superior worker, a caregiver par excellence: modest, soft-spoken, enthusiastic, skilled, efficient, innovative, affectionate, and intelligent. There was a clear distinction between the 'good' nurse and the 'bad', along racial lines. The Bengali nurses, who lagged far behind, were gossip-mongers, quarrelsome, arrogant, and neglected their patients; they worked less and talked more. He went on to argue that if Bengali nurses want to progress in their careers, they must internalize nursing labour as a spiritual task. Similar to European nurses, they must take the initiative of continuously educating themselves, learning

---

[91] The Association of Nursing Superintendents in India (1908).
[92] Noordyk (1921).

newer skills, and take pride in their work. Race explained the disparities in nursing care. It was only the 'pure blood' nurse who could give high-quality care: he was careful in making distinctions between the *phiringi* nurse (Anglo-Indian), and the pure-blooded *memsahib*. The former was the working-class, Euro-Asian woman, who was licentious (flirted with the doctors both during and/or off-duty hours), greedy (took money from relatives of patients), careless (neglected patients), and were foul-mouthed. The Bengali nurse must distance herself from the phiringi and model herself on the memsahib.

Thus, we see essays on nurses and nursing published in the *Nursing Journal of India* from the 1950s that try to institute the ideal nurse. For example, an essay argued that: 'A nurse is not an ordinary person, that should be made very clear to every nurse at the very outset of the nursing profession ... she has to be upright throughout her life....'. Quoting a section of the Nightingale pledge that every nurse takes when graduating, the essay emphasized on the gendered norms meant to govern the life of women offering nursing care: 'How can a nurse say then that her private life has nothing to do with her profession? Has she forgotten her graduation pledge? Doesn't her conscience prick her when she makes such a statement?'[93] The insistence was that not just skill, education, and possession of scientific knowledge, but a carefully crafted gendered being legitimized by class, caste, and racial norms made an ideal nurse.

Despite all such attempts, nursing continued to remain a stigmatized caste-based occupation that drew women who either engaged in distress sale of labour or continued to remain in their traditional occupations as healers and midwives. Occupational closure, via registration, could not eliminate the untrained/partially trained nurse, ayah, or the dai, but it did succeed in devaluing her labour. These women continued to exist in the profession as ancillary nurses, often receiving a few *annas* in return for their services.[94] Middle-class women did not perceive public nursing as seba but rather as a stigmatized and ill-paid occupation. The failure of the medical apparatus to harness women's affective labour without adequate remuneration meant that only certain 'undesirable' women took to the profession. It was

---

[93] Zierbert (1957: 1017–19).

[94] The Association of Nursing Superintendents in India (1905: 21).

slowly understood that, in India, the existing caste-based division of labour prevented respectable women from touching the body and its daily detritus, and given the status of service as a feminine profession, there were no attempts to improve its conditions. Modern nursing, instead of challenging these social norms, adapted itself to existing inequalities. Florence Nightingale observed that in India nursing was facing similar difficulties as in the West, but to a greater degree.[95] In a general environment, where nursing was observed to be the work of a 'servant', and 'needed little training rather than poultice making',[96] the allocation of menial and affective labour to the sweeper/methrani/ coolie woman and medical-supervisory labour to the trained nurse, defeated the purpose of occupational closure. The ideological charge of investing nursing with tropes of seba did not succeed as the stigma of nursing structured by inequalities of class, caste, and sexualities proved too resistive to change. Consequently, this division of labour got further institutionalized with nursing professionals and bureaucrats recommending division of workers into professional staff (ward sisters, staff nurses, and student nurses) and non-professional staff (ayahs, attendants, ward boys, sweepers), each corresponding to ritual duties of caste-based labour. There were even suggestions that auxiliary nursing personnel would do cleaning, sweeping, laundry, and basic nursing service and would be called sebikas.[97]

* * *

We do not have many records of Indian women, who performed nursing professionally at the turn of twentieth century; there are no diaries, journals, or memoirs. We have as records medical men, women doctors, and missionaries writing about Indian women, who entered the labour market as nurses. Most of these documents focused on the stigma, the lack of respectable women in the profession, anxiety about sexuality, and the need for increasing surveillance and supervision over nurses. Investing nursing heavily with the ideologies of seba and spirituality was an attempt to drain it off the stigma of menial and manual labour;

[95] Vallee (2006).
[96] Dolan (1973: 176).
[97] Mitra (1960).

however, it remained an incomplete project. The nursing profession consisted of both the trained professional woman and the supposedly unskilled, untrained low-caste woman with nothing to tell them apart. Increasingly, a division in nursing labour emerged with medical-managerial-supervisory tasks performed by registered nurses, and the rest of of nursing care performed by women from the margins of society with minimum/partial training. This division of labour and a creation of a differentiated workforce survived the restructuring of health services even in contemporary times. In fact, with structural reforms, these divisions increasingly got institutionalized and became the site of increasing inequalities that were both historically and socially produced.

3   The Nursing Labour Market in Contemporary Kolkata

The last few decades have witnessed an overall decline in employment in South and South-East Asia; simultaneously it has also witnessed a feminization of the labour market. However, India remains a contradiction. Contrary to the feminization experienced in other countries, India, with liberalization, witnessed an uneven development for women in terms of employment generation. For some women, hitherto barred professions have opened up. However, for most women, the experience has been of increasing discrimination, precarious employment, harsh working conditions, and a decline in real wages.[1] The ghettoization of women at the bottom of the informal economy, accompanied by an overall decline in women's work force participation, has been the marked experience of the Indian female labour force, however,

---

[1] Mazumdar (2007).

the service sector continues to generate employment for women.[2] The nursing labour market as a sub-sector within the health care service economy is one of the few sectors that has witnessed high levels of employment, yet, it has managed to retain its overall feminine characteristic; however, it is also witnessing increasing stratification and informalization. The contemporary nursing sector has emerged as a segmented labour market, with disproportionate number of women from marginalized caste and class communities over-represented in the bottom rungs. None of this is, of course, new. Scholars have demonstrated that with liberalization of economies women from socially excluded groups continue to be marginalized; in fact, with modernization, there has been a further intensification of their labour.[3] The nursing sector, despite its claims to modernization and professionalization, continues to deploy existing inequalities to produce a deeply segmented labour market.

Despite the attempt to (re)fashion nursing services into a respectable profession, analysis of committee reports and organizational policies show that historically nursing services figured low in health budgets. With the onset of economic reforms (1992), the trends in marginalizing nursing were further intensified as 'curing' was given more emphasis at the cost of 'caring'. With a growing demand for Indian nurses in foreign countries, the profession has emerged as lucrative, however, these opportunities have not necessarily challenged the understanding of nursing care as stigmatized labour. With the migration of women from the Third World to the First World as low-skilled/multi-skilled health workers, racism has further intensified the signifying system, which marks reproductive labour as marginal and unproductive. The nursing profession never expanded at the pace its leaders and visionaries envisaged. However, it remained one of the few occupations that continues to provide employment to a largely female workforce. First-World feminists have termed similar femininized service sectors as 'care work', 'nurturant care', and 'emotional labour', which begs a reconsidering of conceptualizations of both productive and reproductive labour.[4] Closer to home, the question of commodified reproductive labour has been limited to research on

---

[2] Mazumdar and Neetha (2011).

[3] Kapadia (2002).

[4] England and Folbre (1999); Duffy (2011); Hochschild (1983); Smith (1992).

domestic work, sex work, and surrogacy;[5] all three bound together by their levels of precarity, informalization, stigmatization, and marginalization. However, unlike the other three, nursing is seeing a reverse trend: increasing informalization and a fragmentation of nursing care that reflects the complex linkages between the discourse on skills and social identities. The case of nursing raises new questions about how gender, caste, and class are deployed within informality to create and sustain hierarchies. Nursing not only falls under the category of the low-paid, menial, sexually segregated service sector but is also marked and saturated with notions of shame and stigma. In Kolkata's nursing labour market, we see a proliferation of contractual arrangements, and non-standardized employment, which are informal in different ways and in different degrees. This chapter focuses on the changing labour market in nursing as it gradually gives in to informalization and offers myriad employment contracts to workers. Within this framework, I focus on the discourse of skill and its relation with gender, class, and caste.

Privatization of the Health Care Sector in India and Its Impact on Nursing

Contrary to popular understanding that the starting point of the government's retreat from social sectors began with the adoption of the Structural Adjustment Programmes (1992), empirical research has highlighted that the divide between private and public enterprises was always fuzzy. On the question of health, the nature of India's mixed economy permitted both private hospitals and dispensaries to flourish alongside government enterprises. The Bhore Committee (1946) observed that most doctors in the public sector were engaged in private practice and recommended a prohibition.[6] However, this was never enforced.[7] Spurred by the urgings of the committee, the first two Five-Year Plans (1951–61) did promote development of medical infrastructure and increased hiring of manpower but this momentum fizzled out by

---

[5] Kotiswaran (2011); Pande (2009); Ray and Qayum (2009).

[6] This committee was set up under the leadership of Sir Joseph Bhore in 1943 to look into the public health system and the report was published in 1946.

[7] Baru (1998).

the 1960s.[8] In fact, the Mudaliar Committee (1962) openly accepted the reality of public sector doctors, practicing privately, and this admission further institutionalized the convergence between the public and the private health sector.[9] The rapid rate of expansion of the private sector outstripped the public health system, which lead to a collapse of the latter.[10] The process that started in the first two decades after Independence started gaining grounds in the 1970s and 1980s. While budgets were classified under medical education and training, without any distinction made between doctors and nurses, most resources went towards training of the former. Thus, doctors were produced at the cost of training other medical personnel.[11]

Over the decades, the difference between the ratio of doctors and nurses to the population started widening, and hereditary dais continued to flourish in their profession. The project of eliminating and/ or co-opting the hereditary dai, initiated in the colonial period, did not succeed even in Independent India. It was stated that it was impossible as well as undesirable to eliminate the hereditary dai. First, because of the influence she enjoyed in rural society, and second, more importantly, the weakness of the public health system in relation to the burgeoning population.[12] However, the government and international health organizations continued to look upon the dai as the source of all ill that plagued maternal and infant health, especially in the countryside; but they also admitted to their culpability in being unable to eliminate her.[13] While the trained midwife could be incorporated within the folds of modern nursing as an ancillary worker, the hereditary dai stuck out like a sore thumb. Official documents continue to echo colonial views of the Traditional Birth Attendants (TBA), as hereditary dais were renamed, as primitive and harmful,[14] and it was admitted that all attempts to train her into modern practices of midwifery had failed. The significant difference

[8]   Qadeer (1999).

[9]   Baru (1998).

[10]   Gangolli *et al.* (2005).

[11]   Dutta and Narayan (2004).

[12]   Ministry of Health and Family Welfare (1988); Indian Health Survey and Development Committee (1946).

[13]   World Health Organization (1958).

[14]   World Health Organization (1958).

in sheer numbers between trained midwives and the needs of the population assured her continuity.[15] The all-India statistics (2009) on birth deliveries reflected the continuing importance of the hereditary dai: 57.7 per cent of all recorded cases of deliveries was institutional, 17 per cent in the hands of 'qualified professionals', and 25.1 per cent were dealt with by 'untrained functionaries and others'.[16]

The liberalization of the Indian economy included, amongst other things, reducing government expenditures on public health, as well as decentralization, which meant that the responsibility of financing public health care was transferred from the central to the state governments. This, in turn, led to a vicious cycle; the poorer the state, the more it suffered, as it was unable to meet the expenses of salaries and infrastructure. This fitted well with the World Bank's decree on privatization, which gave loans to state governments on the condition that allocation of funds would be made to finance corporate hospitals. Increased tax exemptions, free land, and public private partnership (PPP) were some of the incentives given to kick-start corporatization of health care.[17] In 1995, West Bengal kicked off reforms in the public health sector, by opting for state sector adjustment roles, which had as a condition, government assistance to private players. It was also understood that to improve efficiency and quality, as market theorists claimed it would, ancillary services in government hospitals were to be contracted out to private agencies.[18]

The landscape of the Indian health sector continues to change dramatically, and increasingly, India is becoming a sought-after destination for medical tourists. The health sector infrastructure is growing at an extraordinary rate of two per cent annually, offering advanced surgeries that are ten to fifteen times cheaper than other parts of the world. The National Health Policy of 2002 offered exemptions from income tax, increase in Foreign Direct Investment (FDI) from 49 to 79 per cent in the insurance sector and exemptions or concession rate in custom duty on

[15] The Trained Nurses Association of India (2001).
[16] Family Welfare Statistics in India (2011: Table A.36) (per cent distribution of live births by type of medical attention received by the mother at delivery by residence—all India).
[17] Lefebvre (2009).
[18] Baru (2001).

purchase of medical equipment for private players.[19] The rapid decline in central government spending on health has been matched with a decline in the state government expenditures. West Bengal, for instance, has one of the lowest spending, amounting to 4.63 per cent (2005) of the total share in state budget.[20] By 2006, most of the medical enterprises (85 per cent) in the private sector were nursing homes, with less than 25 beds. While private tertiary care institutions which provided specialty and superspecialty care accounted to about 1 or 2 per cent, corporate hospitals constituted less than 1 per cent of the total number of institutions. The private sector accounted for 82 per cent of all out-patient visits and 52 per cent of hospitalization at all levels.[21] Micro-studies on private practices and secondary-level institutions have demonstrated that even the minimum standards of health care do not exist in these small nursing homes.[22]

Expansion and Consolidation of Nursing: 1947–2015

The professionalization of nursing dates from the establishment of the School of Nursing Administration in Delhi (1943), which ran postgraduate courses on nursing administration for army and civilian nurses. At the time of Independence, there were approximately 190 schools of nursing training set up by the government; however, 80 per cent of the nurses continued to be trained in missionary settings.[23] In 1946, the Bhore Committee pointed out that the standards of training in the 190 schools fell far below average and the nurse-population ratio was cited as dismal.[24] Subsequently, the Indian Nursing Council Act was passed (1947) with a view to regulate the standards of nursing education.[25] Henceforth, nursing in India was governed by this Act, which included uniform training of nurses, midwives, health visitors, and all those who fell under the gamut of nursing

---

[19] Baru (2001).
[20] Berman and Ahuja (2008).
[21] Raj (2006).
[22] Baru (2001).
[23] Healey (2008).
[24] Indian Health Survey and Development Committee (1946).
[25] The Trained Nurses Association of India (2001).

personnel.[26] The Act led to the establishment of the Indian Nursing Council (INC) in 1949, which brought about some uniformity in nursing training. Two courses were established—one was the full course of general nursing, of three years , with an addition of midwifery training of six months (General Nursing and Midwifery—GNM); the second, was the auxiliary nursing and midwifery training (Auxiliary Nursing and Midwifery—ANM), of a duration of two years. In a bid to homogenize and professionalize, the ANM was to replace all other junior grade nursing training that existed in the country.[27] The ANM rank was an attempt to create a para-nursing staff to bridge the gap between the burgeoning population and trained nursing staff.[28]

The various committees on nursing gave recommendations to streamline nursing education and training and to give nursing services the contours of a profession, some of which were implemented but most were ignored. The Bhore Committee addressed both qualitative and quantitative changes required in nursing services; however, the exhilaration that greeted the ambitious targets set by it was soon dampened by lack of implementation. It became clear that the government only wanted to prepare some categories of nursing personnel to staff the hospitals at a nominal cost, and no more.[29] The next two committees, the Shetty Committee (1954) and the Mudaliar Committee (1962), made similar recommendations for strengthening training and education of nurses.[30] The latter, however, went a step further and formally institutionalized the division of labour within nursing by recommending that 'work of routine nature' be done by the ANM nurses. Henceforth, ANMs became 'second-class nurses' who, despite taking full responsibility of the Primary Health Centres (PHCs), demonstrating considerable medical skills, were not given due recognition.[31] A similar plan was proposed for doctors; there were recommendations by the government to train paramedical staff who would function as doctors but would not

---

[26] Raghavachari (1990).

[27] Ministry of Health and Family Welfare (1988).

[28] World Health Organization (1958).

[29] Healey (2008).

[30] Ministry of Health and Family Welfare (1998).

[31] Iyer and Jesani (1995).

be given similar pay scale, recognition, or respect. This would allow an expansion of health care services for the burgeoning population without commensurate increase in expenses. This proposal was defeated by the Medical Council doctor's lobby, which resisted such dilution of standards and qualifications that undermined the profession.[32] Unlike doctors, nurses were unable to come together as an interest group and resist these trends. Therefore, the ANM category got institutionalized within the profession as auxiliary nursing staff, meeting the health needs of the rural population. Gendering of occupations—doctoring (male) and nursing (female)—had a determining influence on the way these two modern professions evolved.

Various types of categories started emerging within the nursing services, which have been recognized by the government. The GNM is a staff nurse and her primary role is to give bedside care and supervise ward attendants. Higher up in the hierarchy are the ward nurses (sisters-in-charge), who are the link between the doctor and the staff nurse and are responsible for the supervision and disciplining of the latter. On top of the pyramid are the matrons and assistant matrons who have dual duty of supervising all nursing students and staff. They are in charge of all matters related to nursing services of the hospital. Parallel to them is the sister tutor, who is in charge of teaching in nursing schools. In hospitals and clinics, there exists another category called the maternity assistants/attendants, who help nurses and midwives during childbirth. At the lowest level are the ward boys, including ayahs, nursing attendants, and orderlies who are employed to do ancillary nursing services under the supervision of the nurses.[33]

Before the Indian Nursing Council Act came into force, nurses registered in one state could not register in another, as certificates issued by one were not recognized by another. This was rectified by the INC, which gave recognition to state councils and examining bodies.[34] Now each school and college of nursing has to register with the state council and then seek INC recognition. There are two registers that are maintained—one at the national level by the INC and the other at

[32] Duggal (2005).
[33] Ministry of Labour and Employment (1961).
[34] The Trained Nurses Association of India (2001).

the state level by the state councils.[35] In 1987, there were only sixteen nursing councils, of which West Bengal was one, and three examining bodies—the South India Board, the Mid India Board, and the Military Examining Board.[36] In 2000, nursing councils had increased to 19, whereas examining boards continued to remain at three. Universities offering degree courses conduct their own examinations.[37] In contemporary times, nursing education has developed lopsidedly: the four Indian states located in the southern region—Kerala, Tamil Nadu, Karnataka, and Andhra Pradesh—have witnessed a rapid growth of institutions (both government and private) offering nursing education, while other states have lagged behind. Linking nursing education, privatization, and employment, scholars argue that the expansion in institutions in the private sectors is linked with international immigration.[38] In recent years, there have been initiatives by the state governments to increase public nursing institutions as well as initiate reservations for men in nursing to respond to the shortage.[39] For example, in West Bengal, in 2013, the embargo on male nurses in the public sector was lifted and men were inducted into the GNM course, to be placed in all departments except for gynaecology and obstetrics.[40]

There are many problems that continue to plague nursing education as well as the profession. On the one hand, BSc (Bachelor of Science) and MSc (Master of Science) nursing degrees are controlled academically by universities, and on the other hand, financial control lies with state health authorities. This means that working conditions and emoluments are not at par with university requirements.[41] The remuneration of nursing personnel is fixed either by the central or state government, depending on the hospital. Even for nursing administrators, pay scales vary from state to state; however, it is not at par with equivalent posts in

[35] The Trained Nurses Association of India (2001).

[36] Khanna (1991).

[37] The Trained Nurses Association of India (2001).

[38] Nair and Rajan (2017: 38–42).

[39] World Health Organization (2010).

[40] See http://www.hindustantimes.com/kolkata/west-bengal-govt-to-start-training-programmes-for-male-nurses/story-IL3VAtZblpS7EQtPuVcPhM.html (accessed on September 2017).

[41] Ministry of Health and Family Welfare (1988).

the departments of health administration.[42] The fact that it is the Indian Nursing Council and not the University Grants Commission that issues BSc degrees in nursing results in its devaluation as compared to medical and engineering degrees; so much so, that the BSc nursing degree is not considered as a qualification for either state or national administrative examinations.[43]

Not just in education, but policies on nursing services vary from state to state. Promotions and opportunities for career growth are bleak. While some states offer deputation for pursuing higher studies, others only permit leave. The scope for promotion is sporadic and a staff nurse can stagnate for 20–25 years at a particular pay scale, and government reports indicate that a large number of nurses retire without having gained any vertical movement within the hierarchy.[44] The state and central hospitals based in major cities have better pay and working conditions than their rural counterparts, while private hospitals follow their own service conditions and pay scale.[45] All these issues get amplified when one looks at private and voluntary hospitals and clinics, where there are no mechanisms for regulation. Nursing staff, already perceived as a subsidiary workforce, have been increasingly affected by the growing informalization and casualization within the formal economy. My fieldwork in medical establishments (both private and public) in Kolkata has revealed that these trends are sweeping in the public sector as well. In recent years, a proliferation of nursing schools, which do not have the minimum infrastructure prescribed by the Nursing Council, has led to a decline in the quality of training.[46] These unregistered schools with their inadequate infrastructure and training churn out nurses whose qualifications are not recognized by the market. Without proper credentials and due recognition, they are employed as casual workers with precarious terms of employment and exploitative working conditions.

While various committees and bodies proposed changes to upgrade nursing into an attractive profession for middle-class, upper-caste

---

[42]   Ministry of Health and Family Welfare (1988).
[43]   Khanna (1991).
[44]   Ministry of Health and Family Welfare (1988).
[45]   Nair and Healey (2006).
[46]   Dutta and Narayan (2004).

women, it continues to remain a stigmatized, low-paid service work. From colonial to Independent India, the issues remain the same. Scholars argue that the colonial state's inability to provide decent working conditions and liveable wages went a long way in stigmatization and low status of nursing, which continued well into the twentieth century.[47] The Bhore and Mudaliar Committees emphasized bad working and living conditions as one of the main impediments; they further pointed out that nursing students were used as substitute labour in hospitals, which hampered their academic learning.[48] Similar allegations were levelled against nursing schools and missionary centres in colonial India. The students were counted as staff right from the day they joined and service was given priority over learning.[49] Most countries have rejected the system of pedagogy, where nursing students are expected to work in hospitals, on the grounds that it hinders learning,[50] however, it continues in India, even today.

Statistics on nurses are hard to obtain. And statistics on informally employed para-nursing staff nigh impossible. While my visits to the health departments, state nursing councils, and archives did not yield any results, conversations with researchers, academics, and public officials reconfirmed that data pertaining to nurse migration, registered nurses, and unregistered auxiliary nursing staff either did not exist or were not made available. Micro-studies conducted in private hospitals and clinics have highlighted that most nurses are unregistered with trainings from unrecognized schools, who are learning on the job. There is a high turnover because of long hours of duty, the nature of work and work contract, and low wages as compared to government hospitals. It has been pointed out that one of the consequences of privatization of health care has been that bedside care has been delegated to Grade IV staff consisting of ayahs, ward boys, and sweepers, employed in large numbers and in an ad hoc manner.[51] As reports on the informalization of employment within the health services industry point out, the central government has increasingly casualized 'semi-skilled' and 'unskilled' jobs. The Eighth (1992–7)

---

[47] Healey (2010).
[48] Indian Health Survey and Development Committee (1946).
[49] Ministry of Health and Family Welfare, Government of India (1988).
[50] Khanna (1991).
[51] Baru (2004).

and Ninth (1997–2002) Five Year Plans witnessed the introduction of outsourcing and contracting of workers in the public sector, and by the Tenth Five Year Plan (2002–07), the contracting out of clinical services was being considered. The period 2000–15 witnessed an increasing trend of hiring contractual staff in Group D levels, particularly as outsourced labour, discouraging any direct contract with the hospital. Group C workers,[52] however, have been resisting casualization on the ground that it would lead to deskilling and thus adversely affect the quality of health care provided.[53]

According to the World Health Report (2006), India had 0.60 doctors, 0.80 nurses, 0.47 midwives, 0.06 dentists, and 0.56 pharmacists, per 1,000 population (all numbers representing percentage per 1,000 population).[54] Till 2015, the number of doctors (allopathic) registered in West Bengal was 61,891, out of which 49,270 were male and 12,621 were female doctors. GNM trained male nurses stood at 1,359, and for women, the number came to 40,961.[55] Given that male nurses were given admission to state institutions only after 2013, it is not unremarkable. However, these figures can be deceptive and misleading as those registered with one state often practice in other states or even those who have left the profession or migrated abroad have not been struck off the list.[56] Given that in the city of Kolkata, private establishments are predominantly staffed by migrant women, working as nurses, which include male migrant nurses, and with no records of women working as attendants, private sisters, and unregistered nurses, these statistics

[52] The classification of government employees under the Central Civil Services (Classification, Control & Appeal) Rules, 1965 is as follows: Group C— A central civil post carrying a pay or a scale of pay with a maximum of over Rs. 4,000 but less than Rs. 9,000; Group D—A central civil post carrying a pay or a scale of pay the maximum of which is Rs. 4,000 or less. See Government of India, 'Central Civil Services (Classification, Control & Appeal) Rules, 1965'. Cited in Basu (2016).

[53] Basu (2016).

[54] World Health Organization (2006) as cited in Hazarika (2013).

[55] The figures are from the active list. State Bureau of Health Intelligence (2017: Tables X.1 and X.2, 245).

[56] I am thankful to Professor Mohan Rao for pointing out this anomaly in health statistics.

do not give us a complete picture.[57] In West Bengal, in 2006, the ratio of doctors to population was 1: 1,961, while for nurses, it was 1:1,646; even in 2015 the gap was hardly breached, as the ratio remains dismal: doctors were 1:1647 and nurses 1:1201.[58]

Trained Nurses Association of India

The Trained Nurses Association of India (TNAI), which has under its jurisdiction, the Health Visitor's League (1922), Midwives and Auxiliary Nurse-Midwives Association (1925), and Student Nurses Association (1929–1930), started with a handful of members, and by the time of Independence, had grown to 2,243 members. By 1971, TNAI had opened local branches in 17 states, however, even in 1997, its membership barely expanded to 63,233 members.[59] The TNAI was recognized by the government as an official grievance body in the nature of a service association and, therefore, allowed to serve in high-level committees such as the Bhore and Mudaliar, make recommendations, and participate in activities of the INC. It functioned like a pressure group or a lobby. In lieu of gaining legitimacy as a service association by the Government of India, TNAI deliberately delinked itself from all union activities.[60] The TNAI effectively became an organization, which could not act as a platform for nurses to unionize or resist state or private organization policies. It steered clear of any strikes and conflicts and eschewed all political activities. The TNAI policy regarding strikes, issued in 1973, made it clear that as its membership did not include the majority of the government employed nurses, they could not be legally appointed as negotiating bodies either at the national or regional level.[61] So, in their own admission, the TNAI could not be considered as a representative voice of nurses in India. The policy statement states

---

[57] Ray (2019).

[58] State Bureau of Health Intelligence (2017: 247) Table X.5: Population Served per Doctor and per Nurse in West Bengal.

[59] The Trained Nurses Association of India (2001).

[60] The Trained Nurses Association of India (2001: 52).

[61] See TNAI website. Policy and Position Statements. Available at http://www.tnaionline.org/policy.htm. Accessed on 10 July 2017.

that it condemned union activities, which redress grievances through strikes, and instead urged nurses to work closely with the TNAI. The policy statement goes on to say, '[M]any nurses, however, have joined unions of paramedical workers, and even Fourth Class employees, where they lose their professional standing and are forced to abide by decisions including strike and controlled by non-professional leaders.'[62] If nurses, deprived of platforms to redress their grievances, joined unions, it would effectively reduce TNAI's claim to be the official representative of the nursing profession. The policy statement required members to discontinue their involvement in agitations that did not align with TNAI's interests. Failing which, the statement added, punitive action would be taken.

The Contemporary Nursing Labour Market, Kolkata

Nursing as a profession has been over-determined by two disparate yet linked phenomenon: the international migration of nurses and the politics of informalization. Migration studies have demonstrated that the sex-affective labour of poor women from the Global South has been pivotal in reproducing the domestic of privileged white women located in the North;[63] and the 'global care chain', which includes skilled care work such as nursing, has been expanding rapidly.[64] As I have argued elsewhere, though there have been concerns of 'care deficit' and 'care drain', the state and central government encourage private corporations to facilitate recruitment and emigration of nurses.[65] Health entrepreneurs, both in India and abroad, recognized the great economic benefit of placing nurses internationally, which has led to the expansion of what hospitals call 'business process outsourcing', that is, educating nurses for emigration.[66] The demand for nurses in USA, Canada, and European countries stemmed from cost cutting in the health sector, which affected nursing services adversely, leading to a decline in middle-class white American/European women choosing nursing as a career, particularly

---

[62] See TNAI website. Policy and Position Statements. Available at http://www.tnaionline.org/policy.htm. Accessed on 10 July 2017.

[63] Parrenas (2000).

[64] Yeats (2009).

[65] Ray (2019).

[66] Khadria (2007).

given stagnant salaries and long, arduous working hours.[67] Service work, particularly nursing, in the Anglo-American world is disproportionately represented by women belonging to immigrant and racial minorities at the lower end; while white, middle-class women occupy the top echelons that mostly include administrative and supervisory tasks.[68] The push factors for nurses migrating abroad are varied: ranging from low wages, harsh working conditions, sexual harassment, increasing costs of private education to stigma, and lack of status. Thus more and more Indian women trained in nursing take to migration.[69] However, the nursing labour market in the West is deeply racialized and nurses belonging to migrant and/or minority communities often face discriminatory practices that exclude them from any career advancement and upward mobility. With international recruitment, immigrant women who have higher qualification than their UK peers often find themselves at a more disadvantageous position.[70]

Along with the international flight of trained workers, the increasing ghettoization of women's labour, the masculinization of the labour market, and the politics of informalization have shaped the service economy. The existing literature on labour has emphasized that processes of formalization in Indian industry, which began in a rudimentary form in the 1930s and gained momentum in the 1950s, led to the exclusion of women.[71] The history of the nursing services is, however, an exception to this pattern; the nursing profession was constructed, in line with global patterns, as feminine and such gendering has survived pressures of formalization. Improvement in wages/salaries and conditions of service did not attract men in any significant proportions into the profession. Even though there has been some induction of men in the profession in different parts of the country, it continues to remain feminized.[72] Given the already

---

[67] Folbre (2006); Smith and Mackintosh (2007).

[68] Duffy (2011).

[69] Chattopadhyay (1993); George (2000); Nair and Percot (2007); Thomas (2006).

[70] Li (2000: 289); Smith and Mackintosh (2007).

[71] Sen (2008).

[72] Even in 2005, women comprised 17 per cent of all registered doctors and 70 per cent of nurses and midwives continue to be women. Rao, Bhatnagar, and Berman (2012).

feminized character of this profession, pressures of informalization have led to greater differentiation within the existing female labour force rather than a change in the gender composition.

Partly fuelled by recent trends, including the liberalization of the Indian economy as well as the politics of informalization and partly by the politics of identity—a differentiated workforce, based on social identities—the increase in the number of workers in nursing has been disproportionately at the informal end of the market. Today, even government hospitals have grown more reliant on unregistered nurses or private sisters, as well as attendants, who represent the most informal and casual end of the workforce. As a result, registered nurses have succeeded in redefining their jobs as more supervisory and managerial, thus gaining status and authority within the nursing hierarchy. However, they have not gained as much in terms of wages and working conditions vis-à-vis other segments within the health care industry. In Kolkata's health care sector, we see today a proliferation of contractual arrangements and non-standardized differentiation on the basis of 'skill' and employment conditions, which are informal in different ways and degrees.

Field Survey: Categories and Respondents

Over a period of three years (2009–2012) I conducted in depth interviews with 100 women in three medical establishments.[73] Based on my research I argue that there are several processes under way in the nursing profession. First, there has been a huge increase in the population seeking institutional health services. There has not been, however, a commensurate increase in employment of trained nurses.[74] The increase in nursing employment or what there has been of it is at the lower two tiers of unregistered nurses and attendants. Registered nurses employed in relatively smaller numbers have pushed forth their agenda of professionalization by participating in supervisory and managerial roles. However, this has not been accompanied by significant improvements in wages and working conditions. Even they work in highly exploitative conditions. Unregistered nurses and attendants at the bottom two layers work

[73] The social and economic profile of the respondents have been presented in the Appendix.
[74] Dutta and Narayan (2004).

in even more exploitative conditions—low wages, long hours, heavy physical and manual labour associated with 'dirty' work, and no social security or collective bargaining power. The three hierarchical tiers of the nursing labour market—formal workers, regular informal workers, and casual informal workers—are produced by the discourse of skills and training.[75] Thus, trained nurses at the top tier of the profession are constructed as highly skilled and are required to meet the demands of critical decision-making, but they share the devaluation suffered by attendants and private sisters.

In my fieldwork, I have observed that the nursing labour market in Kolkata has four categories of workers: registered GNM trained nurses (henceforth referred to as simply registered nurses), unregistered and informally trained ANM nurses (henceforth unregistered nurses), and informally trained private sisters and attendants who have no training. In Table 3.1 I list out the categories with the corresponding levels of training, recognition, and employment opportunities. The categories are grouped together in a manner that reflects, on the one hand, patriarchal understandings of skill and, on the other hand, the nature of the organization.

In my research, I found that the government hospital employed registered nurses (permanent employees with full protection and benefit), private sisters, and attendants (informally employed casual and regular-wage workers). In the private hospital, there are no permanently employed workers—registered nurses, unregistered nurses, and attendants are informally employed, regular-wage workers, and private sisters are informally employed casual-wage workers. The ideology of skill is deployed to differentiate between those categories of workers, who are all informally employed. In the private sector, registered nurses, unregistered nurses, and attendants are employed as regular workers, with three-year, renewable, work contracts and with some

[75] Informal wage employment consists of two types: regular and casual. Regular informal employment means that the worker is employed on a contractual basis and is paid a monthly wage, with some or no benefit and leave. Their contract is renewed every year. Casual informal employment means being hired on a regular basis for a limited period of time and with no entitlements. It mostly applies to daily-wage workers, who operate on a 'no work no pay' basis.

Table 3.1   Categories of nursing personnel and employment opportunities

Category	Qualification	Registration	Employment opportunities	Type of employment
Registered nurses	Recognized GNM diploma (three years six months formal training)	Yes	Public and Private sector	Both formal (government) and regular informal (private) employment
Unregistered nurses	Not recognized (six months to one year of informal training)	No	Private sector	Regular informal employees directly recruited by the hospital
Private Sister	Not recognized (six months to one year of informal training)	No	Public and Private sector	Casual informal employees recruited from outside agencies
Attendants	NA	No	Public and Private sector	Regular informal employees recruited from outside agencies

Source: Author.

leave entitlement and benefits. However, an understanding of the skills of a nurse as against the attendant secures for the former a greater amount of leave entitlement, which is denied to the latter. Attendants have a 'no work no pay' policy and are given only one day off in the week. Private sisters, however, are at the lowest end of the hierarchy— they are employed on a daily-wage basis with no benefit or leave (not even a weekly off), and therefore, are not assured of regular employment around the year. Even working hours are different for different categories of workers, according to the tier they belong to, as well as the policies of the organization. The nursing service in Kolkata, even within the formal economy (both private and government), is a triple-layered labour market—permanent, formal workers, regular-wage, informal workers, and casual, informal workers. This labour market takes on a pyramidal structure, with the permanent formal workforce forming an elite minority and the base consisting of large numbers of casually employed informal workers. Needless to say, each of these layers is not homogenous but considerably fragmented.[76]

Work, Working Conditions, and Wages

In the last four decades, labour studies have been emphasizing on the complex interaction between social identities and workplace hierarchies.[77] Beginning with the categories of race, caste, and ethnicity, the question of gender has also been on the agenda for several decades now.[78] In capitalism, the worker does not lose her/his social identity to become a mere component of the homogenous working class, but s/he carries these identities to be variously construed within categories of skilled/ unskilled or supervisory/manual work. Equally, there is no mechanical translation of social identities into workplace differentiation. In health care services, how is the experience of gender mediated by other social locations—of class, caste, and ethnicity, for instance? And how do they come together in complex interplay? How do they inflect, or do they shape, the triple-tiered pyramid of the profession?

Registered nurses employed in the government sector are located at the tip of the pyramid: protected by labour laws, and represented in the Ministry of Health, they form the elite enclave of nursing care. The general nursing midwifery (GNM) course is for three years and includes an additional six-month internship in a hospital. While government-aided schools of nursing offer stipends to their students, private colleges charge anything between one to four lakh rupees. By and large, public sector hospitals tend to employ nurses graduating from government nursing schools; however, vacancies are rampant. A small percentage of registered nurses thus also work in the private sector—most are an interim arrangement while they wait for vacancies in government hospitals or opportunities to migrate abroad.

Unregistered nurses and private sisters receive their training from unlicensed centres that contribute to the culture of exploitation. These

---

[76] Ray (2016a).
[77] Chakraborty (1989); Chandavarkar (1994).
[78] Fernandes (1997); Lindberg (2005).

centres charge no fees, set up minimum literacy as qualification, and promise immediate employment, thus drawing young women who have dropped out from school or passed with minimum grades to enrol in the hope of a job. The *quid pro quo* is that after finishing their training, the women sign a contract that compels them to work in hospitals for a whole year in exchange of a meagre stipend. The private hospital where I conducted my research runs an unlicensed nursing centre where women are offered a one-year 'ANM' training. Enrolled students are expected to work in the wards as a part of their training. With the completion of the course, they either join the hospital as unregistered nurses, provided they have passed their secondary-level-examination education, or are recommended to an agency who offers employment as private sisters. The agency is run by a registered staff nurse in the same hospital. She collects payments from the hospital and, after keeping her own commission, disburses it to the respective workers. Arati, twenty-eight years of age, Scheduled Caste, and married with two children, took nursing training when her husband could not make ends meet with his meagre earning as a daily-wage worker. Despite opposition from her mother-in law, she travels from the district of Hooghly every day, first to train and subsequently to work as a daily-wage private sister in the private hospital. When she initially applied for training, she assumed it was to become a registered nurse. She narrates her disappointment,

> I trained and joined here. I had thought that I would be a nursing staff, but after training was over, they told me that because I did not pass my secondary-level-examinations, they will not make me a nursing staff. When I enrolled in the course, they did not tell me that without passing school final exams, I cannot be a nursing staff. They run a nursing school here and those who pass out do not get registered. That is why this centre does not apply for a license, so that we cannot register ourselves. Then they can keep us for less salary, knowing that we will not be able to go anywhere else. (Personal interview with the author)

Private sisters, who are employed on a 'no work no pay' basis fill up the broad base of the pyramid. Hired when there is a need and asked to leave when there are no patients, employment opportunities fluctuate in direct relationship with in-patients admission. Sometimes, a private sister can work for 35–40 days without a single day off, and then have no work for a few days or even a few weeks. Usually, the demand for private sisters is so high that they have to negotiate with agencies to get a few days' unpaid leave. Both the hospital and the agency take a cut from the worker's wages for procuring work for them. These agencies function as nursing bureaus, which provide private sisters to hospitals, nursing homes, and residences. A patient pays 130 rupees for a twelve-hour shift; the hospital takes 10 rupees and the owner of the agency takes 10 rupees as commission. The latter takes the money for providing work and the former for allowing the private sister to work on their premises and using their facilities, such as access to toilets and drinking water.

The logic of employing a private sister and its benefits for the hospital economy was explained to me by the operations manager of the private hospital. The private sister is not employed directly by the hospital, which allows the latter to avoid any responsibility. Instead of direct payments from patient-employers to nurses, the billing is done under the hospital's letterhead in a separate column called 'nursing'. This is to avoid any bargaining or demand for extra money and/or tips that could lead to harassment, thus damaging the hospital's reputation. The advantage of including payment of private sisters under the regular bill is maintaining a professional image of the hospital, whereas the disadvantage is that the hospital is liable for mishaps as the payment is made to them. The main reason for keeping a separate column for private sisters and not factoring it into the cost of the bed is to keep the costs down. The manager explains, 'when someone is choosing a hospital to have an operation, they call up four similar types of medical establishment and the first thing they ask about is the price of the bed. That is the yardstick of choosing where they want to get admitted'.[79] So there is constant competition between hospitals to keep bed costs low. Usually, the bed charge consists of housekeeping, food, services of nurses, attendant/ward boy, Resident Medical Officer (RMO), and so on. While some have removed food charges from being included, others have excluded the costs of the RMO in a bid to keep the bed costs low. Private sisters are generally excluded from bed charges in most medical institutions, keeping them as an 'extra cost' incurred by individual patients.

[79] Interview with the operations manager of the private hospital, 12 September 2011.

This segment of the labour force also comprises the relatively less skilled attendant. Like the private sisters, they too are not direct recruits but employed from an agency which provides workers on contractual terms to private establishments. In a slightly better position than the private sister, they are employed as regular casual workers: however, despite being regular informal employees, attendants have no leave entitlement (except for a weekly off). Whatever the reason, failure to report to work is counted as absence without permission, inviting severe economic retribution. If an attendant is absent for one day, two days' salary gets deducted. In most hospitals and nursing homes, the wards are understaffed, with two attendants for ten to eleven patients—the absence of a single attendant can lead to chaos. Being health service providers, medical enterprises cannot ignore a patient's daily needs. In case of an absence, those on duty are 'forced' to do a compulsory double shift. For an attendant in the private nursing home, this could mean three shifts of twelve hours each in a row. Jamuna, Scheduled Caste, aged 25, unmarried, is an attendant in the private nursing home. She took this work as she had neither education nor training to do anything else. Her studies were discontinued after class IV, as her father believed that women should not step out of the house. She would sew, along with her mother and sisters, and after her father's death, she took to working as an attendant in residences. After a couple of years, she got an opportunity to work in the nursing home, and has been employed here for the last seven years. Jamuna speaks of the pressure and stress involved in compulsory double shift. 'Double duty is very painful and they put pressure on us and force us ... it is working for 36 hours straight out. I did duty today, now the extra night and then the regular next day duty. I have to buy food, and then more money gets spent. And even if I do not want to, I am forced to do double shift.' In Table 3.2 I have described the working hours, benefit and wages received by the different categories of workers employed as nursing staff, both in the public and private medical establishments where I conducted my fieldwork.

Braverman in *Labour and Monopoly Capital* (1974) has described this process in very clear terms: the 'degradation' of work in monopoly capitalism in the twentieth century necessitated a deskilling and automation of labour. The separation of the conception

Table 3.2 A description of working hours, benefit, and wages received by the different categories of workers employed as nursing staff (All figures are for 2009–10)

	Registered Nurse	Unregistered Nurse	Private Sister	Attendant
Working hours in a week	48 hours (eight-hour shift for six days)	48 hours (eight-hour shift for six days)	12-hour shift and according to employment demand	72 hours (twelve-hour shift for six days)
Leave	State government leave rules for government employees and casual, sick and privilege leave for private sector employees	Casual, sick, and privilege leave	No leave	No leave except a weekly off
Starting Salaries	Rs 17,355 (for government hospitals) and Rs 5,000 (for private hospitals) per month	Rs 2,800–3,000 per month	Rs 120 per day	Rs 2,100–2,400 per month

Source: Author. Based on Table 12.1 in Ray (2016a: 251).

(management) and the execution (workers) was the driving force of the modern capitalist system. The divisions and subdivision of tasks resulted in destruction of skill and production of a homogenous workforce that could never enter the ranks of the management. This also meant a dual labour market—a managerial and clerical team, as well as a casual, vulnerable, and temporary workforce. The former he describes as a 'range of intermediary categories' who enjoyed a 'privileged market position' and were a 'middle layer' of employment who could never enter the ranks of senior management nor could they be a part of the labouring classes who they were employed to control, discipline, and manage. He included teachers and nurses in these ranks along with supervisors, foremen, accountants, and engineers.[80]

Recent scholarship has also demonstrated that the restructuring of the labour market in liberalizing India has deployed what Braverman describes as a 'dual' labour market. Some jobs, such as the 'secretary'—a classic example of a submissive feminine service provider—has been expanded to include managerial responsibilities, thus breaking out of the feminine stereotype. However, this expansion has not been accompanied by a vertical mobility in the labour market in terms of wages, status, and respect; instead it has brought more responsibility and limited decision-making power.[81] This 'middle layer' within labour market hierarchies is subjected to an intensification of supervisory and administrative responsibilities: on the one hand, they no longer belong to the labouring classes, and on the other, they are not counted in the ranks of those in managerial positions. In our second chapter, we have noted the hierarchies within the nursing profession that often reflected a division of labour that constituted as well as reflected caste, class, and gender inequalities, with women from socially respectable groups in the elite administrative-supervisory-consultant role and women from marginal communities giving the menial-manual hands-on care. While nurses were at the top in this sub-sector, they rarely had any voice or representation in the overall functioning and policymaking of the institutions they served. There were various attempts to institutionalize this dual labour market, but with limited success, particularly in the public sector. The private establishments, however, deployed labour strategies that allowed them to employ maximum women who could give nursing care at the minimum costs.

All nursing staff, whether formally employed registered nurses or informally employed private sisters, have to take care of patients. However, the sheer physical strain and intensity of work varies among categories of workers, depending on the segment of the pyramid in which they are located. For nurses, who are in the higher ranks of the pyramid, actual nursing care has been minimized. They work with medical instruments as well as administer medicine, saline, and injections; and the lion's share of their work is in record-keeping and administration. The

---

[80] Braverman (1974: 405–07).
[81] Fernandes (2000).

expansion of the role of the nurse to include record-keeping and administration has meant that there is no relief from intense work pressure, but the content of their work is markedly different from that of other health care workers located at the lower rungs of the pyramid. In Table 3.3 I have listed out the duties and responsibilities of different categories of nursing personnel employed in both the public and private medical establishments where I conducted my fieldwork.

The ratio of nurse to patient is 1:25–30, while the ideal is 1:3.[82] A ward which has 45 to 60 patients does not have more than 2 nursing staff, when it should actually be staffed by 15 to 20 nurses. So, technically one nurse in a government hospital does the work of almost 7 to 10 nurses. Chitra, in her early 40s, married and coming from an upper-caste, urban, professional family, took to nursing, when she did not clear her entrance exams for medical school to be a doctor. At one point, she harboured ambitions to migrate abroad as a nurse, but met and married her now husband and abandoned all plans of leaving the city. Working as a registered nurse in a government hospital, she describes how the duties of nurses are being remodelled:

Our work is high-pressured. As soon as I come in, I take handover and then check all the patients, and record their condition—who is critical, who needs special medicine, special investigations, and so on. I have to look up the input-output chart, and then there is constant monitoring of patients, administering injections and medicines. Record-keeping takes a long time but it is needed because then the work is recorded, organized, and fewer mistakes are made. However, all of this means that hands-on patient care is neglected and less trained staff are employed to do it. (Personal interview with the author)

The work of an attendant is to take care of patients and keep the ward running. Taking care of patients includes (as noted in Table 3.3) going up and down and across wards and other departments and sections of the establishments. Both the private hospital and nursing home are built in a manner that pharmacies and laboratories are on the ground floor next to the OPD. This means that every time medicines are needed, tests are to be conducted, and reports to be collected, an attendant has to climb

---

[82] Interviews with the matron in the government hospital, October 2009.

Table 3.3 Duties and responsibilities of different categories of nursing personnel

Category	Tasks
Nurses	1. Taking 'handover' from the nurse in the previous shift 2. Accompanying doctors on rounds 3. Noting instructions 4. Providing status reports 5. Administering medicine 6. Examining reports from the laboratory 7. Making notes for doctors 8. Documenting medical conditions 9. Keeping record of un/used medicine etc. 10. Supervising attendants and private sisters
Attendants	1. Administering bed pans 2. Sponging/bathing/turning patients over to prevent bed sores 3. Feeding 4. Taking patients for x-rays/tests etc. 5. Getting reports from laboratory/medicine from the pharmacy 6. Going to cash section when a patient is released, at stipulated intervals 7. Cleaning and maintaining the ward 8. Dusting instruments, nurse's desk 9. Making beds 10. Washing clothes 11. Scrubbing utensils and bed pans etc. 12. Work as aides to nurses—fetching reports, water, passing files, etc.
Private Sister	1. Sponging/bathing/turning patients over to prevent bed sores 2. Feeding 3. Making beds 4. Washing clothes 5. Cleaning and maintaining the room 6. Administering bed pans (contested) 7. Any other work as directed by the patient

Source: Author's fieldwork.

anything between one to five flights of stairs. They are not allowed to use the lift, which is reserved for doctors, administrative staff, and visitors. Sujata, 33 years of age, Brahmin, and married, works as an attendant in the private nursing home. While all of her three sisters are school teachers, she married young, just after leaving school. It was her husband's ill health and subsequent loss of job that made her seek work. With two teenaged children, she runs the home with her meagre salary. Her working as an attendant drew a lot of ire from her family-in-law, who have also increasingly distanced themselves from her. She gives me a graphic description of the sheer physical labour that attendants have to do:

> Giving patients bed pans, getting them ready for surgery, helping them change, giving them water, taking them for x rays ... there is no end to work. Getting the files from the cash and taking it back, requisition for medicines from first to fifth floor ... climbing up and down is so painful, we get so tired, yet they do not let us use their lift. You bring them medicines and then they send you back for another requisition. (Personal interview with the author)

While in the private enterprises everything is located in one building, the government hospital is located in a sprawling campus where wards are spread out in a number of buildings and the laboratory is right at the centre. This means that attendants would have to walk, maybe as long as 20 to 30 minutes, to get reports and medicines, sometimes several times in one day. Private sisters are like shadow workers, an invisible layer existing between the nurse and the attendant. As I have argued elsewhere, they exist because of the paucity of nurses and attendants. Instead of increasing expenditure on labour, by hiring more workers and trained personnel, hospitals and nursing homes employ a 'reserve army of labour' whose costs are borne by the patients. Employed to look after only one particular patient, her tasks remain ambiguous. Whether she will take care of basic medical needs or only give hands-on bodily care remains contentious.[83] Recommended by the nurse, the family is asked to contact a particular agency/centre for a private sister. This, however, is mostly for patients who are lodged in cabins and not wards.

---

[83] Ray (2019).

After finishing my fieldwork, a couple of years later (2014), I went back to the private hospital. While speaking to the administration, I learnt that the 'private sister system' had been abolished. In an incident, one of the private sisters dropped a newborn baby while talking on the phone, which drew the ire of the patient and her relatives. This led to questioning of the credentials and qualifications of the private sisters. However, this has happened only in the private hospital and not in the nursing home or the government hospital. In the wake of this decision, I asked the operations manager how the hospital would manage without the labour of private sisters. The hospital has decided, he said, to increase (unregistered) nurses.

> Private sisters are like an infection, they are spreading all over in almost all hospitals. They need to be routed out; they have no sense of hygiene and cause more damage than benefits. Unregistered nurses, even if they do not have training, are equivalent to a recognized nurse; they get trained by the matron; they are under our direct control and we can supervise them. (Personal interview with the author)

The problem with private sisters is not so much about training and skills, as much as it is about the fact that they are not under the control of the hospital administration. In terms of wages, a private sister can earn upto Rs 3,300 if she works for 30 days in a month, while an attendant earns as little as Rs 2,100 to 2,400, and an unregistered nurse earns Rs 2,800 to 3,000. The advantages of hiring a private sister is, first, that the costs are borne directly by the patient and second in terms of entitlements, no leave or fringe benefits need to be granted. They are in no way the responsibility of the hospital, and therefore cannot make any demands. But as the billing is done under the hospital letterhead, the institution becomes accountable to the patients in case of a mishap, like the one mentioned above. The crux of the matter is that, unlike an unregistered nurse, the private sister is difficult to control and supervise. Being under a nursing bureau and hired only for specific duties, she falls outside the matron's supervisory purview. The on-the-job training that a nurse receives in the ward is not extended, or is relatively less available to these 'shadow workers', who are compelled to remain in the recesses of the cabin.

Val Plumwood has explored some of the mechanics of dualism—foregrounding/backgrounding, relational definition, homogenization, and objectification.[84] Even though the case of nursing does not support any rigid structuring of dualism, some of the strategies that sustain the hierarchical labour market appears similar to those outlined by Plumwood. As a result, the segments within the nursing labour market are sustained in relation to each other and a niche, well-paid, protected pool of registered nurses is produced at the expense of an ill-paid, unprotected multitude of ancillary nursing staff. The circle closes. Attendants and private sisters are considered inferior to nurses and their contributions to the medical enterprise denied or belittled, which translates into low wages and exploitative working conditions. This signifies a supposedly untrained, unskilled, dispensable pool of cheap labour and justifies their subordinate status within the hierarchy. The differentiations within the nursing profession can be seen in context of larger labour processes associated with liberalization of the Indian economy. This pyramidal structure, where the top is constituted of an elite enclave of protected workers and the base by multitude of unprotected, casual workers, is not an isolated phenomenon in the health care industry. It is prevalent in other professions and sectors as well. The ramifications of the discourse on skills, which allows for the coexistence of both registered and unregistered nurses as well as attendant, results in a differentiated and hierarchical labour market. The fragmentation of the economy, where the increasing informalization within the formal economy becomes the discursive site for the ideological constructions of 'skilled labour', gets further compounded, in this instance, by the fact that nursing is a predominantly feminized profession. Subsequently, the result is a greater differentiation within the existing female labour force rather than a change in the gender composition.

* * *

The evolution of the nursing profession was deeply impacted and influenced by the gendered nature of the labour. Considered peripheral

---

[84] Plumwood (1993).

and unskilled, nursing was relegated to the margins in context to professionalization and modernization of the health sector. The lack of opportunities in the sector, coupled with stigma, low wages, and exploitative working conditions, meant that women seeking nursing employment pinned their hopes on the transnational labour market. The paradox of nursing remains: encouraged by the government, more and more private nursing colleges, charging exorbitant fees for nursing training, was opened up with an eye on the foreign market, while locally employed nurses continued to be exploited, and medical establishments understaffed. Spurred by the politics of informalization, medical establishments, both in the public and private sector, look to unregistered nurses, private sisters, and attendants to fill in the gap. The dependency on unregistered ancillary nursing staff is further fuelled by a division of labour, which deploys gender, class and caste to make a case for a differentiated workforce to respond to different needs within health care services.

In most parts of the world, we are witnessing similar trends as 'multi-skilled' ancillary workers are hired to do the lion's share of nursing, particularly the manual-menial-affective components, whereas registered nurses take on the more prestigious managerial-medical-supervisory role.[85] This split by which the work of nursing is divided into the 'skilled', associated with science/management, and 'unskilled', associated with the handling of the body and its daily detritus, has contributed to an overall deskilling of workers. In India, the nurses located at the top of the pyramid take on the role of expert nurse-consultants, administrators, and managers, while workers at the lower rungs of the pyramid deliver round-the-clock bodily care. This has many implications. First, the notion of 'taking care' or 'caring for someone' becomes a truncated experience as the division of labour discourages one section to give hands-on care and the other from any medical intervention, thus contributing to a culture of alienation and disconnect between the giver and receiver of care. Second, the discourse on skills that justify this division of labour, deploy social inequalities, which legitimize such blatant exploitation. This runs counter to arguments that in a modern workspace social identities are dissolved. The interrogation of the labour market, however, can never be complete without investigating the family, and the manner in

[85] Duffy (2011).

which social and cultural capital is (re)produced and circulated to create a feminized workforce, who are compelled to enter exploitative, low-end sub-sectors of the service economy. In the next chapter, I open up the family and its linkages with the labour market to argue that both the private and the public domain work as apparatuses that produce ideal subjects instrumental in maintaining the dominant social order.

4 The Matrix of the Family and the Market

(Hetero)normative Economies

A central preoccupation in feminist thought has been the public/
private binary, a classical entry point into understanding
the ideologies of family and the political economy. The
fascination with spatial boundaries, policing, and transgressions is
indicative of where contestation of power is located. As Anne Philips
observes, the opposition between the public/private is 'identified as
the crucial underpinning to patriarchal political thought.'[1] Questioning
the private/public binary thus became central to the politics of the
first and second wave of the women's movements; however, Black and
Dalit feminists forcefully brought home that the public/private divide
was steeped in caste, class, and racial ideologies and was not useful

[1] Philips (1992: 17).

in understanding *all* women's oppression.[2] In this chapter, I look at the continuities, unities, contradictions, and ruptures of the linkages between the oppositional binaries of public/private, market/home, and masculine/feminine to examine how (hetero)normative economies produce an ideal feminine subjectivity. Feminists have closely scrutinized both the institutions of the market and the family to call out the sexism, racism, and casteism inherent in them, thus arguing against mainstream, neo-classical economics. Women's work constitutes both the spheres that simultaneously reinforce and antagonize each other: the labour market and the family. The binary between productive/ reproductive, work/family, market/home, and exchange value/use value has been conceptualized, grappled with, and thought through to come to an understanding, that both dimensions are marked and constituted by sexual politics, rather than being static, universalized gender-neutral domains.[3]

In this chapter, I explore how the family as an institution produces women as docile, deferential, dutiful subjects who enter the labour market steeped in familial ideologies that work against any transgressions. In India, feminists have argued that the family mediates and controls women's labour, determining her entry into and exit from the labour market, often in response to fertility, marriage, and family fortunes.[4] While it is still very much true, I add that not just in response to family needs, but women's decisions, choices, and their resolve to dis/ continue in the labour market also stems from the kinds of employment available and its conditions. However, there is no one formula or predetermined cause and effect relationship between the market and the family, and while there is a definite link, it is contingent and subjective. Different women respond differently to labour markets, family, and the community. However, there are some commonalities. Most women identify themselves primarily as wives, mothers, and daughters. Families are pivotal to women's understanding of their selves and the world at large; their daily activities, negotiations, perceptions, and perspectives are largely rooted within the hearth.

[2] Chakravarti (2006); Collins (1990); hooks (1984); Rege (2002).
[3] Eisenstein (1979); Papanek (1979); Pateman (1988); Walby (1990).
[4] Banerjee (1999).

I attempt to understand the relationship between the family and the market as a set of relationships negotiated within certain given frames of references. For feminist scholars, the family is an important institution that needs to be opened up and interrogated. How are cultural norms, sexual propriety, and regulation of the female body negotiated in an increasingly complicated cyclic sphere that the public/private distinction entails? Women working as nurses, attendants, and private sisters, with remarkable differences in rank, pay, and working conditions, consistently articulate their identities in familial terms—wives, mothers, and daughters. The central preoccupation of the women interviewed is the survival of the family. The location of different women in different ranks of the labour market is not coincidental but political—women are produced by the family; they are produced docile, obedient, and hetero-normative. To make my argument about (hetero)normative economies and women's exploitation, I have drawn from feminists such as Adrienne Rich,[5] Gayle Rubin,[6] and Monique Wittig,[7] who argue how heterosexuality depends on and perpetuates the gendered division of labour, as well as male appropriation of women's productive and reproductive capacities.

The three-tier pyramidal structure of the labour market (in nursing as well as in other professions) calls for a differentiated workforce, where differently skilled workers fit into its different strata. Drawing from Althusser's theorization of the apparatus,[8] I look at how the family works in fashioning differentiated workers out of men and women. In this chapter, I examine the gendering of social and cultural capital and its (re)production in the private realm. Family becomes one of the sites where such capital is (re)produced, which further places women at a disadvantage in the labour market. In this chapter, I explore women's aspiration, yearnings, and desires and how hetero-patriarchal norms continue to shape and give meaning to such affect. How do women respond to normative structures that define their roles within the family and the labour market? How do they negotiate and make sense of the world that produces them as docile, submissive, and subordinate?

---

5 Rich (1980).
6 Rubin (1975).
7 Wittig (1992).
8 Althusser (1971).

Let's Talk about the Home: Family As a Site of (Re)production

Indian society is in a flux: While traditional understanding of the public/private have been modified to accommodate women's entry into the labour market, particularly for middle-class, upper-caste women, there has also been an increasing surveillance, policing, and controlling of women, their labour, and sexualities.[9] This study is about a subsector in the health care industry, which consists of women trying to find a foothold in the emerging and porous new middle class; it also consists of women casually employed at the bottom of the hierarchy for minimum wages, who endure extreme exploitation and precarious working conditions. It is but understood that the imperatives, urgencies, and conditions of different groups of women entering the labour market are different, varied, and heterogeneous. However, there are certain commonalities: First is the centrality of the family and its welfare in the imaginations, desires, and yearnings of the women. Second, the experience of working in a particularly stigmatized profession with its internal differentiation influences their choices and decisions to dis/continue in their jobs.

The unit of family is a primary, organizing unit of society—it is an apparatus that controls, polices, and produces human beings, following caste, class, and (hetero)sexist norms.[10] It is a site of expression of emotions, affect, and desires. It is also a site of regulation, policing, and control; a place for disciplining, coercion, and restriction; an institution that demands loyalty, obedience, adherence, dedication, and commitment of its members to place it above everything else. The norms that guide the family and the nursing labour market are startlingly similar. A parallel can be drawn between the sexual division of labour in the family, and the sexual division of labour in the modern health care services. The two ancient famous medical treatises in India (*Caraka Sahmita* and *Sushruta Samhita*), where certain reference to nursing can be found, mentions that while a doctor needs theoretical knowledge and practical experience, the helper must be a loyal assistant to the doctor. In fact, for the latter, the stress is on loyalty and obedience rather than knowledge and skills.[11]

---

[9] John and Nair (2000); Rajan (1993).
[10] Beteille (1993); Chowdhury (2007); Rubin (1975).
[11] Leslie and Wujastyk (1991).

Anne Oakley argues that despite modernization and professionaliza-tion, nurses continue to be subordinate to doctors. Early nursing was based on the household model of instrumental and expressive roles: the doctor represented the father; the nurse, mother; and patients, the children. This association still continues, where nursing is not identified with the curative model but that of caring.[12] The similarity between the home and the labour market is not coincidental. By playing on the difference between men and women, heterosexuality is institutionalized, marriages are made necessary and imperative, and mutually exclusive genders created, which drives one to another. 'The sexual division of labour ... creates them and it creates them heterosexual.'[13] So does the labour market. The crowding of women into feminine sub-sectors in modern professions that reinforce their dependency, subordination, and subservience to their male colleagues is not just about sexually segregated jobs: it is also about reinforcing the complementary but hierarchical nature of masculinity and femininity as natural, indispensable, and inevitable.

The gendering of allocation of resources within the household is guided by patriarchal norms and ideological understanding of appropri-ate roles for women. Thus, even when women gain public employment, it has been in response to strategies of family survival—instead of empowering them, waged work is now perceived as an extension of their reproductive labour. With the government withdrawing from welfare programmes, and in the context of a restructured labour market, it is women in their capacity as mothers, wives, and daughters who struggle for the survival of their families.[14] Madhu, 24 years of age, General Caste and unmarried, belongs to a family of landless sharecroppers. Hailing from Ulberia, a municipality in the district of Howrah, she travels to Kolkata on a daily basis to work as an unregistered nurse in the private nursing home. She narrates how she was aware that as soon as she finished her school, she would have to earn enough money to support her family. This expectation is not extended to her male sibling, who is given the resources to study and pursue a technical education (in Kolkata) that is expected to fetch more dividends. She says, 'I always knew that I somehow had to earn money to look after the family. I was

[12] Oakley (1993).
[13] Rubin (1975).
[14] Beneria and Feldman (1992).

the older child and my brother needed to study. I managed to finish my class X and I thought nursing would give me a job, so I underwent training for one year and then joined here. My brother is studying computers.' She contributes all her money towards her brother's education. It has been argued that, given the low age of marriage in India, the typical woman worker was married and with children, responding to familial rather than market imperatives.[15] However, my research shows that a large number of women (38.2 per cent) are unmarried (Table A.1) and thus the entry of young women into the labour market, straight from school or with training, is a departure from the usual trends. However, whether married or single, women continue to enter the labour market in response to family needs.

Madhu is not isolated. The informal economy absorbs women with low education and training, who subsequently find no upward mobility. About 28.6 per cent of the respondents (Table A.2) have dropped out of school to earn money to support the family, and 39.2 per cent of them have passed their secondary level school examinations. While the former are concentrated in marginal, precarious economic activities as untrained attendants, the latter are concentrated in semi-trained/trained nursing categories. Though the levels of school education and the nature of nursing training justify their position in the labour market and corresponding wages, working conditions, and terms of employment, I emphasize the role of the family along with the labour market, which actively produces feminine, (hetero)normative subjects who occupy inferior, subordinate, and ancillary positions in the market and at home. Bourdieu's concept of habitus is useful for us to understand how the family works as an apparatus to produce a docile, feminine labouring body who accepts her 'fate' as legitimate. Habitus is a 'system of lasting, transposable dispositions which, integrating past experience, functions at every moment as a matrix of perceptions, appreciations, and actions....'[16] He goes on to argue that the habitus shapes the aspiration and practices of the individual and the group, who internalize various fundamental conditions of existence into disposition, transforming social and economic 'necessity' into 'virtue', thus submitting

[15] Banerjee (1999).
[16] Bourdieu (1969).

to the existing social order.[17] While investment in male children was the norm (Table A.3), possibly because the gendered nature of the labour market meant that it would fetch more dividends, (hetero)normativity within the household also constituted choices, decision, and resolutions in case of conflicts.

Habitus is not habit, as the word implies, but an embodied disposition that shapes and constitutes us. Young girls coming of age are taught that their lives, education, hopes, and desires are not important but secondary to their families. Radha, 35 years of age, married, General Caste, talks of how her father's job as clerk in the Bata shoe factory could not keep the family afloat, and thus education for the daughters was discontinued. Now working as a private sister in a government hospital, she says:

> We are five sisters and two brothers. How can so many study in one small room? So we sisters did not study. I took training from Red Cross and became a private sister. Our mother and we, the sisters, worked very hard so that we could pay for both our brothers' education. Now one brother is a government officer and the other brother took our father's job after he took voluntary retirement. (Personal interview with the author)

Radha took the option of waged work early in life (and therefore became an unskilled, low-paid worker) so that her brothers could have the education that would place them on a higher position in the labour market. While all the female members of the family (including her mother) 'worked hard', so that the male members of the family could be equipped with the skills required to negotiate the labour market, the constitution of women's labour as 'cheap', 'un/semi-skilled', and 'supplementary' meant that the disinvestment in her education was perceived as a natural course of action in a hetero-patriarchal society. These norms constitute dispositions where women perceive themselves as secondary and insignificant, supporting male desires and ambitions, thereby perpetuating and maintaining the hetero-patriarchal nexus. Consider, for example, Shraddha, who is twenty-six years of age, General Caste, married, and is living in the outskirts of the city. She works as a registered nurse in a government hospital. Coming from

[17] Bourdieu (1990: 54).

an impoverished family of small farmers, she is the only child and was encouraged to think of a career.

> When my Class X results were good, my father stopped me from doing housework and offering tutorials to earn money to pay my fees. A lot of people in the neighbourhood also helped me—they gave me books. My family never opposed my decision to undergo training in nursing because they knew this would ensure a government job and I would be able to help them. (Personal interview with the author)

'A lot of people in the neighbourhood also helped me.... My father stopped me from doing housework and giving tuitions'. This helped shape Shradha's disposition whereby she started believing in her capabilities and the merits of the market. She narrates her struggles in nursing education. Despite coming from a poor family she dreamt of higher education: 'I would really study because I wanted to make my family proud. They believed in me. I knew I had the capability to make it.' The confidence and expectation placed on Shraddha by her family and community, along with material support, allowed her to dream and aspire for a profession that seemed a little out of reach. Though nursing is considered a step down from teaching and remains a stigmatized occupation, for Shradha, working as a registered nurse in a government hospital was a goal that many girls from her background could never aspire for.

While ideologies of love and care make questioning of inequalities within the family difficult, feminists have noted the importance of doing so. Luce Irigaray contends that for a woman, she is a wife and mother in an abstract and universal duty; for men, love for a woman within the home constitutes him as a citizen. Thus, the norm for men and women function differently: while for the former, it is to be a citizen in the civil sphere, for the latter, it is to be a wife and mother, irrespective of her singular desires.[18] The family has been described as 'feudal',[19] feudal, as Spivak explains, in terms of coding of affective value rather than economic—a domestication and internalization of love and affect held together by feudal ideology.[20] Tulika, 50 years of age, Brahmin and

---

[18] Irigaray (1991).
[19] Fraad, Resnick, and Wolff (1994).
[20] Spivak (1994: x).

unmarried, is working for the last fifteen years as a registered nurse for a pittance at the private nursing home. She is aware that conformity to gender roles, as expected from her in her family and society, has led her to miss opportunities in her career, which will never come back. This, however, did not hold for her brothers. Despite a much-coveted nursing training, she could not take advantage of opportunities available to her. However, the same expectations were not set for her brothers, who once established, moved away.

> When I passed the GNM course, my mother expired. To take care of my three young brothers as well as my father, I did not take the government posting. Four years later when I got another chance at a government posting, my father died and my youngest brother was too young. I could not leave him. My other two brothers left home and they now live with their wives. My youngest brother became my responsibility as a part of my household duties. After all, I am the only woman in the family. How could I take a government posting and leave, even if it paid more money? (Personal interview with the author)

Tulika's case is not isolated. Women narrate how male siblings, once established and married, move out of their parent's home and set up separate conjugal households. This means that the responsibility of looking after aged family members and younger siblings fall on the daughter, who in the first place is ill-equipped for the task. Despite evidences pouring in that men do not necessarily take care of their aged parents, the construction of the young woman is still that of a future wife, whose legitimate location is her conjugal household. In Indian society, it is usually expected that women get absorbed into their conjugal households after marriage. Their connection with their natal family is stretched to the point where it becomes customary and ritualistic. However, my research contradicts this commonplace assumption: marriage does not necessarily create a rupture in women's financial responsibilities towards their natal families. Women continue to work even after marriage, so that they can sustain their financial responsibilities in their natal homes. In the face of failure of normative masculinities, where men abdicate their responsibilities as sons and brothers, femininity stretches itself to act as a safety valve. This (re)constitution of femininity—caring and nurturing, ideally directed towards the conjugal family—now includes the natal family that she left behind.

My fieldwork also included migrant workers coming from different states such as Jharkhand, Kerala, Manipur, Orissa, and Bihar who work as registered nurses in private hospitals. Within the age group of 20 to 25, these women are fresh graduates from private nursing colleges, who have come to Bengal looking for work experience as they wait for either government postings or opportunities to go abroad. Their training in the private sector, which is expensive, was funded by loans or contributions from the family and/or the Church. Most women from Jharkhand, whose families have converted to Christianity from Scheduled Tribes, got financial aid partly by the state and partly by the church. Women from Kerala, Orissa, and Bihar are encouraged by their families who recognized the economic dividends of being a nurse in the international market. Annie, 25 years of age, unmarried, and from the Hunda community (Scheduled Tribe) hailing from Ranchi, Jharkhand, trained as a GNM nurse from a private college in Vishakhapatnam and is now working in a private hospital in Kolkata. She talks of how nursing is the chosen profession for most women in her community. 'We are three brothers and three sisters. Two brothers have joined the church and one is still studying. All of us sisters have trained as nurses. The state subsidized my private training and the rest was paid by the Church.' Annie narrates how most women belonging to Scheduled Tribe communities in almost all villages chose nursing as a career. As most of these tribal communities have converted to Christianity, they are supported both by the State, as well as the Church. Nursing is considered an ideal career for women. Kamya, aged 21, unmarried, General Caste, hails from Kerala, trained as a GNM nurse from a private college in Cochin, says,

> My mother is a school teacher and my father works as a guide in Dubai.
> I did not want to train as a nurse. But my mother insisted that there is a
> guarantee of job that will pay well and I can go abroad. My father paid
> rupees two lakh and a bank loan of rupees two lakh was taken. After
> I have gained experience and passed my exams, I will go to Dubai and
> repay the loan. (Personal interview with the author)

Both Annie and Kamya as well as most of the girls who have migrated from other states and are working as nurses waiting to go abroad, say that nursing is the preferred occupation. Given that teachers from South Asia are not in demand in Western Asia, and domestic work remains a stigmatized occupation for 'illiterate' women, most girls take up nursing.

Sexualities and Control: Women and Labour Markets

Work opportunities for women that entail their presence in the public sphere are often structured by gendered norms. The delineation of the private as safe and legitimate and the public as dangerous and illegitimate often guide women's choices and responses to opportunities in the labour market. In most cultures, including India, the legitimate and dominant sexual economy is procreative, conjugal, monogamous, and heterosexual, which codes other expressions of sexuality as marginal, abhorrent, and abject. Even the women's movement(s) have not questioned the rights of those who live outside the conjugal norm.[21] The premium placed on virginity and female monogamy has been seen as central to maintaining and perpetuating caste hierarchy, and adultery/pre-marital sex on part of the woman is seen as a significant crime.[22] Control over women's sexuality is central to women being 'allowed' to work in some places, some occupations and not others. Madhuri, 38 years of age, General Caste, hailing from an urban, middle-class family, got married to a man of her choice while studying for her graduation in Bethune College (an elite girl's college in Kolkata). After her graduation, keeping with the norms of a middle-class, upper-caste Bengali household and the wishes of both her natal and conjugal family, she declined the job offer of a teacher from an elite school in Kolkata. The restraint on women's employment and its articulation in terms of 'danger' to women's chastity is linked to the honour of the family. Thus, sexualized norms of restriction define women's legitimate spaces, which further allow the family/community to establish control. Women's chastity is also intrinsically linked to hegemonic masculinities, where men as fathers and husbands are to ensure the 'purity' of their women. Now going through a divorce with her husband, Madhuri works as an attendant in a government hospital.

> This job is way below my status and education. I wanted to be a school teacher but my husband and parents-in-law did not let me work. I am going through a divorce and I have a 15 -year old son. I applied for jobs in many offices and did not get anything. In desperation, I am working as a *mashi* [attendant]. (Personal interview with the author)

---

[21] Shah (2005: 15).
[22] Chakravarti (1993).

For Madhuri, gender norms, more than education and training, placed her at a disadvantageous position in the labour market. Despite all her caste and class privileges, she is structurally located at the lowest end of this segment of the labour market. The failure of patriarchal arrangements in maintaining ideologies of women's seclusion often leave them in a fix; with the failure of her marriage and her husband's renunciation of the role of the protector, Madhuri is left to fend for herself in a situation she is ill-equipped to face.

Departing from social constructivist theories, post-structuralist feminists argue that bodies are discursively produced and modern subjects are made intelligible by socially articulated norms.[23] The family and the market, functioning as ideological apparatuses, provide a normative framework that produces bodies that are (hetero)normative, which are an effect of regulatory norms that are both concretely material and historically constituted. Thus, one emerges as a subject only to the point that one is socially recognized as one, effectively foreclosing any other possibilities. The regulatory power of gender as a norm makes one productive as well as intelligible and suggests modes of surveillance and discipline.[24] The code of honour and the ideology of chastity are central to control over women's labour. They produce (hetero) normative subjects, who discipline themselves as chaste wives and dutiful daughters within the family, and disciplined and docile workers within the labour market. Thus, control over sexuality and regulation of women's mobility is not just a cultural phenomenon but a structural violence that maintains and perpetuates women's subordination and dependency.

The constitution of the chaste woman, as the submissive worker who internalizes patriarchal norms, has material effects. On being asked of the aspirations, hopes, and dreams of the future, there were varied responses. While some women, mostly working as registered and unregistered nurses, hoped to either get promoted or take up better job offers in other hospitals/nursing homes, those women concentrated at the lowest end wanted to leave the nursing sector altogether. Women with GNM training are confident and self-assured as they wait for better posting, opportunities abroad, or look

[23] Butler (2004).
[24] Butler (2004).

towards promotions; however, for nurses with no registration and unrecognized training, private sisters, and attendants, responses were ambiguous, reflecting fear, uncertainty, and lack of confidence. The lack of any kind of social/economic mobility in the labour market also contributed to women's lack of interest in continuing to work in such low-end jobs. While at the first glance, it seems that women's desire to discontinue in the labour market stems from social and economic recognition at the workplace, a close reading of women's narratives add another layer.

The coordinates of honour/shame exercise tight control over women's mobility by family members, which prevents them from seeking better employment opportunities; in fact, women themselves internalize these fears. To be recognized as a 'good' woman meant to give into fears of possible threat, to not display naked ambition, ready to go wherever a better opportunity awaits, and to adhere to norms of chastity, deference, and submission. The fear of the unknown—of sexual danger 'waiting out there', lurking in places that may offer better opportunities—prevent women from being mobile and quitting one job for the other. None of the organizations where I conducted my fieldwork have any sexual harassment cell, where complaints could be lodged. Sexual harassment (or the threat of it) faced from doctors and ward boys, long commuting distances, odd working hours, and stigmatization of the profession add up to the violence that women working in this sector negotiate on an everyday basis. Bijoya, 42 years of age, Scheduled Caste and married, lives in Konnagar in the district of Hooghly and travels every day by train to work as an attendant in a private hospital. However, she is clear that even if she is offered more money, she will not go to a new place. Her fear of getting sexually violated paralyses any aspirations she may have harboured. 'I have never tried to look for work. I do not have the courage to look for a new place. I have grown used to this place. All nursing homes are not the same; there may be places where a lot of bad things happen.'

What is striking is that while Bijoya is willing to migrate from a rural to urban area on a daily basis, often taking trains at wee hours in the morning, after a night shift or late in the night after an evening shift, she is fearful of a new workplace. Sayori, 27 years of age, unmarried, General Caste, hails from a family of landless sharecroppers and works as an unregistered nurse in the private nursing home. She was one of the few women who spoke of sexual harassment faced by nurses from male colleagues, particularly doctors. She narrates:

> Doctors are very powerful here in these private nursing homes. Most owners are doctors themselves and it is their friends who practice here. In an operation theatre, when a doctor is operating, he will ask for an instrument, reach out his hand, and rest it on your breast. If you move away, he will know you are not interested. If you keep standing, it is a sign you are available. But you cannot complain. If you do, you lose your job. (Personal interview with the author)

Not just ideology but also the threat of violence, if hetero-patriarchal norms are broken, prevent women from exercising their freedom from patriarchal control. Amrita, 28 years of age, Scheduled Caste, and married, is a second generation migrant. Her father left Uttar Pradesh and came to Kolkata thirty years back. He found employment as a sweeper in the same hospital that currently employs her as an attendant. She says,

> Women say they are earning and that is why they are independent. We can never have the freedom of a man; we have certain weakness that can be taken advantage of. If I try to behave like a man, I will be punished by my husband, by society. People will talk, life will become very difficult. No matter how much we earn, we have to watch for ourselves. (Personal interview with the author)

Interestingly, none of the registered nurses expressed any such fears, whether it was going abroad or taking a posting in a city/district they barely knew. When asked, they did not acknowledge sexual harassment at work and blamed the stigmatization of nursing on the misconduct of the individual nurse. For a section of workers, the threat of sexual violence paralyses their search for better opportunities, while for others, the denial of structural sexual violence is essential for their mobility. Both reflect a control over women's sexuality. While for registered nurses, changing sectors (private to government), availing promotions, or migrating to new countries can mean an increased salary and better working conditions, for unregistered and ancillary nursing staff, these possibilities are not open. The latter can only change jobs within the informal economy where increase in salary is marginal—the labour market is constituted in such a manner that their informal accumulation of knowledge is not recognized and thus vertical growth is not possible. For registered nurses, the socio-economic mobility is so rapid that moving to unknown places and migrating to foreign countries seems worth the risk. Thus, familial support in terms of a relative loosening of control over women's mobility is influenced by her earning capacities, which go to benefit the family. The status and visibility of a registered nurse in the medical hierarchy is far higher than an unregistered nurse, attendant, and private sister. The heightened visibility and status (compared to other categories) allows women to take advantage of job opportunities. Normative femininity recomposes itself to include women's economic productivity; however, this does not mean that families loosen their control over women's sexualities.

Tina Chanter, reading Foucault's conception of power, argues that power is not a monolithic, top-down, centralized force, and instead defines power as something that is administered by the subject herself. Instead of it being hoisted on to the subject, it is produced from below. The subjects of modern society discipline themselves. The disciplinarian is also the individual herself as much as social mechanisms that strengthen norms.[25] In a number of interviews, registered nurses responded to queries on sexual harassment, violence, and freedom saying that 'as long as I am good, everything will be all right (*nijeke thik rakhle sob thik thake*). Everything depends on us.' This reasoning that everything is dependent on the will and agency of the subject obscures the structural violence that working women face. In many ways, it even justifies it, and leads to victim blaming. Seemanthini Niranjana argues that putting the onus on the woman is another way of regulating female sexualities. The inside/safe and outside/dangerous binary does not get inverted, instead 'one more layer of the inside—an interior moral sense'—is being posited.[26] Thus the modern subject, the professional nurse, in search of newer and better opportunities, within the country and/or abroad, free from the panoptic gaze of the family, carries the responsibility of ensuring continuity and reproduction of the family honour.

[25] Chanter (2006).
[26] Niranjana (2001: 51).

Reinforcing Norms and Feminine Dependency: Negotiating Work/Negotiating Home

How is gender performed at the workspace? What is the relation between gender identities and aspirations of workers? Gender is an important constituent in structuring ambition and aspiration of women in their workplaces. While the understanding that 'merit' structures and facilitates promotions, career advancements, and increments at the workplace is almost doxic, this section highlights that aspirations, inclinations, and ambitions are as much gendered as well as produced by inequalities of class and caste. Social processes and structures are essential elements in producing gendered dispositions, which create inequalities that are considered legitimate. When I asked my respondents about their dreams and aspirations, 71.2 per cent of the respondents felt that their expectations from the nursing profession have not been met (Table A.4). All attendants and most women working as unregistered nurses and private sisters fall under this category. Some (17 per cent) of the respondents either have no expectations or could not tell whether their expectations have been met. It was mostly women (9.5 per cent) who work as registered nurses, who answered in the affirmative. Table A.5 tabulates distribution of respondents according to their desire for further training. More than 85 per cent of respondents replied negatively. It was a minuscule 5.2 per cent of respondents who worked as trained nurses who answered in the affirmative. Women who work as unregistered nurses, attendants, and private sisters felt that further training was not possible, given their locations in the labour market and/or their subordinate positions at home. Registered nurses largely expressed a desire to stay within the nursing profession but to move up vertically in the hierarchy. But to do so, they need further education and training, which they felt is not possible because of familial responsibilities and lack of spousal support. Only a few women (4.2 per cent) were sure that they will enrol for further studies in the near future. It is easier for trained nurses in government hospitals to attain a BSc or MSc degree as formal employment includes paid study leave and other facilities. However, gender norms act as a barrier. Almost all women are articulate about the sexual division of labour within the household that is resistant to any change and comes in the way of their aspirations. Even if facilities are made available in the public sphere, norms within the private domain curbs growth. However, this dissonance between their aspirations and reality does not necessarily lead to any radical questioning of daily practices or initiate negotiations over the sexual division of labour. Mala, 34 years of age, married, General Caste, hails from an urban middle-class family in Kolkata, and works as a registered nurse in the government hospital. She says,

> I would like to obtain a BSc degree but it is not possible with a child. My husband says he is okay with me enrolling for a BSc courses. But saying it is different and doing something about it is different. Taking some responsibility at home, making some sacrifices—these he will not do. (Personal interview with the author)

The sexually organized social order can only remain stable if women stay true to their traditional roles. This would mean that even if women perform extraordinarily at their workplaces, their roles at home do not change. Basabi, 28 years of age, married, General Caste, hails from a middle-class family from Sodepur, in the district of North 24 Parganas, and works as a registered nurse in the government hospital. She says,

> I feel like studying for a BSc degree and I have started my preparations, but after I graduate, there will be a rural posting. I have enrolled my daughter in an English medium school and I do not want to discontinue that. And my husband cannot handle a child and he tells me that a child needs a mother. Mothers have to sacrifice all the time. My husband wants me to obtain a BSc and an MSc degree and then when I tell him that there will be a rural posting, he keeps quiet. (Personal interview with the author)

The gap between aspirations of women and the realities of a patriarchal society strikes deep. Both Mala and Basabi are keenly aware that patriarchal ideologies of women's roles and duties come in the way of their ambition. Yet, they express their inability to challenge gendered norms that prevent them from achieving their dreams. It is important to flag here that though women working as registered nurses in the public sector do talk of degrees that might help them in their career, it is also understood that the structure of the labour market is such that accumulating degrees do not guarantee any vertical move. The return is so marginal that women prefer status quo. Only one registered nurse, Sumana, amongst all my respondents was able to complete her BSc and was hoping to leave clinical nursing and become a tutor nurse. Sumana,

31 years of age, unmarried, Brahmin, comes from the district of Hooghly. Her father, a shopkeeper, encouraged all three siblings to study and choose independent careers. Sumana, after serving as a nurse in a rural posting in North Bengal, was transferred to the city only a few years ago. She chose not to get married and instead studied for a BSc degree with the hope that she would be able to rise up the hierarchy faster. However, she is disappointed that apart from a marginal increment in her salary, there has been no significant change. She conceded that it was almost next to impossible for women with familial responsibilities to avail the opportunities that the government provides. She traced her ability in achieving a degree to the fact that she was both unmarried and had no duties or responsibilities in her natal family. Her ability to negotiate the labour market was honed by the fact that she is free from familial responsibilities. The primacy of the domestic for women, coupled with the ideologies of femininity, act as a barrier for trained nurses to seek out opportunities. As long as the public sphere is compatible with the private domain, women face no conflict, but when there is a rupture, and one has to be chosen over the other, the latter prevails. Unregistered nurses, however, feel the added burn of knowing that despite having learnt all the work that a registered nurse is expected to do, experience can never replace qualifications. Notwithstanding their (on-the-job) training, they are debarred from promotions, better salaries, and benefits due to lack of a recognized qualification. This ineligibility is exploited by owners and administrators of both government and private hospitals, who hire them for a salary less than one-fifth of a government-employed registered nurse.

The argument that economic dividends influence worker's choices in the labour market as rational agents is belied by some of the narratives. Respect, stigma, fear of the unknown, sexual harassment, norms, and ideologies often play an equal role in decisions within the labour market. This (re)constitution of ideal femininity, where women must earn and yet have traditional gender roles as the bedrock of their identity, is a performance of respectable femininity, which is prevalent even among working-class women. This is reflected in their choices for their children as well. The efficacy of the habitus in constituting subjects lie in the fact that they function beyond the reach of language or free will.[27]

---

[27] Bourdieu (1984).

The gendered habitus of women that constitute her thought, aspirations, and desires, manifest in her choices for her children's future—the (hetero)normative feminine role is the ideal that her daughter must live up to—even if it has failed her.

Almost all women (32.9 per cent) with male children are bringing them up to join the labour market (Table A.6); while among those who have borne female children, 50 per cent are being prepared for marriage (Table A.7). Aspirations for daughters do include economic self-sufficiency but in a feminine profession, to help her marital home accomplish economic security and social mobility. Most women do not want their daughters to join the medical profession, not even as doctors. Teaching is the most desired profession for women and computers/ engineering and the like for men. Some women aspire for established grooms for their daughter, so that they can be housewives, and are saving for a dowry. Daughters are to be educated enough so that they can be employed in 'respectable' professions till they find a suitable groom. Sanchayita, 37 years of age, General Caste, hailing from a middle-class, urban family, and married to a doctor, works as a registered nurse in a government hospital. She strongly feels that her daughters should not have to work. While she herself chose nursing because she wanted a career and was encouraged by her father, she is not sure if she wants the same for her daughters. She says, 'I do not want any of my two daughters to be a nurse. I would prefer them to be housewives. The home gets neglected. They can become school teachers if they want to earn to help their husbands or if they feel that they must be independent.'

Most women think that a male child is a better investment than a girl child; only few did not agree (Table A.3). But without fail, most of those who had children of both sexes and faced financial difficulties withdrew their daughters from school and invested their meagre resources in their son's education. The constitution of gendered dispositions lie within the family. Despite witnessing the failure of patriarchy, and lamenting the lack of education and discriminations faced in their natal homes, women continue to aspire for ideal, respectable feminine roles for their daughters. The (hetero)normative sexual economy that bestows recognition and respect only to those women who are located in conjugal relations and work in respectable occupations for the welfare of their families constitute the habitus that govern women's choices and decisions.

The More It Changes, the More It Remains the Same: Negotiating the Home

One of the most critical sites of mapping evolving gender relations has been the division of labour within the household. Research has flagged that with increasing participation of women in the public realm, no dent has been made in the sexual division of labour within the private sphere; on the contrary, the hope of unpaid household labour being equally distributed among both sexes has gradually dissipated. While working-class women depend on the larger kin system and older women in the family to look after their children while they are away at work, middle-class women depend on paid domestic workers. Women's participation in the public realm has precipitated a crisis in ideologies of gender, and norms are reinforced to ensure that (hetero)normativity is not questioned. Men are not alone in this project, but women and particularly older women in the family are complicit in these often violent processes of regulation and reinforcement of norms. Shraddha, who we met earlier, reported that because her conjugal family is not happy that she is working as a nurse, household work had to be done even more meticulously.

> I am not able to work at home and, thus, I have to listen to a lot of things. Other women in the family, like my sisters-in-law, have to do all the housework and they taunt me. Because I cannot give time at home, they express their anger towards me. I wanted to keep a servant for my share of housework but they did not agree. I cannot even take full responsibility for any chore because we have shift duty. My husband also does not like the fact that I do not do any work at home. These are all indirect pressures for me to give up nursing. (Personal interview with the author)

The refusal to allow Shraddha to hire domestic workers to take care of her share of household work is a means of establishing control over her labour. Employment in the prestigious public health services implied she was relatively better off economically than most women in her social context, however, within her family she is chastised and made to feel inferior and guilty for her inability to give primacy to the private realm. The pressure mounted on her to submit to male authority within the household, give up her job, and focus on the home is to break her defiance in questioning (hetero) normative structures that dictates that she must always give primacy to her role as a wife and mother. Given Shraddha's struggles to train and find employment as a nurse and her father's aspiration for his daughter's career, it is even more poignant that in her conjugal home, she is constantly reprimanded for her success.

Guilt induced by neglect of duties associated with normative femininity (housework, child care), coupled with real threats of violence, work as a disciplining tool that governs lives. Even though employment opens up avenues to explore newer freedom, patriarchal norms clearly lay out boundaries, and transgressions can invite punishment. Therefore, the freedom earned (however limited) is offset by extra vigilance by women to ensure the continuation of gender norms, whether at home or at work. Women's subordinate position within the private and public sphere is reinforced by patriarchal discipline in both realms. As Moyna, 37 years of age, married, Brahmin and hailing from an urban, professional family and working as a registered nurse in a government hospital, says,

> I felt so much guilt, especially because of night duty, that I would try and do everything at home, so that my family-in-law cannot point a finger at me. I would make sure that after duty, I would go straight home and not even stop to have tea. (Personal interview with the author)

A very strong spatial narrative guides women's movements in the public realm. The disciplining of the female body entails that she does not occupy more space than necessary in the public realm. The central preoccupation of women must be the family, and her negotiation with the public realm an extension of that preoccupation. Her everyday activities are choreographed by implicit norms that govern the female body that forbids loitering in public spaces and maintain seclusion. That is, their mobility must be reduced to home and work and back.

Love is Never Enough: Linking Marriage with Employment

Both romantic love and its telos, marriage, are ideologies that sustain heterosexist patriarchies. Further, marriage is defined by patrilocality, patrilineality, hetero-normativity, monogamy, and rules of endogamy/exogamy, whereby the only legitimate union is one that takes place within the boundaries of class, caste, and community. Since the 1990s, discussions on sexualities and desire have become central to feminist critique of family and marriage, whereby the institution of family has been identified as an apparatus that produces (hetero) normative subjects, who sustain the social order.[28] Rinchin has further pointed out that families are also a 'context of violence, oppression and restriction' that forecloses possibilities of other kinds of desires, aspirations, and existences.[29] My discussions, conversations, and interviews with women working in different ranks of the nursing labour market, more often than not, veered towards the institution of marriage and its inevitability. Given my 'single' status, conversations of how I was 'allowed' to stay unmarried foregrounded the compulsory nature of heterosexual unions, the unavoidable and inescapable institutionalization of romantic love. My respondents spoke of conjugal relations, aspirations for a life partner, the inevitability of marriages, fear and insecurities of dowry—all of which they relate to their economic and social status. Marriages are essential for steering resources to maintain, perpetuate, and reinforce heteropatriarchy, and are, therefore, key to sustaining the public/private binary in an increasingly complex society.

The institution of arranged marriage is prevalent but with alterations. Women chose their partners but parental consent plays a crucial role. A significantly large number (41.2 per cent) of women married with consent of both families, while some (20.2 per cent) faced objections (Table A.8). Some of the objections were grounded in rules that forbade marriage beyond caste and community boundaries; others were miffed for transgressing class norms. Some women also faced opposition from prospective in-law because they worked as nurses or attendants. No one that I spoke to faced objections on the grounds of being a waged worker per se. It could also be that women I met, interacted, and interviewed were those who were 'allowed' to continue to work after marriage. Most women (47.8 per cent) felt working as nursing staff made it more difficult to find a groom in the marriage market (Table A.9). It was mostly women working as trained nurses (13.8 per cent) who felt that being a nurse worked as an advantage when it came to looking for a match, particularly for those from the states of Kerala, Jharkhand, Manipur, and Orissa. Chhaya, 45 years of age, General Caste, hails from a family of professionals who had migrated to the city twenty years back and is working as a registered nurse in the government hospital. She felt

---

[28]   Menon (2012).
[29]   Rinchin (2015).

that she got marriage proposals because she worked in the government sector; being a nurse was incidental. On the contrary, Ramala, 27 years of age, General Caste, hails from a family of impoverished farmers, working as an unregistered nurse felt that both being a nurse as well as an informal worker went against her. 'So many marriage proposals did not materialize because "first a nurse, and on top of that, private job". My sister-in-law also works as a private nurse; that is probably why my in-law agreed to this marriage.'

For some, working as a nurse is an impediment to a good alliance; for others, it is the key to social and economic mobility. As much as the nature of the work influences choices and opportunities in the marriage market, work contract also have an influencing role. Sometimes nursing itself did not prevent marriage proposals but the nature of work contract did—the vulnerabilities faced by workers in contractual employment and the consequent effect on the stability of the family seemed to play a decisive role in women's worth in the marriage market. Women working in the government sector get more desirable marriage proposals than women working as nurses in the private sector. A government job is desirable, whether a staff nurse or an attendant. Most registered nursing staff in the government hospital felt that their husbands married them because they were in public employment. The plenitude of marital opportunities and prospects for women in government employment, despite being in a largely devalued occupation, speaks volumes about the perceived potential of women's economic contribution to the conjugal family.

Social and economic motivations played an important role in choosing partners for both men and women. While nurses working in government services aspire to either marry doctors or other well-established professionals, unregistered nurses, private sisters, and attendants aspire for a man who has a 'steady job' or is self-employed. Marriage is seen as a route to social and economic mobility. Jaya, 23 years of age, Scheduled Caste, living in Bongaon in the district of North 24 Parganas, and working as a private sister in the government hospital, wants to marry a man who has a contractual job and is not paid wages on a daily basis like her. 'I want to marry someone who is earning 10,000 rupees at least and who is in a contractual job. Not this—"no work no pay".' With the fragmented nature of the labour market that prevents vertical growth, particularly for women located at the lower end, marriage may be the only way of gaining some kind of social and economic stability. The imperative to marry was partly social and partly economic. Women at the lower end of the hierarchy were articulate that only marriage could give them some financial solvency and stability, which their precarious jobs with exploitative working conditions could not. They also realize that their lack of education/training meant that there was no possibility of finding employment that could give them the stability that they crave. Marriage could possibly be the only viable way out of the quagmire that they found themselves in.

Conversations on autonomy, romantic love, and marital unions also reflected traditional conformism. Pierre Bordieu writes, 'The constraints surrounding every matrimonial choice are so tremendous and appear in such complex combinations that the individuals involved cannot possibly deal with them consciously ... marriage strategies are the product of habitus.'[30] Women often said that they did not care much for caste and community identities in choosing life partners but further reported that they were married into their own social groups. Some women did flout such conventions and transgressed norms to marry men of their choice; most women chose to maintain status quo. However, most marriages are arranged according to strict caste and class rules. Working as nurses/ attendants is a transgression of both middle-class and upper-caste norms; yet, the boundaries of such norms are stretched to accommodate paid labour. But when it comes to conjugal alliances, such norms are strictly adhered to. Caste plays an important role in deciding life partners. For instance, some women said that they do not observe the caste system, yet their families are looking for alliances within their caste and class groups. Caste rules can be bent to accommodate paid menial work but remain inflexible when it comes to establishing marriage alliances. Kakoli, 22 years of age, Brahmin, who works as a private sister in a government hospital, insists she will only marry within her own caste. Yet, when asked whether working as nurse is not a transgression of caste norms and a loss of caste status, she responds 'I am a sebika and I am not breaking any caste rules by doing this kind of work, so why should I marry outside my caste?' The trope of sebika is used in imaginative ways that allows women's paid labour to be accommodated within caste rules without questioning its dominance.

[30] Bourdieu (1976: 141).

However, for some women, paid work has given them the bargaining chip to transgress caste, class, and gender norms to marry men of their choice. Women reported defying familial authority to marry men of other castes. Anima, 40 years of age, Scheduled Caste, working as an attendant in the private nursing home, proposed and subsequently married her (now) husband. Being of a lower caste than her husband, she met with resistance from her family-in-law. However, being employed gave her the confidence to pursue her husband.

> I met my husband through a common friend four years back (previous to marriage); we travelled in the same train. When I got my job, I went up to him and proposed marriage. I did not realize that I would face so much backlash from his family, but because I am earning I am able to fight back. However, the salary is too meagre to make much of difference. (Personal interview with the author)

All women (across caste, class, religion) expressed a fear of dowry, expensive gifts, and exorbitant wedding celebrations. It did not matter whether their jobs were permanent, contractual, or daily-wage. A few women working as registered nurses and belonging to tribal communities outside Bengal followed the customary bride price, which they admitted was nothing but symbolic. A minimum of 10,000 rupees had to be given to the bride's father. Women from Jharkhand reported that almost all women who belong to scheduled tribes were nurses and it was the most popular profession for women. Nurses were in great demand in the marriage market, and women were encouraged to take up nursing from when they were in school. This partially explains the demand for nurses as brides in Ranchi. Annie, who we met earlier, says,

> Whole of Ranchi and Jharkhand, in every Scheduled Tribe household, everyone pays bride price. My service as a staff nurse will increase bride price but we do not ask for more. It's not in our customs to increase bride price because the girl is earning, but because I am working as a nurse, I can ask more.

Scholars have argued that the transition from bride price to dowry was due to the increasing masculinization of the labour market and the subsequent marginalization of women. The erosion of women's employment opportunities and her gradual confinement within the domestic realm led to a devaluation of women's productivity, which spiked dowry practices all over the country, even in castes and communities that traditionally practiced bride price.[31] The presence of bride price in certain tribal communities, even if it is practiced symbolically, demonstrates how the devaluation of women's labour may not have been as pervasive or uniform as made out to be. In this case, globalization and an international market for service work has seen a resurgence of women's traditional labour. Annie asserts that her employment as a nurse and her plans to migrate abroad legitimizes her demands of higher bride price, even if local norms and customs prevented her from doing so. What remains incontestable is the link between dowry/bride price and women's employment.

However, this was not the case with Hindu families. Hindu nurses working in Kolkata, even as government employees, could not say no to dowry. Though they were politically against dowry as they perceived it as a crime against women, they acknowledged that gold, exorbitant celebrations, and gifts for the groom and his family are demanded and given. The agitation against dowry and existence of laws against the practice possibly may have influenced what is considered as dowry, but has obviously not eradicated it. Working class women did not seem very affected by public discourses on dowry and its legalities, and freely admitted that without cash being given, there would be no marriage—the amount could vary anything from Rs 50,000 to 2,00,000.

Most married women expressed their inability to leave their marriage despite conflicts which ranged from mutual incompatibility, domestic violence, extramarital affairs, and gambling to alcoholism and unemployment of their spouses. The most cited reason is the difficulty of living outside the institution of marriage as a single woman. The welfare of the family, which depended on a double income, also prevented women from rocking the boat. The stigma of a divorce or separation and the threat of violence worked as a powerful tool of social control in keeping women within the conjugal home. The retribution of breaking a norm could break a life. Patriarchal disciplining with the family, workplace, and communities ensures the nexus of hetero-normative patriarchy. Aparna, 45 years of age, General Caste and working as an attendant in a

---

[31] Banerjee (2002).

private hospital, observed that nurses would come to hospitals beaten up, because husbands were jealous and suspicious. So I ventured to ask her why women did not leave violent marriages despite having enough money of their own. She felt that the threat of violence faced by single women if they leave home outweighs the fear of violence they faced at home.

> Men can marry again, but once a woman is married, very few will accept her. To break a marriage is not difficult but to survive without marriage is difficult. You tolerate the pain that you are going through in your husband's home, everyone will support you. But if you leave, they will speak very badly about you. Even in the hospital, your colleagues will assassinate your character if they know that you do not live with your husband. The boys in the neighbourhood will taunt you, and maybe even attack you. At least if you are married, you are physically safe, no matter how painful it is. (Personal interview with the author)

* * *

In this chapter, I have traced how (hetero)normative economies structure women's lives, their choices, aspirations, and desires. The repressive discourses on family, honour, and chastity produce (hetero) normative subjects who occupy submissive, docile, and gendered roles, within the family and the labour market. Understanding the family and the labour market as historically and discursively produced provides us with an access point in understanding the interlinkages and the complex manner in which the two interact. Women's employment and the deployment of their labour has been a crucial territory in understanding evolving gender relations. While the picture has been dismal, given that historical and contemporary studies have demonstrated the ghettoization and marginalization of women in the public realm, the question of how it affects women's roles, duties, and bargaining power within the household is much more complex.

I suggest that there are no linear cause-and-effect relationships between the public and the private realm, as some models on power relations within the family suggest. The economically determined position, arguing that women's empowerment emerges from her gainful employment, has already come under critique. Instead, I argue that the resilience of patriarchy stems from the constitution of the subject according to repressive (heterosexual) norms operating both in the family and the market, which makes the gendered division of labour inevitable and imperative. It is in this context that I examine everyday practices, choices, yearnings, and aspirations of women, to argue that the production of the affective economy reflects the manner in which social and cultural capital is (re)produced within the family. The production of the normative subject—chaste, obedient, and submissive, who locates herself first within the private and examines the public with the lens of the former—is central to the efficient functioning of the social order. This patriarchal structure based on hierarchical inequalities is reproduced over generations. As the nature of labour market changes, feminine norms are stretched to include supposedly emancipatory agendas of waged work; however, patriarchy recomposes itself to accommodate this new femininity. In the next chapter, I examine everyday politics of labour based on hierarchies to argue that the workplace is an important site in producing identities and subjectivities. The production of the universal category called 'woman', equally exploited by the market and the family, is displaced, as I bring in other social identities to argue that women equally participate in divisive politics. In the next chapter, I look at women as social and political agents, who produce contradictory and contested fields, so as to secure marginal gains for some at the expense of others.

5 (Re)producing the 'Other'

Spatializing (Un)touchability, Dirty Work, and Inequalities

The question of the 'self' and the 'other' is fundamental to understanding human subjectivities, particularly for feminists who are antagonistic to traditional accounts of subjects, given that Cartesian dualism (in the Western philosophical canon) posits the subject as rational, unified, and non-corporeal.[1] Postmodern feminists, in particular, have argued that the subject can no longer be conceived in terms of an atomic self, disembodied and transcendental, but as mired in and produced by power, culture, and discourses. The jettisoning of the subject who enjoys a 'view from nowhere' to a subject produced by her context is a crucial step in acknowledging and recognizing hierarchies based on gender, caste, and class. (Re)thinking the subject from a post-modern perspective is also crucial in dismantling the classic notion of

[1] Llyod (1994).

a subject with a universal inner core, prior to any marking. This notion of an essential humanism that constitutes the core of a subject is central to the making of the universal category 'woman', which obliterates and erases other markers, for instance, caste, class, ethnicity, race, and sexualities. This lack of vigilance towards differences that constitute the experience of the female has been a central concern to both postmodern and post-colonial feminisms.[2]

Simone de Beauvoir draws attention to the question of the 'other'. She argues that the Self cannot be constituted as the subject without at once setting up the Other over against itself.[3] Given the slipperiness of categories, its incompleteness, and leakiness, it is everyday life that sustains inequalities, differences, and distinctions—the boundaries that mark the 'self' and the 'other' are never rigid, unyielding, static, or inflexible. On the contrary, boundaries and borders are porous, permeable, irregular, and prone to disintegration. Differences that are socially constructed and discursively produced and norms that create universals often in the interest of powerful groups, divergence from which carry negative and oppressive meanings, affect lives in real and material ways. Given that the relationship between social identities and occupational hierarchies remain untouched in some sectors (such as manual scavenging) but are coming under considerable strain in others (including nursing), what are the everyday rituals and practices that are performed, which contaminates and sanitizes space that is inhabited by differently ranked bodies offering similar kinds of labour? The nursing segment that I have studied is wholly composed of women; however, it accommodates women from different class and caste groups. In this chapter, I displace popular and teleological narratives of the congruence of class and caste and hope to locate the complexities of intersecting identities and the social stratifications it effects. In a workplace that is fraught with anxieties about identities and the subsequent disruption and unsettling of social order that it foments, the need to (re)produce boundaries take on urgency.

This chapter seeks to understand how notions of defilement, hygiene, pollution, and contamination ceaselessly work to structure women's experiences of working in a caste-based occupation, as well as their articulations of shame, humiliation, and pain. A hospital is a locus of

[2] Nicholson (1994); Mohanty (1991).
[3] Beauvoir (2011).

struggle between order and chaos, health and sickness, hygiene and dirt. As Douglas argues, reflecting on the notions of dirt, purity, pollution, avoidance, and transgression is central to understanding the durability of social structures and the relationship between order and disorder.[4] Historically, nursing is a caste-based occupation, a service offered by women belonging to marginalized communities within Brahmanical patriarchy. Yet, as I have demonstrated earlier, it is not a homogenous sector; rather, over the years, it has increasingly witnessed a differentiated workforce. This undermining of rigid occupational structures has generated anxieties centred on social identities, which are reflected both in everyday politics of discrimination, distinction, distancing, and intolerance as well as in the ideologies of socio-spatial politics. Organized spaces are not autonomous and systematic units but emerge from social frameworks and are thus simultaneously social as well as spatial.[5] Workers are produced by the spaces they work in, as well as co-produce them. I argue that space is not a grid by which we analyse exclusions and marginalization but is constitutive of the latter.

How does a woman working as a nurse/attendant/private sister in a small nursing home or a larger corporate hospital experience her labour? How does she negotiate social structures that constitute her as an unskilled, inferior, powerless unit of labour? How does she elucidate her identity as a worker? And, how does she perceive the signifying system that exploits her labour and confers on her the status of an inferior worker? How do women negotiate social identities that enjoy complex relationships with labour? Women working at the lower end of the hierarchy, engaged in cleaning, healing, and medicating human bodies manually and with bare hands, are not necessarily from the *Dalit-Bahujan Samaj* but women from higher castes reduced by poverty to seeking jobs that are ritualistically impure. The co-existence of women from different castes in a similar segment, formerly meant for women of lower castes, leads to anxieties of social disorder, chaos, and threatens to break down the caste system. How are borders created, rituals enacted, and spaces demarcated that allow separation, classification and codification of labour? The labour that goes into healing human beings include, as we have noted, labour that is devalued, disrespected, and stigmatized:

---

[4] Douglas (2002).
[5] Lefebvre (1991); Soja (1980).

the intimate corporeal labour that is required to heal ailing bodies is labour that requires contact with blood, bodily fluids, vomit, faeces, and other kinds of pus that violates body surfaces, which keep the notion of 'self' and 'other' intact. It is ritualistically impure labour. The discussions on stigma associated with nursing points to the routine humiliation and shame that women experience in being nurses and nursing aides across ranks. Experiencing humiliation and shame are not just *effects* of labouring in symbolic and ritualistic impure occupations but constitute subjects; as the Dalit experience of the 'walking carrion'[6] further (re)produces the practice and ideology of untouchability in a purported modern workspace. This chapter explores how processes of labour and gender inequality articulate with other structures of subordination (such as class and caste) to shape lived experiences of work and livelihood, exploitation, and struggle.

Dirt and (Un)touchability: (Re)casting Caste

The anti-caste movement and ideologies of Dalit liberation, spearheaded by B.R. Ambedkar, had as its underlying theoretical and political premise sharing of power as a precondition for Dalit liberation.[7] Yet, despite political democracy, contemporary India did not see a dissolving of caste relations, particularly in the labour force. The promise of the 'Nehruvian model' to bring in development and establish an egalitarian society, lay in tatters, and economic exploitation as well as impoverishment, continues. Reservations in government services did help the Dalit community to gain a foothold in education and services, but it could not dislodge the stranglehold of middle-class, upper-caste communities on public resources.[8] In fact, the promises of modernity in dissipating discrimination remains hollow, and as scholars argue, modernity and discrimination coexist. Deshpande contends that it is in the interest of the globalized capitalist entities to maintain and reproduce discrimination and inequalities in the labour markets. While the benefits of liberalization have predominantly been absorbed by the upper-caste elite, it would not be an exaggeration to

---

[6] Introduced by Naipaul as cited in Guru and Sarukkai (2012: 209).

[7] Omvedt (1994).

[8] Omvedt (1994).

argue that the downside—increasing casualization of jobs and/or unemployment—has as its first victim, the Dalit woman.[9]

It is argued that in urban landscapes, untouchability has lost its edge, given the teeming population, the anonymity, and the consumption of public spaces that erases social markers of identities, as well as political assertion and growing consciousness of the Dalit community; untouchability has become a 'dead issue'.[10] However, there is a strong corpus of literature that argues against this thesis, claiming that not only is untouchability alive and kicking but it has also been reinvented and remodified to suit capitalist modernity. This section focuses on 'untouchability' as a practice, as an ideology that stratifies the workforce, irrespective of the worker's identity. This is neither a new nor a unique phenomenon. Scholars have emphasized how tasks are assigned according to caste identities in modern factories,[11] and sectors such as domestic work deploy existing notions of caste ideologies (purity/pollution) to discriminate against employees.[12] Not just employers and establishments, but workers themselves deploy strategies that exclude social groups based on existing inequalities, such as caste and gender, to secure small gains, for instance, better wages.[13] The nursing sector is a small ghetto in the modern service economy, which has retained its largely gendered characteristic but accommodates all kinds of castes. It is one of the few caste-based occupations that have witnessed professionalization and, consequently, an internal stratification on the basis of skill, training, and knowledge. The shared experience of poverty by women has played a decisive role in breaking the caste codification of nursing labour (particularly semi/untrained labour) and the struggles of women working as nurses, attendants, and private sisters to respond to the marking of nursing labour as a low-caste occupation has led to varied outcomes. One of the most crucial result is that of the split in nursing care between medical and manual labour. Second, the constant reinforcement of caste (as well as class) boundaries between ranks of workers. The simple caste-class nexus that was prevalent even a few decades back has lost its power, undermined by

---

[9] Deshpande (2007).

[10] Deliège (2010).

[11] Lindberg (2005).

[12] Froystad (2003).

[13] Harriss-White and Prosperi (2014).

poverty, agricultural crisis, increasing loss of jobs, and masculinization of the workforce. In the medical institutions in contemporary Kolkata, it is this breaching of caste norms that cause a lot of anxiety and conflict. The caste distribution amongst the respondents demonstrates that both the General Caste and Scheduled Caste categories are more or less equally divided (Table A.10) with 45.7 per cent and 43.9 respectively. However, a further break-up amongst ranks of workers shows that most registered nurses belong to the General Caste category (17.7 per cent), with migrant women from Scheduled Tribes comprising more or less the rest (4.5 per cent). Private Sisters and attendants make up for most of the Scheduled Caste workers with 14.6 per cent and 22 per cent respectively. There were some women (5.1 per cent), particularly among the attendants, who showed discomfiture in revealing caste identities. Given the historical relation between low-caste communities and certain service work, I did not pursue this line of questioning any further.

The ideological force of caste lies in its power in constituting groups, determining the quotidian life of its members—purification rules, marriage and food rules, legitimate occupations—which ensures the identity of the group and assures its continuity. To achieve a more insightful understanding of why caste associations with certain labour have persisted, one needs to turn to the ideology of the caste system and the practices of untouchability. Scholars such as Uma Chakravarti argue that the caste system has evolved to maintain Brahmanical purity, that is to protect the upper castes from doing any impure labour, which is exclusively done by the lower castes. Thus, the purity of the upper-caste body is constituted on the exclusion of the lower castes.[14] Both Sarukkai and Guru contend that the sacred, pure 'self' can only be maintained in relation to the despicable 'other'—the untouchable.[15] Guru argues that the Dalit body conceptualized as the 'walking carrion' and/or mobile dirt is essential for the practice of untouchability; the ideology of untouchability just does not make a person invisible but also unimaginable: it 'cancels out a vast section of people from the social interaction, both in terms of time and space.'[16] 'Dirt' is central to the imagination of the labour performed in the hospitals and nursing homes. Almost all respondents,

[14] Chakravarti (2006).
[15] Guru and Sarukkai (2012).
[16] Guru (2009: 212).

particularly those located at the lowest end of the hierarchy, characterized their work as 'dirty work' that is disrespected and stigmatized.
V. Geetha argues that the untouchable is associated with what is waste,
trash, refuse, leftover, and the polluting excess that needs to be taken care
of by the labour of the untouchable. In this context, untouchability is an
essential element in a social order that works against the coeval existence
of human beings.[17]

Barnani, 28 years of age, Dalit, widowed, hails from a family
of landless labourers from Konnagar, in the district of Hooghly.
Desperately seeking employment, she found a job as an attendant in
the private hospital and lives in a rented accommodation next to her
workplace. Her two children are brought up by her natal family, and she
works to send money home. She feels that it is only because they work
with body and bodily waste that they are held in such contempt by the
nurses and the management. 'They are disgusted by us; we clean human
faeces and urine. They do not want to touch us. For them, we touch dirt
and therefore, we are dirt.' The most commonly used word to explain the
work, nature of work, and to describe the worker is *nongra*; nongra can
be literally translated as dirt, as well as dirty. Both used as a noun (dirt)
and an adjective to describe someone/something (dirty work/dirty
woman), nongra remains an important lexicon in describing as well as
producing worker's subjectivities. The contact with human waste, and
thus dirt, is an embodied experience. The difference between labour and
the personhood of the worker gets blurred as contact with dirt (as part of
providing service) is an embodied act. Touch is an intimate gesture that,
at one moment, threatens to collapse the boundaries between self and
the other, and, at another moment, reinforces differences. Untouchability
is one of the most potent weapons in maintaining caste identities and
consequent economic and social exploitation. Anupama Rao urges us to
understand how untouchability as a category of the quotidian shapes,
politicizes, and redefines the caste system that is integral to the constitution, maintenance, and reproduction of the Hindu society.[18] I argue that
the political, spatial, and symbolic violence of untouchability draws its
legitimacy and strength by (re)enacting the historical violence that is
embodied in the Dalit body in current modern capitalist organizations.

---

[17] V. Geetha (2009).
[18] Rao (2011).

Where impure labour is performed by both Dalit and Brahmin women, the practice of untouchability constitutes newer inequalities, by deploying older stratifications to (re)produce stigmatized existences. The body of the woman located at the lowest end of the labour market is not just a marginalized, static body on which violent acts are enacted, but is brought into being by an affective economy of humiliation and shame. To make sense of the violence that surrounds the body of this woman, compelled to labour in a caste-based occupation, is to bring in the question of power and hegemony: How are borders reinforced in an environment where the very fluidity and slippery nature of tasks allocated unsettles borders and brings it to a crisis? The survival and reinforcement of boundaries depend on symbolic and ritualistic violence embedded in contact zones.

Women narrate experiences of being held in contempt by those who are senior in rank. While nurses complain that doctors are dismissive and disgusted by their very presence, attendants and private sisters complain of similar treatment by women of higher ranks, such as nurses and ward managers; in fact, even more acute. I argue that not just the Dalit but even the upper-caste but impoverished woman compelled to work in a 'dirty occupation' is considered contaminated, impure and the despicable other. She becomes the 'walking carrion'—her inherited caste purity is lost, never to be salvaged. The ideology of caste, with its deep-rooted material base in occupational closures, ensures that once an upper-caste woman labours in a low-caste occupation, she embodies the characteristic of the lower-caste woman. Ritu, 22 years of age, Brahmin, who works as an attendant in a private hospital, narrates the impoverishment of her father (a landed farmer) and her migration to the city from the district of Murshidabad in search of a job. Her uncle brought her to the hospital promising her the job of a receptionist but she was offered the position of an attendant instead. Unable to go back home empty-handed, she was compelled to work, 'cleaning faeces and vomit':

> The doctors and sisters here treat us badly; they behave like we have leprosy. They move away from us as if we are untouchables. The way they look at me as if I am an animal, they treat me like I am not a human. I am a Brahmin and my grandfather was a priest. It is only because we are poor that I have to do this work. And here I am treated like some lower caste just because I am cleaning dirt and touching fluid and blood. (Personal interview with author)

The treatment of the Brahmin woman as the 'leper', the untouchable', derives from her labouring and coming into contact with ritualistically impure matter. The upper-caste body can only maintain its purity by ritualistic and symbolic practices; the performance of unclean labour on an everyday basis, where the body comes in contact with waste, refuse, and all that is impure, further points to the inability of the person to maintain caste purity. Feminist economists have argued, in the context of gender, that work segregated as women's work was devalued and denigrated in modern factory spaces, but when men took over the same jobs, it was perceived as skilled labour, leading to a hike in wages and improved working conditions.[19] But in the case of nursing labour, where the workforce continues to be feminized, upper-caste women performing labour segregated for Dalit women does not revalorize the labour. On the contrary, they descend to the bottom of the caste hierarchy. I argue that the practice of segregating Dalit bodies to perform unclean and impure labour exists because work plays a pivotal role in producing the worker, as well as the untouchable body. And the practice of untouchability is central to this production. Sarukkai argues that tactility is a way of being in the world, and the practice of untouchability is almost always connected to borders and boundaries that cannot be transgressed.[20] Borders are essential to social arrangements. Policing borders to maintain caste hierarchy takes on paramount importance given the threat of transgressions with the collapse of feudal relations, no matter how incomplete. These transgressions that render rigid borders that are porous and fluid open up possibilities of a reconfiguration of traditional hierarchies based on caste, class, and sexualities. Borders exist because of accumulated meanings, histories of hierarchies, and memories that operate on an economy of difference. The rejection of the upper-caste body engaged in impure and dirty labour from social spaces, and the disgust and revulsion that it triggers, is set off by a deep rooted anxiety and panic of the possibility of caste hierarchies being displaced. The violent response to upper-caste women performing impure and dirty labour is a process of otherizing, both a rejection and a reminder that they have lost all claims to caste privileges and their bodies are now constitutively impure.

[19] Banerjee (1991a).
[20] Sarukkai (2012).

An analysis of women's experiences and affective responses to labour-ing in a devalued, derogated, and impure occupation demonstrates how borders and boundaries are created, and how its limits are challenged. The study of emotions, particularly shame and humiliation, and rejection, is a key to understanding ideologies and power structures that produces the self and the other. Sara Ahmed reminds us that emotions are not something we possess, but instead, they are active constituents of body surfaces, boundaries, and effects.[21] Thus, emotions are bodily changes that are affective responses central to creating borders between the self and others. Sulekha, 44, Christian, married, got the work of an attendant in a private nursing home after working many odd jobs. Hailing from the district of Howrah, with a sick husband, who got employed off and on as a gardener, she dwelled in extreme poverty. Sulekha's neighbour worked as a security guard in the hospital and put in a word for her to the hospital management. Working in the ICU for eight years, Sulekha is a familiar face, and often helps nurses in their medical work. However, she insists that 'nurses are disgusted by us. If they sit next to us, their feel their honour will be compromised. They even ask us to wash our hand before taking water from us.' The expulsion of the body that incites hatred and repulsion, and yet, whose presence is necessary to hold the system together is an abject body. Julia Kristeva reminds us: 'It is thus not lack of cleanliness or health that causes abjection but what disturbs identity, system, order. What does not respect borders, positions, rules. The in-between, the ambiguous, the composite.'[22] Abjection is thus a necessary process for the self by which it banishes all that threatens it; however, this banishment is never complete. The abject exists within the system as either tamed or disciplined or outside the system as oppositional ele-ments that threaten its very foundation. The abjection of both Dalit and upper-caste women dealing with human waste and refuse in the hospitals and nursing homes is sustained by the quotidian. What does everyday humiliation and pain do to us? How does shaming produce bodies and subjectivities that internalize caste norms? The meanings that have accumulated by historical rules that govern food, contact, and touch are reinforced when upper-caste nurses refuse to take food or water from the hands of Dalit women or even ask them to wash hands before they

[21] Ahmed (2004).
[22] Kristeva (1982: 4).

serve water or hand over a pen. While upper-caste women insist that it is an innocuous act to maintain hygiene, women working in the lower ranks insist it is disgust that prevents them from establishing contact. Not touching or establishing contact draws from traditional and historical associations of caste-based labour and untouchability—the 'walking carrion' who contaminates by mere touch. Some of the Dalit women working as attendants narrate how they are openly called derogatory caste names, such as *dom* (untouchable caste). The question is how effective are these injurious speeches, these processes that produce abject bodies. Judith Butler argues that the subject is constituted in and by language; hate speech injures because it does not just name but constitutes the subject by drawing upon existing norms, rituals, and practices, a power that is derivative—it gets its meaning from prior action, that is, citationality.[23] Butler goes on to discuss the question of agency and the impossibility of predetermining the meaning of hate speech. However, in this context, the act of naming and interpellation of a subject as an object of disgust, an abject body that needs to be expelled from the social and the political, has resonance given the field that the subject is embedded in. Historically, Dom is an untouchable caste that performed the most menial and impure labour—disposal and cremation of dead bodies. Hate speeches and injurious acts (the refusal to touch) draw their power and legitimacy from norms, rituals, memories, and the lived reality of the body's abjection. Ahmed argues that naming something as disgusting is performative; it draws from previous histories and memories and generates the object it names.[24] Thus, both the self and the other are brought into being through the performative of disgust or any similarly intense affect. These names/acts assign meanings that are already circulating within the symbolic and given the existing stigmatization of the labour, the precarious location of the worker, and the rules and rituals that govern interaction amongst different kinds of people, citationality ensures the efficacy of interpellation, that is, it constitutes subjects by naming. Basabi, whom we have met earlier, narrates how women working as attendants are Dalit women who live in slums, and have no character, education, or training. 'These women are nongra; they are *kharap* (immoral). We do not mix with such women, but here,

---

[23] Butler (1997a).
[24] Ahmed (2004).

because of the nature of the job, we have to.' The principal of a famous nursing school in Kolkata insisted that you cannot call unregistered nurses and private sisters as 'actual' nurses: 'They are like the servants we have in our houses. They are dirty and unhygienic. They have germs under their fingernails, and with the same hand, they feed patients. They are unsafe. They are not nurses—yesterday they washed utensils, and today they are taking care of patients.' Compare this with some colonial records on the dai: 'the dai never has the slightest hesitations in putting her unclean hand into the uterus ... in goes her dirty hand, which perhaps has just been cow-dunging a floor or attending a case of puerperal fever....'[25]

Putul, 35 years of age, General Caste, hails from a family of small farmers. Widowed with two children, she migrated from the district of Purulia with the hope of an 'office job', only to be offered the work of an attendant. Expressing her helplessness in the face of adversity, she confides in me that she can never tell anyone the work she does in the nursing home. Expressing her shame, humiliation, and pain, she, however, does not question the ideological and material basis of this division of labour; instead she has 'fallen' in her own eyes and in the eyes of society.

> This ayah's work is done by chotolok. There is no respect. How can I ask others to respect this work, when I have fallen in my own eyes! If I studied a little bit more, I could have been a nurse, but today I am nothing more than an attendant.... Of course, the nurses look down on us, they do not want to eat with us, touch us, they do not even want to sit with us. I come from a high-caste family, but because I lost my husband, I have to work like this. (Personal interview with the author)

This failing of both patriarchal and caste ideologies whereby upper-caste women are compelled to labour in supposedly impure occupations is perceived as an individual misfortune. The subjective experience of being treated as a chotolok is justified as the division of labour is never questioned. Falling in one's own eyes, the compromise of one's self-respect and the feeling of shame, rejection, and humiliation experienced by the body now rendered untouchable, further constitute subjectivities that nullify the possibilities of any emancipatory politics that could have emerged

---

[25] Victoria Memorial Scholarship Fund (1918).

from the modernization of a hitherto stigmatized occupation. The feeling of shame, particularly in this context, acts to produce a subject who is docile, embarrassed, and wounded. Reena, 34, unmarried, General Caste, took employment as an attendant in a private nursing home out of sheer desperation, because there were no other jobs available. While she started to train as a nurse in an unlicensed centre, she quit midway because of illness in the family. Having lost both parents to poverty and ill-health, she lives with her brother and sister in a rented accommodation and is the main bread earner of her family. She narrates that it was sheer poverty and desperation that made her take to working as an attendant. She says,

> No one does this work unless they are compelled. Those from 'proper' families cannot do this work—cleaning human faeces—is this work? Women from lower-caste families do not have a problem, they are used to it. I could not adjust to it; I would cry when I would scrub bedpans or wash bed sheets defiled by vomit. Sometimes I think, where was I born and where did I land up? (Personal interview with the author)

Women from General Castes working at the lower end of the hierarchy are thus faced with a loss of status, which they attribute to luck, fate, loss of land and/or male authority. There exists a clear and unmistakable correlation between rank and hierarchy, with the degree of cleanliness, purity and impurity of the tasks allocated. For a Brahmin woman, the menial nature of the work of an attendant in a hospital setting is a transgression of caste, class, and gender norms. Cleaning blood, excreta, and bodily fluid is seen as a loss of middle-class, upper-caste respectability, and waged work itself of femininity. The shame associated with losing rank and purity, the humiliation and drudgery associated with reluctant acceptance of demeaning labour, constitutes subjects that do not fight for 'self-respect' but accept it as their 'fate'. The acceptance of such events as 'fate' is an attempt to a partial replenishment of dignity. Butler argues that the subject is a 'belated metalepsis', a 'subject effect'. It comes into being and is constituted by various discourses.[26] Emotions such as humiliation and shame interpellate subjects by drawing on histories, cultures, and

---

[26] Butler (1997a: 50).

memories to constitute a woman who is compelled to accept herself as an inferior and abject being. As Disha, 27 years of age, Scheduled Caste and married, says, 'I feel so proud to work in a hospital. I have a job and I am not dependent on anyone. But the way they treat me here, I feel ashamed to do such work'.

Nurses too face similar contempt and disgust, though the practice of untouchability does not materialize in such harsh terms in their everyday lives. Most nurses belong to the General Caste category and have secured a relatively higher (arguably in this context, cleaner) position in the nursing sector. Not just employer-establishments but workers themselves have participated wholeheartedly in such divisive politics to ensure some gains, at the expense of others. These politics of labour are constituted by gender, class, and, in this context, overwhelmingly by caste identities, to maintain a stranglehold over some pockets of labour and thus claim dignity and enhance status. This is not unique to nursing; it is a phenomenon observed in other sectors as well.[27] Without the regular cleansing and purification acts that are performed by women located at the bottom of the hierarchy, nurses cannot maintain themselves as repositories of medical knowledge, focusing on cleaner and prestigious administrative tasks and basic medical interventions. However, registered nurses complain that they are perceived as uneducated, low-caste women, who have taken to the medical profession due to poverty or distress. Despite their relatively higher status, they remain vulnerable to the stigma associated with women in the service sectors. Hema, employed as a registered nurse in a government hospital, relates how she faced caste discrimination because she works as a nurse. The second of seven siblings, Hema, 34 years of age, Brahmin, hails from an urban, professional family, and was encouraged by her father to choose an education that would secure her a career in public services. Impressed with the nurse's uniform in a visit to a hospital, she chose to study nursing in Ramakrishna Mission in Kolkata. With her father's early death, she and her eldest brother took up the responsibility of bringing up their younger siblings, which also meant that she put off all marriage proposals. Single and with a BSc degree in nursing, Hema rues her choice of career because of the stigma associated with it. She narrates,

[27] Harriss-White and Gooptu (2001).

People hold nurses in contempt and are disgusted by them. They think that this job is dirty or that women who do it come from chotolok families. Once after duty, I was returning home in a bus and another female passenger started chatting with me. When I told her I was a nursing staff, she moved away from me; she physically distanced herself from me as if my presence disgusted her. They believe that nurses are Scheduled Castes. Maybe it was true in the past but now women from good families with academic qualifications enter nursing. (Personal interview with the author)

The physical distance that the woman passenger put between Hema and herself was not just to protect caste purity but also to purify the physical space that she was compelled to share with low-caste bodies due to urban configurations and public transport system. The practice of untouchability was not just to evade contact with someone who is perceived to be constitutively impure, but to cancel out the person's presence from the social space, to exclude, to eject. Nursing, even at the top level, is considered dirty work. Despite protests by registered nurses that they no longer have to work with bodily impurities, the tenacious hold of identities with memories, traditions, and culture accumulate meanings that are hard to displace. Hema felt that it was the presence of low-caste attendants and unregistered nurses that led to this association. The historical association of nursing with untouchability could not be successfully broken if 'these untrained uneducated women' continued to be counted as nurses.

Nursing labour continues to be identified as impure labour offered by women from Scheduled Castes or other marginal communities. Sonalika, 31, unmarried, General Caste, hailing from a family of shop-keepers in the district of Hooghly migrated to Kolkata, first to train and then work as registered nurse in the government hospital. While she saw an advertisement for nursing training and decided to pursue it as a career, encouraged by her parents who are proud of her prestigious government posting, she feels that the work is stigmatized and does not get due recognition. She says, 'My own sister refuses to take nursing training; she thinks the work is dirty'. The perception of dirt and/or untouchability is not restricted to the public sphere. The family is also a site where such discriminations are practiced to marginalize, exclude, and disparage members of the household who have transgressed norms. While the home is theorized and imagined as a stronghold of personal liberty, autonomy, affect, and solidarities, feminists have noted how the home-family-private have been sites of violence and injustice.[28] Béteille argues that the family has survived as an institution only because individual members have been willing to sacrifice their interests to perpetuate its well-being and continuity.[29] Punishment and rewards are meted out to members of the family based on who upholds, preserves, and violates the precepts and norms that maintain the sanctity of the family-kinship-community. Women belonging to higher-caste families lament the treatment meted out to them by their kin, based on corporeal contamination, due to their labouring in low-caste occupations. Sohini, 29 years of age, Brahmin, hails from a family of small farmers and sharecroppers in the district of Hooghly, and took to working as an attendant in a private hospital when her husband stopped working after prolonged illness. While her family-in-law is relatively well off, they refused to help her and she had to find ways to support her immediate family, including her 5 year old son. She says,

> My larger family avoids me. They do not tell me anything but I know what they are thinking—a Brahmin girl is working as an attendant in a hospital. My own family members have stopped talking to me. They avoid me. So now I avoid them. (Personal interview with the author)

Annapurna, 40 years of age, Brahmin, hails from an urban, professional joint family. It was her husbands' retrenchment from a private company and subsequent mental health problems that led her to look for jobs in order to keep the home running. Working as an attendant in a private hospital, she faces ostracism from her family-in-law who, however, do not offer to help her financially. She says,

> My sister in-law avoids me at home because I work as an attendant in a hospital. She is a teacher in an English-medium school. They do not allow their son to come to my room or talk to me. They do not mind if he goes to my other brother or sister in-law, but they do not like it when he comes to me.[30]

Reservations in the public sector have entailed Dalit women accessing highly competitive government-funded nursing schools/colleges and

---

[28] Rao *et al.* (2005).

[29] Béteille (1993).

[30] Ray (2016b: 67).

subsequently getting employment in the public sector. Dalit nurses did not complain of facing overt caste discrimination within their workplaces, being protected by their status and relatively higher bargaining power. However, being located in a segregated labour market almost always identified as a caste-based occupation implies that they were unable to overcome social prejudices and were equally or maybe more vulnerable to bigotry. Reservations in nursing services have had uneven and paradoxical consequences: while it gives access to lower-caste women to a sector that has recently seen caste mobility, it also entrenches and reinforces the caste and class stereotypes that are associated with this sector. Equally, Dalit women getting jobs in the upper echelons of nursing services through affirmative policies have engendered a backlash, as reservations threaten to tear into the fabric of elitism that cloaks public health services. As witnessed in anti-reservation protests, all fractions of the upper castes come together in opposition to subordinate groups when they lay claim to educational, social, and political privileges. Attempts of nursing leaders to delink nursing from lower-caste, working-class women get defeated as reservations breach the very walls built to keep the latter out. Latika, General Caste and working as a registered nurse, feels that there are too many women from lower castes who are entering nursing services: 'They come in through reservations. They will gossip, have illicit relationships, will not work and just sit around. That is why government nurses have such bad reputation.'

Spatializing Inequalities: 'A Place for Everything and Everything in Place'

In this section, I enquire into the role of space in maintaining and reproducing power relations. Space is not just a passive 'place' but an active constituent of social relations.[31] In the previous section, I argue that while Dalit women have always been subjected to untouchability, even those who are 'high-born' but compelled to labour in low-caste professions, are marked as the outcaste/untouchable 'other'. In this section, I bring in the question of space and its constitutive role in teaching women labouring in 'impure' professions 'to know their place'. Society is

---

[31] For a detailed understanding of how space constitutes subjectivities, see Jameson (1991); Lefebvre (1991); Soja (1989).

socio-spatially organized to sustain hegemonic ideals and power and these forms of oppressive practices are given context by the organization of space. Untouchability is not just socially but also spatially constructed. The segregation and partition of space, forming exclusionary enclaves, is not just to contain the threatening other but also to constitute and (re)produce the marginal as one. In effect, one can argue that space functions as a signifier that produces meanings and conveys to us how to act and what our worth is. Certain spaces, such as pockets of the city, are regulated and policed in a manner (explicit and/or implicit), which clearly lets certain section of the population know that they are unwelcome—'out of place'.[32] Cresswall details how places reproduce meanings, in very natural, self-evident, and commonsensical ways and thus exclusionary acts embedded in our everyday lives are (re)produced in banal, doxic practices.[33] In this section, I explore how spaces constitute subjects.

The constant emphasis on dirt and the feelings of disgust and revulsion that it inspires, manifesting in the practice of untouchability, is a crucial way of not just hierarchizing bodies but also space. Sara Ahmed argues that emotions such as hate, fear, and disgust constitute the body: 'Pulling back, bodies that are disgusted are also bodies that feel a certain rage, a rage that the object has got close enough to sicken, and to be taken over or taken in. To be disgusted is after all to be affected by what one has rejected.'[34] Hema's experience of being rejected by a co-passenger on the basis of her occupation is not just a social division of labourers, but also a ranking and grading of space that aims at maintaining and reproducing social order. The practice of untouchability that almost *all* women working at the bottom of the hierarchy are subjected to is an attempt to maintain and reproduce boundaries that are threatened by close proximity of differently ranked bodies. While in factories or other modern capitalist organizations, caste-based segregation is more explicit and visible, the organization of labour and the division of tasks is relatively more unstable, fluid, and porous in medical establishments, making markers of caste relatively inconspicuous, indiscernible, and indistinct. It is left to norms, culture, rituals, and daily socio-spatial

[32] Donald (1992).
[33] Cresswell (1996).
[34] Ahmed (2004: 85–6).

practices to make obvious social identities, ranks, and hierarchies. Space is not just a container, it actively constitutes and structures relations and processes that produce gender, class, and caste identities. Thus, one can argue space is central to formation of power and hegemonies.

The practice of untouchability, as we have noted before, cancels out bodies marked inferior from social spaces, thus reinforcing the social order. Barnani talks of many incidents that are examples of bad treatment meted out by nurses. She narrates an incident when there was a *bandh* (strike) and all private buses were taken off the road. The private hospital had arranged for cars to transport administrative and medical staff, including nurses, but they had excluded other workers, such as security guards, sweepers, drivers, private sisters, attendants, and ward boys, who were expected to report to work at their own risk. When her night shift got over on the morning of the bandh, she witnessed the hospital car ferrying nurses back home, who had just finished a shift with her. Noticing a vacant seat, she requested a lift and was rebuffed.

> There was a bandh one day, and the hospital car was going to Howrah railway station. I asked them to give me a lift part of the way. The sister-in-charge said, 'Do we have to travel in the same car with fourth-grade staff?' What would have happened if one day the hospital car would have given me a lift? (Personal interview with the author)

The refusal to share space with a fourth-grade staff is a reflection of how space is used to exclude unwanted, purportedly inferior bodies; simultaneously, the exclusion of such bodies constitutes the car as a space that signifies and reinforces both 'superior' class and caste and a marker of conspicuous consumption. Such bodies cannot be done away with inside the wards. With their fluid spaces which allow continuous movement of different ranks of workers, these wards make segregation unstable, identities precarious, and hierarchies contentious. Thus, the contained space of the car becomes a significant tool in reinforcing power, identity, and hierarchies. The denial of a tentative appeal for sharing space in a critical situation is not just to teach a fourth-grade staff her 'rightful place', it is also a rejection of any solidarity or alliance based on a shared identity as a worker. The employer-establishment having already discriminated on the basis of rank between workers, by denying non-economic aid to some and providing it to others, is further appropriated and reinforced by a section of workers themselves.

Barnani gives another example of how the ideology and practice of the caste system segregate spaces: at one point the nursing staff refused to share the table with attendants in the common dining hall. Bringing to work the notion of purity and pollution, the matron passed a rule that attendants can only eat during a particular hour and should not share the table with nurses during lunch hour. As noted before, neither are all attendants Dalit nor are all nurses upper-caste. However, the temporal-spatial segregation of eating constitutes a rank of workers as untouchables and the other as 'pure' castes. As a protest, all attendants refused to enter the dining hall and insisted on eating in small groups in changing rooms. To settle the score, they refused to clean the tables after the nurses had finished lunch.

> As we do not enter the dining room anymore, we have refused to to clean the table. We are the ones who clean the table and yet they do not let us use it; now go and see the condition of the dining hall. They [nurses] sit in that dirt and eat. (Personal interview with the author)

Food is particularly contentious, as prescriptions about what one can eat and with whom, inform caste boundaries and identities. Food practices, thus, are inherently political. When I asked the matron about this order, she told me that it was difficult if everyone took a lunch break at the same time, thus, the order. Admitting to caste inequalities and segregation implicates one as pre-modern, a charge many organizations evade or deny. However, social identities are inherent and deeply embedded in the manner in which spaces are used, produced, segregated, and codified. Dining in public spaces is a key to unravelling caste restrictions, where not just commensality but social relations and networks across caste groups become possible;[35] a ban on inter-dining, reflecting upper-caste norms, constitutes the dining hall not as a static space but as a producer of meaning. A prohibition on entry in a space meant for food consumption is not just about where one can or cannot enter, it is loaded with meanings, given the histories and customs associated with food consumption. Spaces where 'untouchable' bodies are prevented from entering is at once constituted as a sterilized, purified space that only upper-castes bodies can freely occupy and, at the same time, constitutes those bodies that occupy

[35] Caplan (2008).

it as pure and clean. Everyday practices, reflected in the codification of space, constitutes and signifies bodies that may or may not belong to any such empirical category.

This is also evident in some other common spaces in medical establishments—apart from the government hospital (both architecture and lack of security makes it impossible), both private establishments have an injunction against attendants and private sisters using the elevator. What is the effect of this seemingly innocent technical apparatus on the distribution and codification of spaces and people? The elevator has been analysed as a disciplinary element in the history of buildings, both in Europe and America, to the extent that it makes verticality accessible and distributes spaces, as well as protects the elite from the contamination by the plebeian.[36] However, in contemporary residential complexes and office spaces, elevators function as dispersal of individuals according to hierarchy. The existence of back stairs or the service elevator in almost all modern gated residential communities and hotels separates the domestic workers/ service providers from the elite residents and guests. The obvious class dimensions where the need to invisiblize, segregate, and deny the existence of the large population of men and women servicing and providing for elite residents is reflected in the sanitizing of space for the consumption of middle classes. In hospitals and nursing homes, nurses, doctors, members of the management, patients, and their visitors can access the elevators; attendants, private sisters, and ward boys have to use the staircase. Only when they are visibly accompanying and assisting a patient are they allowed to use the elevator. Among arguments forwarded by the management, the most common is that of efficiency and to keep the elevators free for those who need it the most—patients, doctors, and visitors. For instance, the managing director of the private nursing home said that 'if attendants and ward boys start to use the elevator freely, it would make it difficult for the hospitals to function.'[37] However, in both the hospital and nursing homes, it is the attendants and ward boys who are most mobile. Their duties include going up and down five floors many times a day, fetching reports, medicines, transferring files, and so on and so forth. Doctors and visitors come to the wards only in stipulated hours,

---

[36] Bernard (2014).

[37] Interview with the managing director, private nursing home, January 2012.

nurses are statically located in the wards, and members of the management communicate between wards and floors via telecom. Sujata, whom
we met earlier, says, 'Getting the files from the cash section and taking
it back, requisition for medicines ... we are constantly on the move from
the first to the fifth floor ... climbing up and down the staircase is so painful, we get so tired yet they do not let us use the elevators'. The uneasiness
that many in the elite ranks feel in sharing intimate space with those
of lower social orders is reflected in the squeamishness nurses express.
Anjana, 28 years of age, married, General Caste, and one of the few registered nurses in the private nursing home says, 'Are we now expected to
share elevators with sweepers? Will a doctor do it? Will the management
do it? Then why should we?' In an oligarchic workforce, the elevator
becomes an apparatus that weeds out the working-class rank and file
from the elite service providers. Additionally, laying claim to the elevator
space allows a rank of workers to a shared sense of entitlement with
middle-class managerial and medical staff.

Massey argues that space is 'one of the axes along with which we
experience and conceptualize the world'.[38] The contemporary economic organizations, particularly with their increasing flexibility and
casualization, exemplify the importance of space in constituting relations between employers and workers on the one hand and between
workers themselves, on the other. The systems of allocation of people
to different spaces, each having different levels of surveillance and
control, constitute not just identities but also social hierarchies. The
production and reproduction of spatial inequalities helps understand
how places (as the locus of everyday life) are shaped through a flow of
signs and meanings. Starting from access to changing rooms, toilets,
and even drinking water, registered and unregistered nurses employed
privately on contract, as well as attendants and private sisters employed
on a daily-wage basis, are denied basic amenities. Ramala, whom we
met earlier, and who is currently working as an unregistered nurse in a
private nursing home, says:

The nurse's changing room is tiny, next to the canteen boys' toilet. There
is no fan and water seeps in from the toilet and soaks our clothes. The
canteen boys can peek into our room. We do not even have a safe and

[38] Massey (1994: 251).

secured bathroom. In these private nursing homes, the nurses are most neglected, but even this tiny space is not open to private sisters or women attendants—they are considered *tuchchha* (insignificant). (Personal interview with the author)

Nurses in the government hospitals are provided with a chamber, a private toilet, and a bed to rest in, if they feel too exhausted, but women working as private sisters or attendants do not have access to these rooms. They have to dress in overflowing, unclean toilets, or find covered corners to furtively change in and out of their uniforms. Asha, thirty-five years of age, Scheduled Caste, hailing from a family of menial workers, took to working as a private sister in the government hospital, before her marriage. She continued to work to support her husband who is employed in the construction industry. She says, 'We requested the nurses to let us change in their rooms, and we even assured them that we will not use their toilets, but they refused. They do not care that we have to change publicly, our honour is not important'. The constitution of bodies as chaste and honourable, in need of privacy and protection, is directly linked to identities and occupations. The normative middle-class, upper-caste body needs segregated spaces that are exclusive for their use, protected from the contamination of the body of the other. Given the constitution of Dalit female bodies as promiscuous, and available[39] this spatial segregation in their everyday lives is essential to maintain and reproduce caste and class boundaries; particularly, in an organizational space that witnesses constant challenges to borders and boundaries. Anna Lindberg had similar observations regarding cashew nut factories in Kerala, where tasks traditionally perceived as 'dirty', such as shelling nuts, undertaken by Scheduled Caste women, had the worst working conditions. These factories had mud floors, were congested, lacked adequate lighting, and had no fans. However, the work environment of the more prestigious sections, such as the grading section populated by Nair women, were far better. Thus, she concludes that though cashew nut factories contributed to breaking down caste barriers, in their everyday socio-spatial politics they maintained and even perpetuated the associations between low castes and dirty work.[40]

[39] Balmurli (2009); Malik (1999).
[40] Lindberg (2005).

The organization, division, and allocation of places into spatial units that signify class and caste boundaries also co-produces them.

The hospital space has its own organizational logic revolving around ranks and hierarchies. Nurses, private sisters, and attendants do not sit, talk, or eat together. Social distinctions are rigidly maintained and friends are usually made within ranks. Attempts at rupturing such carefully orchestrated distinctions are promptly rebuked. My visits to the hospitals during the night shift, when the place is relatively quiet as opposed to the buzz of activities through the day, made it easier for me to observe how space has been neatly divided and compartmentalized. Though each of the three organizations is distinct in its architectural and spatial arrangements, there remains a certain continuity in the usage of space. Nurses sit at the largest and most conspicuous desk (maybe the only one on the ward/floor), which is strategically placed to allow a bird's eye view of the whole ward. Sometimes a floor can have more than one ward and then the nurse's desk is placed in a manner that allows for supervision of multiple wards. It is usually non-specialized wards (general) that share a single floor, where the nurse's task become more of supervision of attendants and ward boys rather than keeping a hawk eye on the medical condition of the patient. An ICU would have a circular nurse's table right in the centre of the ward, allowing each patient to be monitored from that one location. The spatial arrangements differ from establishment to establishment and beds are arranged according to the size of the floor or the ward. A circular nurse's table is useful in a smaller ward (private nursing home) where every conceivable space has been used to put in beds. On the contrary, the ICU in the government hospital has fewer beds, and therefore has a nurse's table on one side with a view of the whole room. These spatial arrangements can be deeply contested and a potential source of conflict. Any attempt to challenge these spatial arrangements is seen as a challenge to power, authority as well as hierarchies. For example, in a ward, the nurse's desk signifies authority, knowledge, and power— attendants or private sisters who pull up a chair and sit by the nurse's desk are immediately reprimanded. The reprimand is not necessarily verbal: a gesture, a look, a tone of coldness in the voice is enough to put a woman of lower ranks back 'in her place'. What may be an innocuous act of sociability is perceived as an act of transgression and challenge to rank and authority. The nurse's desk is indeed intimidating. Papers piled up, files being sorted at different stages, records of medicine, linen and instruments, a duty roster with names and respective shifts hanging on the walls or chalked on a board, a constant coming and going of medical and administrative staff. It gives an impression of grave activity. The separation of nurses, private sisters, and attendants, where there is a social veto against the latter to even stand near the desk unless they have specific tasks, is not just a practice of social distancing. It is also a mechanism to inhibit women's access to information and prevent any exchange or flow of knowledge between skilled workers and those located lower in the hierarchy.

Scholars argue that spaces are embodied and different bodies experience space differently; for instance, gender becomes a key axis by which a 'gender-space' is produced crucial to the maintenance and reproduction of the social order. Thus, the dialectic between gender and space needs to be constantly reinforced, regulated, and policed to ensure that there is no erosion of hegemonic ideals. The control of women and their access to public spaces has been central to such projects, or to put it differently, gendering of public spaces is essential to maintenance of the dominant social order.[41] For instance, during the night shift, ward boys (men) usually occupy the lounge, the outer space that guards the entrance to the floor or ward, often sleeping stretched out on the couch. Their bodies flowing, the demeanour relaxed: their inhabitation of space foregrounds how bodies are constituted. Gender stratifies space and the latter constitutes gender. Seemanthini Niranjana alerts us to how the body and its inhabitation of space becomes the medium through which the 'female' is constituted and equally, norms by which women's use of space is governed.[42] Not just gender but also caste and class. Women workers of lower ranks, such as private sisters and attendants, do not sit on chairs or sofas. They are expected to stand by the patient's bed or sit on the floor of the ward or the cabin. Though the attendants and the ward boys have similar wages, work, and working conditions and occupy the same status in the hierarchy, men rarely sit on the floor, and women on chairs. Neither the ward boys nor the attendants sit at the nurse's table. The difference in the way men and women occupy similar places gives us an insight into how space and gender mutually construct each other. While men sleep at night, stretched out on sofas or other similar habitable places, women doze sitting in a corner of the ward with their heads down. While the former physically takes up

[41]   Ranade (2007).
[42]   Niranjana (2001).

as much as space as possible, the latter shrinks into herself, a movement that is inward, trying to be inconspicuous, invisible, and discreet. The different ways bodies occupy spaces, the constitution of the body in public spaces that is marked by gender, has already been noted.[43] However, gendered spatial arrangements also affirm gender roles, and thus the sexual division of labour. While in the hospitals and nursing homes there is no sexual division of labour on paper, practices in the wards differ. While the work of an attendant (on paper) blurs cultural understanding of what is masculine and feminine work, and both male and female attendants are supposed to do similar work for male and female patients respectively, actual practices in the ward redraw boundaries. A social veto on men doing an attendant's work, which de-masculinizes them, allows an informal sexual division of labour to operate which, however, is not written in hospital policies. The private/public divide operates where women take bodily care of patients including male patients, and male ward boys run personal errands for doctors and nurses, take patients for tests, push trolleys, lift patients bodily, and anything that is perceived as a 'man's job'. The link between spaces, labour processes, and gender stratification work in manners that are complex and intriguing. Hospital wards are flowing spaces, and the work of an attendant, unlike a factory worker, is not fixed to a spot. They move between wards, buildings, wings, and floors as they ferry patients, fetch reports, bring medicine, and so on. The constant movement, flux of bodies, makes surveillance over time and movement difficult. Whereas with women, access to space is informed by the public/private divide, implying that they spend their free time indoor, in the wards, men freely access spaces outside wards, buildings, and hospital campuses. Chaitali, 36 years of age, married, Scheduled Caste, hails from a family of menial daily-wage labourers from the district of Hooghly. Married off at the age of 15, and facing intense domestic violence in her in-law's home, she migrated singly to Kolkata to work as a domestic worker. After gaining employment as an attendant in a private hospital, she now lives with her daughter in a rented accommodation. Chaitali believes that men do not make efficient workers, particularly, in this segment. She says:

Women work efficiently. Men, they cannot do any work efficiently. If they are cleaning urine, that is all they will do. Women will do everything

[43] Phadke, Khan, and Ranade (2011).

neatly and in order. Men will do some work, and then they will say, 'We are just coming from downstairs' or 'We will smoke a cigarette and come'. (Personal interview with the author)

Women rarely loiter in corridors, parking lots, lobbies, or outside the hospital campus; on the contrary, men make a habit of idling, socializing, and bonding with other men in these areas, rendered masculine by excluding women. This has three implications: women are marginalized in important communication and information networks; secondly, they find themselves doing more work than their obligations; thirdly, men are coded as bad caregivers—impatient, careless, and indifferent—and thus better at doing more masculine things. Bodies are always already gendered, and simultaneously interlocked with caste, class, and cultural particularities. The different ways bodies occupy spaces in different cultural contexts act as signifiers of their worth, capabilities, and constitutions. Post-structuralist feminists perceive the body not as a pre-given, raw matter that is civilized, ordered, and moulded, but as a lived body in its specific sexual and cultural difference constituted by interlocking systems of meanings, significations, and representations.[44] Grosz argues that the feminist investment in conceptualizing, interrogating, and defining the female body is intrinsically bound up with questions of agency, space, and mobility that is accorded to women.[45] The conceptual linking of women's bodies with biological roles renders them as vulnerable, passive, caring, and nurturing. This coding whereby masculinity is identified with the mind and femininity with the body, insidiously works in structuring gender stratifications in the public sphere: in this context, where women attendants and ward boys have commensurate responsibilities in the wards, misogynist perceptions of appropriate labour creep in, in most crafty and cunning ways. Shikha, thirty-eight, married, Scheduled Caste and working as an attendant in the government hospital, resonates what Chaitali says:

At night, they [ward boys] are sitting downstairs and smoking and the nurses will call us. When male patients pass bowel, we have to clean it. You cannot let a patient lie in his dirt. Male patients will object

44 Gatens (1996); Heinamaa (2003).
45 Grosz (1994).

and complain to nurses that why are women touching us. But the nurses will not say anything because they are the ones who are sending the ward boys outside to get food and tea. (Personal interview with the author)

The very spatial arrangement, while reflecting demarcations, actively form and produce structural hierarchies. The conceptual binary of the public/ private divide that signifies men as producers rightfully belonging to the public space and women as reproducers belonging to the private, operate in insidious manners. The hospitals and nursing homes are workplaces, located in the public sphere, and women's access and habitation in this sphere, though mediated by gender, class, and caste, locates her as a worker, albeit an inferior one. However, this insidious sexual division of labour where men are given chores that make their absence conspicuous in the wards, which is a site of (re)productive labour, reinforces binaries that are humanly constituted and socially produced. Whereas in India, particularly amongst working-class and/or Dalit women, the public/ private binary continues to be far more porous than for other communities, it still remains embedded in familial ideologies. As Saraswati Raju argues that 'place' acts as both a mediator and a context in which one must place the linkages between women's employment and spatial location. Spaces and patriarchies mutually constitute and reconstitute each other differently in different places.[46]

Gender and class come together to maintain status quo on sexual division of labour, even when these are contrary to organizational norms. Despite complaints from male patients that ward boys are not doing their jobs in terms of taking bodily care, nurses turn a blind eye. Ward boys are useful in terms of running personal errands for nurses and doctors, and the concession is being exempted from certain distasteful duties in the wards. To compel ward boys to perform their duties would mean giving up the comforts of an 'errand-boy'. Both nurses and ward boys do not want to perform menial bodily services, which would possibly declass and feminize them respectively. Middle-class nurses connive with working-class men to ensure that privileges gained by both the groups through the grids of gender and class are not forfeited in the wards.

[46] Raju (2011).

The hospital space provides the order, the matrix in which unrelated bodies are brought together in a mutually constitutive and discursive relation, where both space and corporeality are fleshed out. I neither posit the hospital as a 'place' or the worker as a 'body' in a prior moment that determines one or the other but argue that their constant interaction produced spaces that are constituted on the inequalities produced by the axes of gender, class, and caste. Foucault has argued that discipline maximizes forces of the body by increasing utility; at the same time, it diminishes it, by increasing obedience. 'Discipline is above all an analysis of space: it is individualization through space, the placing of bodies in an individualized space that permits classifications and combinations.'[47] These techniques of disciplines are intimately linked to uses of space.[48] In my fieldwork, I observed that work is neatly divided into shifts, different for different categories (nurses, attendants, and private sisters), a combination of which ensures that optimum nursing care is given with minimum staffing. Nurses, attendants, and private sisters have spaces allocated in the wards and cabins and attempts to step out of it are rebuffed by immediate supervisors. Spaces are coded as dangerous (lounges, changing rooms, corridors) and useful (nurse's table). Ranks are strictly maintained—matron, sister-in-charge, and staff nurse amongst registered nursing staff, as well as between categories of nursing personnel—nurses, attendants, and private sisters. These spatial (re) organizations of bodies are not just about allocating places to people but actively producing spaces as well as subjectivities. How do subjects see themselves? How do they see each other? How are spaces inhabited and lived? What are the traces of space in corporeality? A section of the workforce that occupies supervisory roles observe everything; not just raw materials and instruments, but the behaviour, attitude, and skill of

[47] Foucault (2007).

[48] The art of discipline is organized around four techniques. Enclosure (gates that opened and closed at appointed hours), partition (each individual was allocated his own space), coded spaces (specific spaces were coded dangerous or useful), and rank (where individuals were located in the classification system). The instruments used by disciplining powers are hierarchy (need for specialized personnel for supervision), normalizing judgements (where every deviant behaviour is brought under a norm), and examination (what makes the normalizing and the hierarchizing punishable and rewardable) (Foucault 1991).

the men and women who labour in the wards. The operation of disciplinary power allows for a definition of good and bad behaviour that is oppositional, and individuals are mapped between the two. Women workers, especially those at the lower end, occupying ranks of attendants and private sisters, find themselves increasingly under the scanner: behaviour (rude, insolent, and argumentative) and attitude (lazy, thievish, and immoral) is examined to peg women workers as either good or bad women and/or workers. Norms are both spatially and corporeally produced within disciplinary fields, as women are expected to conform to normative constructions of 'good' women as well as workers.

The supervision of the workforce is done at many levels. At one level, there are security guards, ward managers, and representatives of the management, and at another level, nurses keep an eye on private sisters and attendants, while they themselves are subjected to supervision by seniors in the hierarchy. As much as spatial organizations are meant to produce subjects who internalize their own oppression, the hawk-eyed vigilance on workers points to the failures and incompleteness of such projects. That the subject is never completely and totally determined by discourses and norms, and hegemonic projects contain elements of coercion and domination, are demonstrated by the policing, surveillance, and scrutiny that workers are subjected to. For instance, no lateral communication is tolerated. It is almost as if there is this fear lurking that if bodies group together publicly, they may collectively arise. Whether in the government or in the private enterprise, the management cannot tolerate women in lower ranks sitting together and talking. During the night shift, guards will ask women to disperse, nurses will ask attendants to spread out in the wards and not sit together. Ritu, whom we met earlier, talks of how nurses separate friends during working hours, by assigning them duties in different wards. Any attempt to meet during lunch hours or free time is checked. 'The security guards will not let us sit together. When they come on rounds, they will tell us to disperse. Even the sisters cannot stand it when two attendants get close.' Not just the attendants but nurses, ward managers, and the security guards too come under such supervision. In the private nursing home, representatives of the management come in late at night unannounced to see if all the employees, including the ward managers and the security guards, are at their duty stations. No segment of the workforce is exempt from supervision, not even the supervisors themselves.

Space, time, and work are arranged within the hospital and nursing homes in a manner that is sensitive to management and organizational strategies. Attendants and private sisters cannot be seen together, sitting and talking. Nurses, however, sit at the nursing table and can work, talk, and rest. This also gives them a vantage point over the whole ward. The nurses' station is located in such a manner that every movement in the ward can be observed. Attendants must ideally sit away from each other. Private sisters are confined within the cabins of the patients and cannot leave the room, except to use the bathroom or fetch drinking water.

Attendants complain that nurses cannot tolerate them sitting or even putting their heads down, while they themselves take similar liberties. The very nature of the work of nurses and the attendants, which functions on the duality of technical and manual labour, is the benchmark of work productivity. Nurses sitting at the desk with record books can talk, ponder, or sleep—it fits in with the understanding that a nurse's work is administrative and includes record keeping, which essentially means that she stays at her desk. An attendant or a private sister's work is manual, which means she takes bodily care of patients. Sitting, dozing, or talking to other workers signifies that she is cheating on both time and work. Sumita, 24, married, and practicing Vaishnavism, hails from an urban lower middle-class family. Her father worked in the railways and encouraged her to train as a nurse as it would be easier to gain employment. It was not lack of resources but awareness that made her enrol in an unlicensed centre. Now working as a private sister in the private hospital, she narrates how nurses insult private sisters on a regular basis:

> They do not like attendants and private sisters sitting and talking to each other. They will keep saying, 'Stay in the ward next to the patient. Do not come and sit at the nurses' table.' Even if someone is sitting with her head down, they will threaten to complain that you were sleeping. They will speak to you very insultingly, 'Have you come to work? Why don't you sit at home and rest?' (Personal interview with the author)

The nature of the work requires nurses, attendants, and private sisters to be in the ward throughout the shift with no official lunch break. The absence of any of the staff for even some time can become a source of conflict. The nature of medical care is such that if a patient needs help, it cannot be denied or delayed. The absence of a staff in any of the rungs of the hierarchy at a particular moment essentially means that the staff from the next level has to fill in. With less than minimum staff, this leads to a tug of war, especially between the private sisters and attendants, whose work is almost similar. Nurses face similar clashes with doctors. If a nurse is absent from her post when a doctor comes for a round, it is the latter who has to administer injections and perform intravenous cannulation. And if a private sister is absent when a patient needs a bed pan, it is the attendant who has to fill in. For optimum functioning of the medical enterprise, there is a need to ensure that everybody stays in their place. Shilpi, 27 years of age, unmarried, General Caste, took nursing training straight after school, when her father's business started to fail. Coming from the district of North Dinajpur, she migrated to Kolkata to train in a government school of nursing and served in a hospital in North Bengal for several years. She was transferred to an urban posting only recently. She narrates how shortage of nursing staff and arrogant behaviour of doctors adds to her stress of working in a hospital:

> In the ward, sometimes there is only one nurse. I am alone on duty, and if I go to the bathroom for five minutes and the doctor comes and sees I am not there, he will not even ask about my whereabouts. He will start shouting that the nurse is not at her station. The whole hospital will get to know that in so and so ward, the sister was absent during her duty. (Personal interview with the author)

* * *

The hospital economy is held together by different levels of workers who are located unequally. The subservient, humble location of a set of workers is vital for the well-being and interests of others , who are located in a relatively superior grade. This comparative and marginal well-being is fiercely guarded, and strategies that reinforce inequalities, discriminations, and marginalization are deployed: in this context, caste norms of tactility and being are used to cancel out sections of workers who may demand social and economic recognition that would eat into the privileges of those located at the top. Space remains crucial to the constitution of subjects. The spatial division of labour and the workers are central to the constitution of subjectivities and social relations. Given that dirt, disorder, and chaos are central to the imagination of the hospital space, it creates anxieties of transgressions, infractions, and violations of existing norms, borders, and boundaries, based on caste identities.

The hegemony of the social order is thus dependent on the politics of reproduction and boundary maintenance that counters any form of unsettling. Doreen Massey asks, 'Who is it *really* that is hankering after a notion of place as settled, a resting place? Who is it that is worrying about the breakdown of barriers supposedly containing an identity?'[49] (Italics in original).

In this chapter, I have examined how a modern workspace, which purportedly defies traditional links of social identities with occupational hierarchies, is organized to reinforce and maintain social inequalities. In fact, in some contexts, it even exacerbates existing inequalities. Given the nature of the labour performed and the heterogeneous workforce, it is hard to maintain a division of labour—borders and boundaries become increasingly fuzzy, messy, and complicated. Central to this chapter is the argument that workers are produced not just by oppressive capitalist processes, but by deploying tactility, being, and space to produce subjects that are abject. The division of labour, whether in the household or the modern factory space, is correlated with degrees of inherited purity by those who perform it. However, these divisions are increasingly being corroded with considerable overlaps, spillover, seepages, and contradictions.

[49]   Massey (1994: 122).

6   (Re)producing the 'Other'

Stigmatized Lives, Unruly Dispositions,
Sexual Transgressions

The quotidian, as we have observed, plays a constitutive role in producing subjects. It is in the everyday politics of labour that practices of affirmation and contestation are played out. Hierarchies based on sexualities, class, and caste are aligned and realigned as women workers struggle to have a social identity both within their workplaces and families. This chapter seeks to understand how hierarchies based on axes of class, caste, and sexualities are (re)produced. How is 'otherness' created and sustained? The construction of certain workers as the 'other', reinforced and maintained by everyday practices, is embedded in material realities that reflect organizational strategies as well as labour market processes. As argued in the previous chapter, representations are not reflexive but *constitutive* and therefore have a real and material impact. Historically, working-class lives and cultures have been represented as marginal and inferior and are constituted through regimes of representation adopted and 'normalized' by the dominant groups. Stuart Hall argues that representations play a constitutive role in the construction of identities, and a politics of representation must take on board that it is discursively produced. Thus, categories are constructed through representations and are not something that lies outside it.[1]

The chapter asks many questions: How does stigma work to produce subjects who accept denigrating working conditions, precarious employment, and gross inequality? Given that the subject is never fixed but is always becoming, how do class, caste, gender, and sexualities intersect to discursively produce workers who are labelled inferior, thus legitimizing exploitation? Class is a contentious category: while there have been various attempts to define it, it resists classification. I ask how is 'class' lived. What are the forms in which class finds expression in everyday lives? What is the role of sexualities—sexual dispositions, practices, and norms—in justifying the division of labour within a sub-sector of the health care economy? While certain cultural meanings assigned to hierarchical binaries (male/female, middle-class/working class, Brahmin/Dalit) are not just acceptable and commonplace, more detailed understanding of how these formations have emerged at a given point of time at a critical juncture, is required. Feminist anthropology has brought into focus that women's access to and occupation of public spaces is mediated not just by sexualities, but also by caste and class.[2] The previous chapter has detailed how social identities and spatial politics are deployed to legitimize exploitation; in this chapter, I argue that caste, class, and sexualities work in tandem to produce subjects who find it difficult to question universal norms. However, these axes of inequalities are sometimes so inextricably woven together, both in domination as well as resistance, that it is an impossible task to disentangle the threads. The messy entanglements produced by intersecting identities provide ideal grounds for the making of the self, which is deeply rooted in a constituent other—whether it is man/woman, master/slave. The otherization of a section of a population, whether in context of class, caste, gender, or sexualities, needs modes of otherizing. Stigma is a

[1] Hall (2005).
[2] Dube (1997).

tool par excellence in classifying population, preventing social mobility, and objectifying a section of population as a resource. Foucault argues that biopower—which is characteristic of modern society—is the integrated exercise of simultaneous technology of disciplines and the normative regulation of populations. It does so by applying itself to the 'everyday life categories of the individual'.[3] Biopower, thus, intensifies an individuals' relationship to herself and her own self-governance. It produces subjects: 'It is a form of power that makes individuals subjects ... subject to someone else by control and dependence, and tied to his own identity by a conscience or self-knowledge.'[4] In this chapter, I ask how are differences created, sustained, and reproduced. What are the ambiguities, overlaps, and contradictions that threaten the dominant social order and what are the frames of references that try to appropriate such seepages and contradiction within the symbolic? And how do these identity politics intersect with labour processes that produce a highly heterogeneous labour market? How do social identities, cultural capital, and the discourse on skills intersect to legitimize exploitation and precarity? A study of dominant groups can give us an insight into how the other is constructed. Bourdieu flags 'taste' or cultural competency as an important tool of stratification that clearly marks out groups.[5] This chapter looks at how clothes, cosmetics, jewellery, and sexual practices operate to mark groups as dominant or marginalized. The exaggeration of differences between subgroups is situational, contextual, and contrastive: in this context, where nursing is itself stigmatized as unskilled, servile, and corporeal labour, the need to culturally distinguish between categories of workers, to assert differences within subgroups, takes on an immediate urgency.

Nursing Labour: Stigmatized Labour and Disrespected Work

The word 'stigma' originated in the late sixteenth century, it means 'a branding, a mark made on the skin by pricking or branding, as punishment for a criminal or a mark of subjection, a brand in extended usage,

[3] Foucault (1990).
[4] Foucault (2001: 331).
[5] Bourdieu (1984).

a mark of disgrace associated with a particular circumstance, quality, or person. The word comes via Latin from Greek *stigma* "a mark made by a pointed instrument, a dot"; its plural form gives stigmata."[6] Stigma is thus a way of dividing, classifying, labelling, and regimenting a population. Foucault's contribution in understanding how the marginal other is produced is useful for us to understand the political and ideological drive behind stigmatizing a section of the population. In *Abnormal* (2003), Foucault theorizes the marginal as different from the abnormal, as the former plays an important role in the social symbolic. They occupy a liminal space in society either due to devaluation, or their objectification as a resource meant for the well-being of the dominant group that further enables society to perpetuate and reproduce unequal relations.[7] The ground for this objectification is made possible through stigma. Stigma may be experienced in an individual level or as a group, and in this section, I am concerned with the latter: when, institutionally and structurally, a subsection of the population is stigmatized and denigrated for the advantage and convenience of a few.

The larger devaluation of nursing as an ancillary staff in the health care industry, being a handmaid to the doctor, reduced to a semi-skilled worker, slightly better than a domestic worker, speaks volumes on how labour is gendered. In this section, I argue that stigma plays an important role in the devaluation of nursing labour; stigma is not an effect of devaluation, but it plays a *constitutive* role. Stigma also produces highly gendered subjects, who accept the devaluation of their labour, skills, and knowledge. The triple–tier nursing labour market with its increasingly complex division of labour performed by a differentiated workforce cannot be maintained only by organizational strategies. It requires consent and compliance, obedience and submission to social structures and labour processes that justify the pyramidal nature of the labour market. As much as nurses submit to their construction as subordinate and subservient to medical men, private sisters and attendants submit to the construction of their labour as ancillary to 'trained' women in medicines—that is, the nurse.

Goffman contends that persons with a stigma are considered less than fully human and subject to all manner of discrimination which reduces

---

6   Knowles (2005).
7   Foucault (2003).

their life chances.'[8] Stigma requires a level of stickiness—when something sticks, refuses to go away, smears, homogenizes, and takes away from one's notion of self. Stigma is essentially a negative attribute—like shame, it detracts from a person's worth and produces subjects who are yielding, passive, and submit to power, reducing a person to what Goffman calls a 'tainted and discounted one'.[9] Almost all the respondents (95.7 per cent) feel that nursing is stigmatized while only a handful (4.2 per cent) perceive it otherwise (Table A.11). Most trained nurses feel that nursing is stigmatized because it is perceived as unskilled labour. Tista, 42 years of age, General Caste, and married, hails from an urban family of professionals. She took to nursing because she was attracted to the ideology of seba. She points out, 'nursing is stigmatized because people do not know the training and education required to become a nurse. They think anybody can become a nurse.' The emphasis on 'anybody can become a nurse' is repeated again and again in various interviews. All registered nurses emphasized on the degree/diploma that a nurse has to earn; unregistered nursing staff insisted that they too have come into service after training, though unrecognized. Nursing staff, both registered and unregistered, argue that knowledge and training differentiate them from the 'uneducated, lower-class, Dalit women', who historically worked in hospitals and nursing homes.

The discourse on skill, identity, and stigma in context to women's reproductive labour produces subjects who comply with normative frameworks that constitute some labour as respectable, and others not. Harking back to colonial India, a clinical instructor in a college of nursing observed, 'In the past, nurses were widowed, distressed women and low-caste prostitutes who had no other livelihood options but to take up nursing, which has led to such a stigmatization of the profession. People do not see what kind of education a nurse has to go through before she starts practicing.' It is not just skills and education but also social identity of the woman that constitutes dispositions conducive to acquiring knowledge that goes into the making of a nurse. Even government-employed nurses are affected by this devaluation, despite receiving the best salaries and work contracts in this segment of the labour market. Tista continues: 'My parents-in-law never looked at my profession happily.

---

[8]   Goffman (1963: 102).
[9]   Goffman (1963: 3).

In fact, they look down on it. They do not understand the education, the training, the selfless service that goes into this job. They have never respected my job my service.'

Classical political economists consider labour as work that falls under the purview of economic activities that bring in wages for goods and services produced;[10] thus, professional nursing is a service offered in exchange of wages and should ideally fall under the rubric of work. Ronald Meek argues that traditionally, the social status of the producer as well as skill and intensity of the labour determined the value of the commodity; however, with the advent of capitalism, the status of the producer became irrelevant (with society being neatly divided into working class and the bourgeoisie) and it was only skill and intensity of labour that mattered.[11] However, stigmatization of surrogates and sex workers, for instance, points to the centrality of caste and sexualities in constituting the value of the service provided,[12] which further complicates arguments that overemphasises class, overriding all other differences in understanding work, its value, and the social status of the worker. Deploying the labour theory of value, Marxist feminists have argued that the devaluation of women's paid labour stems from an insistence on its unproductive nature and thus their focus has been to emphasize on the value produced by reproductive labour.[13] However, John argues that in a society riddled by caste, public labour represents stigma and humiliation and thus cannot be valorized like other forms of paid labour. She argues for a 'stigma theory of labour', which goes beyond gender and class, and brings in a caste analysis of why certain labour is almost always tied to the Dalit labouring body, more so, if it is a female Dalit body.[14] As I argue elsewhere, the convergence of various factors—the nature of work, discourse on skills, the relation between social identities and occupations—constitute labour as degrading and humiliating.[15] The focus on training, education, and degrees possessed by women labouring as nurses and nursing aides speaks directly to

[10] For a further discussion, see Brennan (2006).

[11] Meek (1956: 76–7).

[12] Kotiswaran (2011); Pande (2009).

[13] Barrett (1980); Walby (1990).

[14] John (2013).

[15] Ray (2016b).

the discursive construction of such labour. The central theme in this context is 'lack'—a lack of knowledge, skill, education, or disposition to become a skilled worker. This lack is a constitutive element in the imagination of the professional nurse. One can thus argue that the struggle of nurses to mark their profession is primarily defined and determined by a lack. To be recognized as a worker is to transcend gender, caste, and class markers; to rise and transcend one's corporeality and to become an unmarked worker. In the previous chapter, I have demonstrated that even those women from upper-caste communities, possessing academic and technical nursing qualifications, are treated as 'untouchables' because of their close proximity and contact with ritualistically impure matter. The constitution of a body as stigmatized, incapable of intellectual labour, and synonymous to nature, as opposed to culture and modernity, is central to the devaluation of women's labour, particularly caste-based labour. As Annapurna, whom we met earlier, argues that it is the nature of the work and the stigma attached that does not allow her the identity of a worker, 'Society attaches a lot of stigma to this service. This has so little salary. People will say she works as an attendant and yet she is so vocal'.[16]

The attempt to re-signify labour that was almost always marked by class, caste, and gender led to occupational closure, thus being accessible only to those women who possess cultural capital to qualify as a registered nurse. However, the failure of occupational closure lies in the division of labour within the health care industry. To transcend the stigma associated with low-caste labour, marked by dirt, filth, and pollution, performed manually, required a disassociation with some aspects of nursing labour—the corporeal and the hands-on bodily care. The logic is circular: modernization of nursing envisaged an expulsion of chotolok woman from the profession and bringing the bhadramahila on board; however, historically, gendering of the profession, meant its continuing marginalization in health budgets. The non-allocation of public funds for nursing meant that the scarcity in nurses had to be dealt with by a differentiated workforce, which included women from all strata of society. The continuation of the chotolok woman in the profession, even if placed in the margins, leads to cartographic anxieties of spatial and social transgressions. It also

[16] Cited in Ray (2016b: 67).

implies that the process of de-stigmatization, as envisaged by the professionalization project, could not be achieved.

Registration of nursing has not eliminated the chotolok woman; on the contrary, it has just rendered her vulnerable. Professionalization has not prevented the working-class, lower-caste woman from becoming nursing staff; it has only created newer hierarchies and modes of exploitations. The discourse on skills that constitute bodies as in/capable of intellectual labour draws from social identities, as much as taxonomies of labour that resist classification of reproductive labour as 'work'. Given the social and cultural processes that refuse to grant recognition to women's work as skilled intellectual labour, qualifications and degrees become pivotal to the nursing sector in establishing itself as a profession. Caught in a vortex where increasing gatekeeping means fewer women from lower social strata are able to enter the profession, the nature of nursing care proves to be a quandary. The imagination of nursing labour as dirty means women from higher social groups are unwilling to take it up as a profession; it also means recruiting women from groups that are traditionally associated with such impure labour as ancillary nursing staff to conduct the most essential components in healing processes.

Cultural Capital and Skills: Occupational Gatekeeping

The debates on the emergence of the middle class will be useful for us in understanding the antagonism that semi/untrained women employed as nurses/nursing aides face. The middle class defies easy classification. Recent scholarship has defined the middle class as a group of people who have risen in power and prestige due to their access to scarce resources such as education and occupational skills; but all agree that the middle class is a heterogeneous group that resists taxonomy.[17] It is understood that the emergence of the middle class is bound up with the development of capitalism, where as a social group they provided various services for the maintenance of the system. In Bengal, the emergence of the middle class was tied to the ownership of land, as colonial rule disintegrated native industries.[18] The introduction of English education to help the British run the colonial machinery with ease meant that it was this class that

[17] Bardhan (1984); Deshpande (2003).
[18] Mukhopadhyay (1998); Tripathi (1994).

by sheer dint of possessing cultural capital, took to modern education. Thus, English education became the key ingredient in the formation of the Bengali middle class. The distancing from land, manual labour, and the inclination towards services, preferably in the public sector, marked the disposition of this new class. However, even the bhadralok was not homogenous—there were more or less classified into three subgroups: higher or propertied middle class, middle class, poor but honest middle class. But all of them possessed education, which ensured their entry into the ranks of the bhadralok.[19] Even in contemporary times, the entry to the ranks of the middle class is contingent on taste, refinement, education, and ability to hoard cultural capital, whether through institutional means, social networking, or gatekeeping.[20] As E.P. Thompson pointed out, class is not a component of social structure, static and ahistorical, that presupposes a 'class consciousness'—on the contrary, class consciousness is a way experiences are culturally articulated in traditions, rituals, institutions, and customs. It is a culturally constituted, historically specific phenomenon: 'class is defined by men as they live their own history....'[21]

As I argue elsewhere, trained nurses focus on the training and education that goes into the making of a nurse to emphasize on the skilled nature of their labour. And this cultural capital is zealously guarded. The GNM diploma is not just evidence of competence (embodied cultural capital) but a marker of the extent of professionalization that the service has achieved, which allows its holder certain entitlements.[22] The presence of unregistered nurses and nursing aides, though necessary to maintain the medical/managerial consultant status of the registered nurse, poses a problem in terms of how the service continues to be perceived and stigmatized. The coexistence of the purportedly skilled bhadramahila and semi/unskilled chotolok woman in the same sub-sector implies that the stigmatization of the labour as corporeal, menial, servile, feminine, and primitive is shared by all members. The need to mark and distance a 'trained' nurse from an 'untrained' one takes on more urgency. No one is more affected in this struggle than the private sister—semi-trained

---

[19] Mukhopadhyay (1998).
[20] Bourdieu (1984); Fernandes (2006); Fernandes and Heller (2006).
[21] Thompson (1966: 11).
[22] Ray (forthcoming-b).

like the unregistered nurse but gaining employment in the category of a private sister implies that her body becomes a site of contesting claims, negations, assertions, and resistances. The presence of the private sister poses a double bind: private sisters are essential for the cabin system as the minimal recruitment of registered nurses makes systematic surveillance and monitoring of patients at an individual level impossible. Possessing minimum education and unrecognized training in nursing, they challenge the very basis of medical knowledge, the very foundation of 'cultural capital' legitimized by institutions. The injunction against their performance of medical tasks stems from intra-conflict between ranks of nursing personnel, whereby registered nurses came together to prevent private sisters from performing medical labour and accessing further knowledge than what they already possess. This delegitimization of knowledge of women, made vulnerable by the discourse on skills and classification of labour, justifies their exploitation and marginality. While unregistered nurses take on responsibilities, duties, and obligations similar to that of a registered nurse, the 'private sister' is considered fair game by both. In private sectors there are either no registered nurses or just a handful of them; most of them are migrant women with GNM training, employed to meet government needs. The unregistered nurse performs the same duties, occupying the same position of authority and power, and taking similar responsibilities as that of a government-employed registered nurse, for one-third of the pay (see Chapter 2). The private sister in both public and private health services occupies a liminal position. She reminds the unregistered nurse of the fragility of her claim on power and authority as well as exposes her claims to skill and knowledge by highlighting that both have received the same training in duration and in intensity. For the registered nurse, she is the abject body, the chotolok, who by the dint of her caste, class, and sexuality tars and stigmatizes the profession as a whole. Her claims to similar knowledge and training as the nurse threatens to tear into the carefully built hierarchies within the profession and jeopardizes the efforts of the nurse to enter the hallowed corridors of intellectual labour. She must be put in her place.[23]

The injunction against private sisters on performing medical tasks is an outcome of the nurse's struggle to prevent plebeian women from accessing medical knowledge; it is to ensure that she remains where

---

[23] I have argued this in detail in Ray (forthcoming-b).

she belongs—the corporeal, the menial, and the manual. The hospital administration does not allow private sisters to engage in any medical or technical work, despite possessing certain training—whether it is administering medicine, injections, catheters, or undertaking intravenous cannulation. And just by removing medical interventions from their work, their identities as nurses crumble—the private sister becomes more of an attendant and less of a nurse. In the context of an economy described as highly global, knowledge-driven, and increasingly competitive, the image of who can be a nurse depends on the degree she can distance herself from manual labour and engage in medical tasks. In a context where skills are socially constructed, highly gendered, classed, and marked by caste, the fragile base upon which nursing claims its right to a profession, draws its authority from occupation skills legitimized by institutional degrees. Thus, Sumita, whom we met earlier, says, 'We have come to do nursing but our work is similar to that of an attendant. They clean vomit and faeces and we do the same. We have been reduced to the status of an attendant.'

Given that the nursing labour market is dependent on women from 'inferior' social groups, particularly for the construction of the 'trained' nurse, the attempts to prevent the former from entering the nursing profession takes a grave turn. Though knowledge functions as one of the major sites of symbolic violence, there are others that make for easy targets to show up hierarchies and buttress privileges, for example, the nurse's uniform. Given that in the Anglo-American world, institutionalized healing was primarily offered by religious bodies, the nurse's uniform is said to have been influenced by monastic orders and their strict injunction against showing flesh. White robes were particularly seen as symbolic of humility, cleanliness, and purity; and in later times, adopted as a marker of discipline and regimentation. It was argued that a uniform was 'advantageous on the grounds of economy as well as neatness and its effect on a corps of nurses is the same as on a company of soldiers'.[24] Goffman correctly points out that uniforms are signs that carry social information and possibly could mean different things to different groups—from communicating status to control and stigma.[25] The nurse's uniform, like other professional uniforms, constitutes the body

[24] Stimson (1936: 370).
[25] Goffman (1963: 47).

that it inhabits—a professional class marked by specific set of skills and, in this case, ideal gendered subjects. Otherwise resistant to any form of activism, the nurse's union in the government hospital strongly opposed the donning of the nurse's white uniform and cap by the private sisters.[26] The significance of the uniform in bolstering the claims of nursing as a profession came to the forefront when a collective opposition emerged against the private sister wearing the white dress and cap so typically associated with the professional nurse. Chhaya, whom we met earlier, led the movement. She says:

> The cap is the main dignity of the profession—there is a capping ceremony and only after that can we wear a cap. We have to take an oath before we are allowed to don the cap. Unauthorized nurses and hospitals abuse this. How can people disregard nursing caps like this? Without registration, one cannot wear a cap. How can an unauthorised ayah wear the same uniform as a nurse with a PhD degree? This is against our dignity. (Personal interview with the author)

The rituals of initiation into the nursing profession are emphasized by registered nurses—the 'oath', the 'uniform', the 'cap' that distances a legitimate from an illegitimate nurse; rituals that take on a sacrosanct nature, whose non-observance violates the spirit of nursing. The cap and the uniform signify the nurse's dignity, her new-found position as a medical professional in the global economy. These rituals are not just about policing entry into professional nursing; it also constitutes the nurse. Women entering the nursing profession take the 'Florence Nightingale Pledge' in a ceremony marked by solemnity, gravity, and formality. Only after they have sworn the oath emphasizing purity and faithfulness, and pledge to 'maintain and elevate the standard of my

---

[26] In the government hospital, a nurse's bureau was started by a minister's wife (of the then ruling Left Front), for subcontracted women with primary education, but with a six-month to one-year nursing training in unlicensed centres, to work as private sisters in the wards. In a unique display of solidarity, government nurses backed by faculty members from nursing colleges went on strike demanding the removal of non-registered nurses. This dragged on for almost three years ending in a resolution where these semi-trained private sisters were reinstated, but were stripped both of their uniform and the title of a nurse. Instead, they now wear brown saris and are called by a different name.

profession'[27] can they wear the nursing cap. The strict policing of entry into the nursing profession is not just about gatekeeping. It is equally about making each individual nurse responsible for raising the bar of who can enter the rank of professional nursing.

The presence of unregistered nurses, staking claim to this newly established image and possibly succeeding, has to be violently routed. While the everyday practices of labour in the wards necessitate the presence of private sisters and attendants, the uniform of the nurse is the most visible symbol of her cultural capital. An unregistered nurse wearing a similar uniform not just threatens/destabilizes knowledge claims of the trained nurse, but also blurs the distinction between registered and unregistered nurses, thus threatening class and caste distinctions. Within the medical hierarchy, the nurse's uniform is one of the most visible markers that symbolically shields relatively powerful groups from being clubbed together with the subordinates. Jhilum, thirty, unmarried, General Caste, hails from an urban family of service workers. Unaware of the difference between registered and unregistered courses, she trained in nursing from an unlicensed centre after reading their advertisement. Now working as a private sister in the government hospital, she argues that once private sisters were stripped of their nurse's uniform, they became targets of collective symbolic violence.

> When I had a uniform, the Group D staff would never say 'change the urine bag'. They would call us didi (elder sister) and address us as *apni*. Now they speak to us like we are their servants—they address us as *tumi*. Even doctors address us as tumi.[28] Where there is no respect, no honour—how can one do such work? (Personal interview with the author)

[27] The Nightingale Pledge, http://www.truthaboutnursing.org/press/pioneers/nightingale_pledge.html (accessed on 10 July 2017).

[28] In *Bangla* language, there are three ways of addressing a person: *apni*, *tumi*, and *tui*. *Apni* is usually reserved for someone who is older and respected. It is a formal way of address that takes into account the status of the addressee. *Tumi* is a more informal form of address used for the same age group or when the addressee and the speaker have reached a level of intimacy. *Tui* is an extreme form of informality used with children, amongst friends, or in certain contexts to convey disrespect and disregard. It can also be used to humiliate the addressee.

The connection between uniform and respect came up in almost all interviews. Almost all private sisters in the government hospital who were 'stripped' off their uniform believed that other workers, nurses, administrative staff, patients, and even doctors stopped respecting them when they stopped wearing the white uniform. The trained nurse is a figure built on violent exclusions. However, no one group is static in its (dis)privileged position; it keeps shifting and changing, and at different junctures, one or more identity becomes more important than the other. While registered nurses occupy a privileged position vis-à-vis attendants and private sisters, they become the 'other' in relation to doctors. The power struggle between doctors and nurses also rotates largely around education and qualifications. Education justifies the doctor's status as an expert-consultant, the nurse's status as his handmaid, and the semi-trained/untrained nursing aide as a menial, unskilled labourer. Medical knowledge, that is science, is projected as a masculine discipline and exclusively a doctor's domain; however, medical service cannot function without the collaboration of nursing personnel, whether trained or untrained. Inherent within this collaboration is the contradiction of initiative and personal ambition. As long as personal ambition or initiative is sought to be contained internally within each of these professions—for nurses amongst other nurses and for doctors amongst other doctors—it is acceptable. Professional competition between a nurse and a doctor is not seen as possible or legitimate. The symbolic violence that is inherent in these exclusionary definitions of nursing and doctoring is based on an education system that gives legitimacy to doctors as experts of scientific healing and nurses as ancillary medical workers. As the doctor's position is determined by skills and degrees (though in general, there is supposed to be no competition between doctors and nurses), when nurses achieve higher degrees, it becomes difficult to maintain the absolute hierarchical superiority of the doctors. And this is in part because, despite the rigid separation of nursing and doctoring within the medical profession, as middle classes, they participate in a general shared hierarchy of degrees institutionalized by academic authorities. Thus, if a nurse goes on to get an MSc or a PhD degree, and the doctor does not have an MD (Doctor of Medicine) or equivalent, it could become a source of conflict and power struggles. Doctors (or even others in the management) rebuke any medical initiatives taken by nurses: 'You want to be a doctor?' 'You think you know better than a doctor?' Nayantara, 42 years of age, married, General Caste, has been working as a registered nurse for the last twenty years and narrates how doctors routinely humiliate nurses: 'Doctors taunt us. We have studied similar subjects so we have some medical knowledge, but if we point out something in the wards, they will say something sarcastic, particularly in front of patients to humiliate us.' However, the medical labour market that allows semi-trained nursing personnel to perform certain tasks also gives similar opportunities to nurses, to contest their labour as purely emotional or affective, that is devoid of scientific knowledge. Nayantara continues, 'Doctors come for a few hours. No matter what they say, if any urgent medical decision needs to be taken, we (nurses) do it. Though technically we are not supposed to be taking medical decisions, most of the time doctors are not available, so we have to use our experience to deal with the situation. Then how can you say that we have no scientific knowledge.' As with all other professions, the need to build borders, establish boundaries, and regulate entry and exit is imperative. Given nursing's fraught history of emerging from a caste-based, plebeian occupation, and administrative or governmental indifference to what they perceive as semi-skilled feminine ancillary care work, it is left to the everyday politics of labour to make visible the markers that constitute a professional trained nurse in the new, global medical economy.

Working in Hospitals

When I started going to the hospital in the middle of the night for my field work, I was greeted with curiosity and suspicion, from both security guards of the gated community where I live, as well as well-meaning neighbours and relatives. 'What do you do at the hospital in the middle of the night? Who are the women who stay at night in the hospitals? Why can you not go during the day?' One of the security guards took the initiative to ask the driver of the rental car whether I actually went to hospitals and not somewhere else. The amount of explanations that I had to give and the negotiations with the community I lived in made me ask my respondents, 'What does it mean to work in a hospital? What does it mean to "work nights"?' The hierarchical order of jobs, the 'unproductive' nature of the labour, informal employment, and the workplace are embedded in power structures, discourses, and norms that produce the hospital space as 'kaajer jaiga' (a place of work). Women's work and their employment patterns must be located at the interstices of patriarchal norms, new forms of production, and the (re)organization of capitalist labour markets. Increasing poverty, desertion by male members, and changing norms of obligations and responsibilities are tweaking traditional and spatial conceptualization of the private and public, of home and the workplace.

In the previous chapter, I argued that menial and manual labour, such as nursing in public hospitals, embodies humiliation, which adversely constitutes the identity of the worker. In this section, I try to understand women's perception of their workplace, the hospital and the nursing home, as a space that grants them the identity of a worker. Not just the nature of work, but the location or place, terms of employment, wages, and working conditions constitute the status of work and the identity of a worker. For example, paid domestic work, with its minimum wages and exploitative working conditions, remains a caste-based labour that precludes any identity as a worker. Scholars argue that the spatial location of paid domestic work marks it differently from other kinds of labour, given its location on the cusp of modernity and feudalism.[29] Given that a large section of urban women find employment as domestic workers, and given the similarities, continuities, and overlaps between nursing (at the lower end) and domestic work, is the hospital a legitimate workplace? How different is it from (someone else's) home as a workplace? Is hospital work, particularly for those located at the lower end, perceived as the work of a domestic worker?

Historically, hospitals were accessed by the poor and the wretched, cared for and cured by the distressed and the outcaste.[30] However, in contemporary times, even those women engaged at the lowest end, working as ayahs, are quick to point out that hospitaler kaaj (working in a hospital) is better than jhier kaaj (work of a servant).[31] Rekha, 38 years of age, Scheduled Caste, took to working as an attendant after marriage, when she had no other option. Married into a family of menial workers, her husband's earnings were not enough to support the family. Living in

---

[29] Qayum and Ray (2003).

[30] Arnold (1993).

[31] The word jhi is a derogatory term used for domestic workers, particularly for those who engage in the most menial and manual labour.

a rented accommodation, she and her husband both sought work in the service economy, and she strongly feels that working in a hospital is far better than working in someone's home. She says, 'This is a workplace. I do not feel disgusted, but if I had to do the same work at someone's house, I would. There is no respect. The work may be same, but still this is a hospital. If I worked in someone's home, people would say, *jhier kaaj kore* (she does the work of a servant).' The location of work plays a constitutive role in defining the worker's identity. As Rekha argues that the work of an attendant is similar to the work of a domestic worker, however, the spatial constitution of the hospital gives the worker a sense of identity that is barred to someone engaged in similar work. This echoes amongst all the respondents in the research project. The most prestigious work is office work—work of a clerk, peon, and administrative help—labour-intensive but clean; but given that they lack the minimum education required, hospital work is the next best. Tapati, 40 years of age, Scheduled Caste, only started working after her husband disappeared one day leaving her with two pre-teen children. After spending many years bringing up other people's children in private residences, she found employment as an attendant in the nursing home. Tapati also feels that working at someone's home is not work: 'Taking care of children in someone's home is not work—*eta kaaj noi* (this is not work)—working in a hospital may be looked down upon but still this is work.' Or as Kajal, 35 years of age, married, Scheduled Caste, who also took to working as an attendant in the private hospital when all other options were closed, says, 'There is more respect in this than washing dishes in someone's house. This is a hospital, it is a workplace.' Given that the menial component of nursing care and domestic labour, overlaps in a significant manner, spatial location marks labour in ways that are conspicuous, and of consequences.

What constitutes a space as a workplace? The imagination of modern workspaces, that is places where work occurs—with its discipline, punctuality, rhythm of shift jobs, uniform, and movements guided by the hour of the clock—acts as an invisible structure in determining women's experience of labour, employment, and their everyday lives. How does the workplace and terms of employment stigmatize women and their labour? I think above and beyond economic, social, and technological factors that constitute labour as stigmatized, trying to understand the politics of location makes for an interesting access point in understanding how subjects are constituted. Chaitali, whom we met earlier, complains bitterly of the stigma associated with hospital work. But on being asked whether she would prefer to work at someone's home, the answer is an empathetic no. 'Working as a house nurse[32] is of course better in terms of wages, but there is no respect in working in someone's home. There is a lot more respect in working in a hospital, than to work in someone's house. Here there is a routine, work hours—*eta to kaajer jaiga* (this is a workplace)'.

Even if it increases her wages, Chaitali does not want to move out of the hospital space. The stigma associated with reproductive labour, particularly in someone else's home—jhier kaaj—works in non-rational ways to influence the choices of women. Capitalism's 'rationalism', where it is understood that workers freely choose to seek work that is advantageous to her/him in terms of wages, is contradicted by the worldly beliefs and practices of social actors. Althusser displaces the base-superstructure model to argue that the economic system does not necessarily have a dominant role in influencing culture, but a number of factors, including politics and ideology, contribute in varying degrees.[33] This theorization helps us to understand why women continue to work in hospitals, even if other workplaces make more economic sense. For women, who have always found work in the manual, menial, stigmatized sub-sectors of the service economy, how do respect, recognition, and status play out in real and material ways? What are the practices that make spaces workplaces? What are the rituals, relationships, and structures within spaces that make one workplace more legitimate and desirable than others?

The physical separation between home and work (even if it is someone else's home) helps in delinking commodified reproductive work from its domestic shackles and makes it more respectable. It is not just paid employment, but all the markers of a profession—uniform, shift, office space—that gives attendants and private sisters a sense of being a part of a professional workforce. As Sujata, whom I introduced in the second chapter, sums up, 'If I work in someone's house, people speak very badly about me. At least here I have a fixed time, a workplace and

---

[32] A house case/house nurse is when semi-trained nurses or untrained ayahs work in residences taking care of sick, elderly people or children.
[33] Althusser (1969).

uniform.' Even the nature of the organization, whether it is government or privately owned, bestows status on workers. A government job has more value, even if the work is daily-wage, than a regular, contractual job in a private establishment. Kajori, 42 years of age, unmarried, General Caste, and working as a private sister in a government hospital, for the last fifteen years, says that though she gets offers to work as an unregistered nurse in private clinics, she refuses to leave. 'I could have joined a smaller nursing home as a regular nursing staff, a regular contractual worker. But the respect I get when people get to know that I am working in a government hospital, I do not want to lose that.'

Working in a hospital allows some accumulation of social capital. This is also true of other kinds of commodified reproductive labour, such as domestic work; however, some of the women felt that working in an establishment rather than a private residence allows them to know more influential people. Tinni, 37, married, and living in the slum behind the hospital, worked for twelve years in 'house cases' as an attendant when her husband fell ill and lost his eyesight. An acquaintance introduced her to a contractor, who placed her as an attendant in the private hospital. Tinni believes that her job in the hospital puts her in contact with senior doctors, who otherwise would not be accessible to the urban poor. Therefore, while her work per se may be demeaned as menial, with no economic or cultural value, her location in the labour market—in a corporate institution, rather than someone's home—puts her within the circulation of social capital and makes her an important resource for the larger family and community.

> When I worked in house cases, people would avoid me; my relatives would not speak to me. But when I joined a big hospital, suddenly I became someone's elder sister, someone's sister in-law. Not because I had a better salary, but in case they need my contacts. In case they get admitted and need me to introduce them to some senior doctor. (Personal interview with the author)

An initial glance shows that the overwhelming response to give up current jobs if the financial situation at home improves is affirmative (74.4 per cent). However, the sub-categories are telling. All women working as private sisters and attendants would like to leave their jobs; in contrast, those women who are adamant that they would not leave their jobs even if family income increases, belong to the category of registered nurses (17 per cent), with only a few belonging to the unregistered nurse category (Table A.12). As Mala, whom we met earlier, says, 'Even if my family income increases, I will not give up my job. There is a dignity in a government job, even if it is just a GNM nurse.' Contrast Mala's response to that of Rituparna's. Rituparna is twenty-two years of age, General Caste, hailing from a family of service workers. She works as private sister on a daily-wage basis, in a private hospital.

> In this hospital, I will never get a proper posting, so my father keeps telling me to leave the job and get married. Nursing is so stigmatized, and then working in a private hospital as a private sister is something my family is against. My father says that you are not even a permanent staff, then why are you continuing? (Personal interview with the author)

Some of the private sisters working in the private sector are willing to leave their existing jobs, and join smaller nursing homes, where they will be employed as regular, unregistered nursing staff, removing the word 'private' from their designations. This would imply less salary, but an enhancement in status. This vertical move would facilitate a horizontal move as well, that is, from the bottom of the pyramid, they would come up to the middle. The increase in recognition, respect, and status that this move would facilitate, far outweighs the loss of wages suffered by the worker. Those who are employed in the government hospital, however, are still hoping for a policy change that would make all contractual work permanent. Sushmita, 47 years of age, unmarried, Scheduled Caste, joined the government hospital as all her other options had dried up. Her father's sudden death, when she was eighteen, brought an end to her education, and she took to tailoring and other odd jobs to be able to provide for her teenage siblings. Working as a private sister for the last twenty years in the same hospital, she hopes, that her service will be regularized. She says,

> We are still hoping that the job will become permanent or, at least, a fixed pay. This 'no work no pay' is very humiliating. I am only staying, hoping that something will change. I am tired of the disrespect. I do not want to leave a government hospital, but if nothing changes, then I will join a small nursing home for a fixed pay as a staff nurse, even if it is lesser money. (Personal interview with the author)

Women's narratives of experiencing humiliation and shame, because of their employment in a devalued sector, does not just point to the nature of work as embodying stigma but also nature of work contracts and of establishments. Precarious working conditions affect bargaining power adversely. The hierarchy is uncontested: in terms of respect, status, prestige and salaries, permanent government jobs are top of the line. Anuradha, Scheduled Caste, 45 years of age, married, and working as an attendant in a government hospital, feels that the contractual nature of the work adds to the devaluation: 'Because I am a Group D staff on contract, people look at me as if I am a piece of dirt. But if I am a permanent staff, they would give me respect. It is because we are not employed on a permanent basis, people do not respect us.' Madhuri, whom we met earlier, also feels similarly. She says, 'If I am a permanently employed staff, then the respect would be more. First, it is dirty work, and then contractual job, and with such low salary, which is why there is so little respect.' The contract of service then is not just a mere piece of paper laying out terms and conditions but also a signifier. It signifies the status of the worker. Contractual work at private hospitals and nursing homes are seen as equivalent to permanent jobs; though hire and fire is possible, it is not a general practice and there are certain job securities. It is daily-wage workers, designated as private sisters, whose conditions are the most insecure and exploitative. As Malati, 42 years of age, widowed, Scheduled Caste, working as a private sister for more than fifteen years in the government hospital, says, 'Even a Group D staff can speak to us insultingly, because we are not permanently employed staff. They are uneducated and untrained, yet they give us no respect.' Sumita, whom we met earlier, says, 'Staff employed on contract still gets some respect. We are on a daily-wage basis, and you see how the attendants talk to us—when someone amongst us becomes a regular nursing staff (unregistered nurses), their attitude changes.'

Some of the private sisters in the government hospital claim that on the virtue of being paid on a daily-wage basis, they are reduced to menial workers, and they face insolence and disobedience from attendants who refuse to recognize their authority. While it is commonplace to see hierarchies being built on the basis of skill, education, or qualification, terms of employment can re-signify those hierarchies. So, even if a private sister is more qualified than an attendant who has no training, the terms of employment reconstitute these hierarchies.

Stuart Hall rejects Marx's notion of culture as passive and secondary, to argue for its active, constitutive role in society.[34] The framework of reference, the moment of naming, and the figures of speech used in everyday language constitute workers. The stigma associated with working in the lower ranks leads to women falling back on deception to be able to gain status and respect in society. Some of the women who work as private sisters and attendants in nursing homes and private hospitals report that their families and communities back in the districts are unaware of the work they are doing. They do not deny working in hospitals; instead, they claim to be nursing staff. The comparative advantages of working in a higher rung in the hierarchy outweigh the disadvantages of working in a particularly stigmatized sector. Poulami, 22 years of age, unmarried, Brahmin, and hailing from a family of landless sharecroppers from the district of Howrah, travels to Kolkata every day to work as an attendant in a private nursing home. She says: 'Attendants and nurses do not get any respect in society. But a nurse is better off than an attendant. People in my family know that I am working in a nursing home. They do not know that I work as an attendant. They think I am a nursing staff.'

Women are constantly negotiating the relationship between workplace hierarchies and social identities. Lying to their families and communities about the nature of the work to escape stigma seems a common phenomenon, especially for those women who have migrated from the rural countryside to urban cities in search of work. Equally, there are women who are located at the bottom of the hierarchy, who couch their pride and defiance as workers in ideologies of wife/motherhood. Naila Kabeer, in her study on women workers in garment factories in Bangladesh, notes how women negotiate cultural meanings of purdah, to fit in with economic necessity. While not challenging the official discourse on purdah, women contest its meaning to justify their decisions to work in a factory.[35] Women rationalize their choices of working as a menial worker in a hospital, using ideologies of maternal altruism, especially in the face of failure of kin to assist them in times of economic distress. While it is understood that the ideology of female seclusion (as a marker of class, caste, and gender norms) are increasingly coming into conflict with the daily reality (that is, women's compulsion to earn),

[34] Hall (1958).
[35] Kabeer (2000).

it is offset with another ideology—sacrificing mother, responsible sister, and dependable daughter. Sree, 26, General Caste, married and hailing from an urban, working-class family of service providers, took to working as an attendant in the private nursing home after her husband's illness and failure to provide for the family. She says:

> We are working because of our children. This is *nichu kaaj* (lowly work). But we do it, because we are mothers. When people in society know that I work as an attendant, they are dismissive, and they insult me, which is why I do not go to any relative's house. I have to live. If society has to accept me, they have to accept me like this; otherwise they can go to hell. (Personal interview with the author)

Jaba, twenty-six years of age, Scheduled Caste, found work as an attendant in a private nursing home, when her husband asked her to leave home with their two daughters. Now living in a rented accommodation, she is the sole breadwinner and guardian of her children. She narrates how it was the failure to provide a son that led to the dissolution of her marriage, and laments that nobody from her extended family or community stood by her in her time of need. Though she feels that the work is derogatory, she justifies her employment by displacing the community's right on her body and her labour. When the community has failed in providing sustenance and support, they have also lost all right to question her decisions. It is a breakdown of feudal community ties, where benevolence and patronage are responded to, by conformism to norms.

> This line is stigmatized. Society looks down on whoever does this kind of work. They think this is nichu kaaj. I do not care who says what. I have to run a household. Is anyone feeding me? Is anyone helping me? As long as I am not stealing or doing *kharap kaaj* [bad work], I do not care what they say. (Personal interview with the author)

In almost all interviews, when women are justifying their labouring in tainted occupations, they insist that at least they are not performing kharap kaaj. I have translated kharap kaaj literally as 'bad work', but it means work that is sexual, dishonest, and against the norms of the dominant social order. Working-class women have always had to fight the stigma of immorality, greed, thievery, and prostitution. Whether it is empirically grounded or not is unimportant, but the constitution of the female labouring body as almost always marked by immorality determines not just the subjectivities of the women working outside their homes, but also has serious material consequences. Link and Phelan argue that stigma and its consequences are dependent on the degree of one's access to social, economic, and political power.[36] It goes without saying that women located at the upper end of the hierarchy, though tarred with the same brush, are able to manage the effect as well as resist the consequences of stigmatized lives.

Nursing is also stigmatized because of close proximity with male colleagues of all social ranks and identities (from doctors to ward boys) as well as night shift. Not just transgression of sexual norms and propriety but contravention and violation of caste and class endogamy also fuels the dominant imagination of women working in hospitals as aggressive, seductive, and promiscuous. While women in other professions do work in close proximity to men, even at night, such as the IT sector and flight operations, nursing as a profession has been peculiarly marked out for its immoral overtones. The inability of registered nurses, who are located at the lowest strata of the middle class (with minimum education, working in stigmatized occupations, no autonomy or decision-making power, and relatively low wages), to fight stigma in the absence of social and cultural capital, demonstrates their failure to enter the ranks of the 'New Middle Class'.[37] As a response, some of them deploy occupational strategies that carve out new roles for registered nurses; others demonize and blame a section of the nursing staff located at the bottom layers, who take the windfall of the stigma. Moni, 27 years of age, General Caste, married, and working as a registered nurse, is scathing in her criticism of attendants and private sisters: 'First, people do not know what nursing is. Night duty and then menial work adds fuel to the fire. Then there are these women (attendants and private sisters), who have relationships with doctors and ward boys, and the whole profession is stigmatized.'

[36] Link and Phelan (2001).

[37] Fernandes and Heller describe the New Middle Class (NMC) as 'new', not in terms of its social composition, but by the ways in which this fraction has sought to redefine its identity through the language of liberalization. They describe the NMC as 'not a unified category' and considered sociocultural inequalities, such as those based on caste and language, as an integral part of the process of middle-class formation. Fernandes and Heller (2006: 497).

Chotolok Cultures: Thievery, Immorality, and Sexual Transgressions

Norms are both imposed as well as self-defined. This section focuses on norms of sexualities, gender, class, and caste, in the making of one's own identity. How is the 'deviant' that legitimizes and justifies objectification, exploitation, and negation produced? When categories are porous, how is the normative gendered, classed, sexualized, and caste body marked out? If class is understood as 'class-in–practice', 'defined by its politics and everyday practices through which it (re)produces its privileged position',[38] what are the discursive projects that produce newer subjectivities that simultaneously draw on historical inequalities as well as newer forms of discriminations? The question of gender, caste, and sexualities is intrinsically linked with class, as subjects are almost always overdetermined by various intersecting social identities. My focus in this section is to trace the various beliefs, norms, and practices that constitute subjectivities in keeping with Foucault's theorization that subjects are not antecedents to discourse but produced through them.[39] In this section, I focus on sexual practices to identify how women who refuse to live by hegemonic gender, sexual, class, and caste norms are identified as chotolok women; or to put it differently, chotolok women are those who are unable to transcend their sexualized bodies marked by caste and class to fit into the hegemonic ideal. This hegemonic ideal is governed by the universal norm, which reflects the culture, practices, and customs of the dominant social group. As Foucault argues, 'The norm is something that can be applied to both a body one wishes to discipline and a population one wishes to regularize.'[40] The ascription of degeneration, promiscuity, aggression, and coarseness as internal and intrinsic to chotolok cultures—symbolized by women, who work in the lower ranks of the labour market—legitimizes the objectification and appropriation of their labour. I have argued elsewhere that the construction of the ideal nurse as a pristine, pure, self-sacrificial gendered subject, as against the large number of women with various degrees of training and recognition, who took to providing nursing care in different ranks

---

[38] Fernandes and Heller (2006: 497).
[39] Foucault (1984).
[40] Foucault (1997).

and capacities, was linked to the regulation and control of women's sexualities.[41] Given that the registered nurse and the unregistered nurse/private sister/attendant share close proximity, the need to put physical and moral distance is integral to the re-definition of the self, which also necessitates a redefinition of the self's relationship with the other. The key to otherization in this context is to delineate and highlight differences that produce dominant and subordinate cultures. The regulation of female sexuality, for instance, is a site of strong cultural contestations. In Bengal, the decline of 'culture' was linked to the bhadramahila taking to the public sphere.[42] The term 'bhadramahila' is not just the female counterpart of bhadralok but rather an ideal woman possessing certain spiritual and moral qualities—a desexualized, duty-bound gendered subject.[43] Even in contemporary times, sexuality is coded by class and caste, which while imposing ideals of hetero-normativity on the working-class Dalit woman, produces her as the abject other. In this context, one can argue that class and caste is, at best, experienced less as a political 'consciousness' and more of a 'lived identity'.

Historians have noticed how workers have been variously labelled as dangerous and branded as criminals to facilitate repressive labour legislations and increase surveillance and techniques of discipline.[44] In this context, the attribution of certain characteristics, such as thievery, aggression, promiscuity, and irrationality, to women labouring at the bottom of the labour market, reinforces their labour as corporeal and manual, thereby delegitimizing any claim to knowledge that they may have acquired over the years. If one takes identities as fluid and subjects as always becoming rather than fixed and foundational, one recognizes identities as an effect. Taking a cue from Judith Butler, that the cultural and economic cannot be seen as a different sphere, and the system of significations as secondary and trivial to political economies but instead constitutive of it,[45] I examine how behaviour, gestures, clothes, cosmetics, and sexual practices of the labouring poor—private sisters and attendants—are brought under scrutiny. This is done to discursively

[41] Ray (forthcoming-a).
[42] Chowdhury (1997).
[43] Bannerjee (2001).
[44] Nair (1998).
[45] Butler (1997b).

produce an inferior body—irrational, carnal, aggressive, and primitive—
that refuses to assimilate in the daily rituals and rites of the modern
workforce, thus legitimizing and justifying the exploitation of their
labour.

Take, for example, thievery. The practice of checking bags when
workers exit the premises after a day's work is constituted along class,
caste, and gender lines. While in the private hospital, only attendants
have their bags checked, in the private nursing home, both nurses and
attendants are subjected to checks. No bags are checked in the government hospital. In all establishments, male employees including ward
boys and cleaners do not have their bags checked, nor do female ward
manngers or the sisters-in-charge. The managerial logic for this is that
attendants and the nurses deal with stocks, which is difficult to account
for on an hourly basis. However, attendants and the nurses are quick
to point out that the ward secretaries, managers, and the ward boys
have equal access to stocks, yet they are not brought under the same
surveillance. Such signifying practices that denote certain workers
as thieves, and certain as trusted, respected, and valued cleaves the
workforce in lines that represent intersecting axes of inequalities. The
representation of some women embodying thieving attributes is essential to the ideological project of the pyramidal labour market—while
employer-establishments formulate such policies, it is approved by
those who are exempted from its reach. Resistance to such surveillance
methods is a submission to its power. Most attendants argue that as
medicines frequently get stolen, either the nurses or the ward secretaries are held responsible, since they are the ones who are 'educated'.
The checking of bags of attendants and some unregistered nurses in
the private enterprises carries with it the resonance of middle-class suspicion and a general cultural perception about the dishonest nature of
working-class women. However, some feel that the process of checking
bags also protects them from being falsely accused, as medicines and
other miscellaneous items continue to get stolen despite such security
measures. Thus, middle-class nurses and managers cannot be exempted
from suspicion. However, nurses, ward secretaries, and even the management continue to blame attendants and working-class attitudes, for
pilferage in the hospitals and nursing homes. One incident of a nurse
being caught stealing a room freshener, and another nurse lifting injections from the ICU is referred to by almost all attendants in the private

nursing home to underline the reality that pilferage is not restricted to particular classes or segments of the profession. Chaitali, whom we met earlier, says:

> We are always blamed for everything. As if we are all thieves and dacoits. Our bags are checked, but see, it was the nurses who were caught stealing. Medicines keep getting stolen, and they always blame us. But we are not educated, so how will we know which medicine to steal? No matter how much they say that it is the attendants who steal, everyone knows but does not admit that it is the nurses and ward secretaries who keep stealing medicines, because only they know which medicine is for what. So, let there be checking and let them explain the stealing. (Personal interview with the author)

The crafting of identities is almost always dependent on sharp boundaries, between the self and the other: in this context, the practices of the other, becomes the marker that consolidates boundaries, the policing of which requires constant acts of repetition. Clothes, for instance, are not just innocent apparels that cover bodies, but signifiers of class, caste, and other social identities. Women located at higher ranks, such as nurses or even ward managers, speak of consumption of clothes, cosmetics, and jewellery, by women working as attendants and private sisters, as a demonstration of their immoral, dishonest, and vile nature. Mallika, 45 years of age, married, General Caste, working as an unregistered nurse, speaks of private sisters and attendants in her nursing home, as 'women of bad character'.

> Look at their clothes. Every day they will wear a new sari, carry expensive phones. They complain that they earn so less, then where do they get so much money from? They are either stealing or indulging in baje kaaj. (Personal interview with the author)

Baje kaaj, in this context, would imply sexual labour that is remunerated. The charge of thievery and promiscuity/prostitution, is a peculiar characteristic that marks the chotolok body. Lack of education, aggression, coarse language, high-pitched tone, and shamelessness are some of the markers that differentiate a chotolok woman from a bhadramahila: public, sexual, unfeminine, ideally located in public spaces, as against the ideal upper-caste, middle-class feminine body inclined to the private realm. Women working in the lower ranks (attendants and private sisters) insist that their clothes, cosmetics, and jewellery, even during off-duty hours, come under the scanner, unlike a nurse or a female ward manager. Jaba, whom we met earlier, is defiant:

> Who said that because I am an attendant, I cannot dress up? The nurses will discuss which attendant is wearing what dress, how much cosmetics we are using. They will even notice if an attendant wears five different saris on five days of *pujo* [festivities]. Nurses dress up so much themselves, yet, that is not a problem; but they cannot stand it if an attendant who works in a lower post wears good clothes and comes to work. (Personal interview with the author)

Bodily markings functions to distinguish one class from another—the middle-class trained nurse from the working-class attendant/private sister. Paid employment allows women to buy certain consumer luxury items that erase class distinctions, at least in the imagined field that the body occupies, which brings working-class attendants/private sisters closer to middle-class nurses. The 'theory of leisured class' puts forward that because conspicuous consumption marks class, 'aspirational classes' cement their status through conspicuous consumption.[46] Pierre Bourdieu argues that individuals increasingly distinguish themselves from others, not according to economic factors, but on the basis of cultural capital—which includes education, appreciation of the arts, consumption, and leisure pursuits.[47] Thus, the discomfort generated when supposedly chotolok women wear clothes and jewellery that is also bought by bhadramahila nurses arises from an anxiety of breaching of social differences. Charu Gupta argues that for Dalit women, historically, humiliating dress restrictions marked their bodies as inferior, polluted, and promiscuous. Thus, clothes are also a marker of mobility, a symbolic act, and an assertion of identity that transcended their historical past.[48] Anupama Rao, too, makes a similar point: not just 'good clothing, footwear, jewellery, and bodily comportment—standing erect while speaking, refusing to contort the body in an obsequious fashion—was critical to Dalit self-fashioning'.[49] The notion of the self is sustained

[46] Thorstein (1934).
[47] Bourdieu (1984).
[48] Gupta (2016).
[49] Rao (2011: 67–8).

by the quotidian, thus transgressions of everyday rituals, customs, and norms invites fury that contradicts the seemingly innocent nature of the act. Trained nurses perceive women working in lower ranks as lazy, argumentative, and unethical. In spite of running the wards, sometimes, singlehandedly, they are perceived as women, who lack cognitive capability to become an efficient nurse. I asked Swarupa, 57 years of age, Brahmin, married, who has been working as a registered nurse for the last 30 years in the government hospital, what her opinion was on the phenomenon of private establishments hiring nurses without registration. She remained dismissive of their knowledge and skills. Linking knowledge with social identities and inferior dispositions, Swarupa says,

> Most of these unregistered nurses have no training, and you can make out from their work. They do not know anything. Most of them come from nichu jat, nichu ghar (lower castes and lowly families), they have no education, and that shows in their character and in their work. They will not listen, and they will not learn. Even the attendants—they come from such lowly families, they fight all the time instead of working. How will they learn? They do not have the character to do so. (Personal interview with the author)

Similar views resonate amongst nurses in all three medical organizations that I visited. Attendants do not work; they are argumentative and lazy with no sense of responsibility; they need to be coaxed and cajoled, to do their share of work, otherwise they will scream and shout in the wards, disrupting discipline and endangering patient's health. Unruly, undisciplined, and defiant, attendants are attributed childlike qualities that needs to be worked upon and brought within a regime of modern-day work discipline.

Not just thievery, aggression, coarse behaviour, or loud gestures, but the process of othering draws extensively from sexual practices. Carnality, promiscuity, and sexual availability are equally attributed to caste, as much as class. Working-class, lower-caste women, in precarious employment, are reduced to immediate bodies and perceived as incapable of intellectual labour, which then legitimizes their disposability. Historically, lower-caste women who labour in the public realm have been constructed as sexually licentious and publicly available.[50] The

[50]   Rege (1998).

constant focus on sexual practices as both an effort to establish hegemonic norms as well as contestations demonstrates the centrality of
sexuality in organizing the political economy. Women's employment
has almost always been interlinked with sexual control, violence, and
honour; thus, the need for a section of upper-caste, middle-class women
to define and distance themselves from the labouring masses, particularly in a stigmatized occupation, takes on urgency. Sexual practices and
disposition are thus one of the markers that draw demarcating lines
between the hegemonic subject and its deviant other.

The development of class and of class distinctions, which has caste
and sexuality equally embedded in them, draws much of its strength
from cultural as well as social capital. Promiscuity and prostitution are
two tags that have stuck with nursing. Even in colonial India, or the
Anglo-American world, nurses were conflated with prostitutes (see
Chapter 1). The overarching response was (a) to blame the 'servant
class' that came into nursing and subsequently, (b) attempt to block the
entry of such women from entering the nursing rank. The anxiety and
stigma of promiscuity created even more consternation, as it pointed to
women's complicity in sexual encounters, unhindered by any economic
compulsions, reflecting a lack of propriety. Not just gender, but the
process of otherization is based as much or equally from sexualities.
If gender refers to the differences between male and female, sexuality
is a broader term that refers to 'to all erotically significant aspects of
social life and social being, such as desires, practices, relationships and
identities'.[51] The otherization of the sexualized, working-class Dalit body
can be best understood by the study of those in power: the constitution
of female Dalit bodies as public, sexual, unfeminine, associated with sexual liberty and promiscuity, made for both a case of sexual exploitation
as well as a foil to construct the ideal upper-caste, middle-class, female
body—not engaged in remunerated labour, in seclusion, and leading
normative, sexually regulated lives. The increasing presence of the poor
but respectable deserted woman/widow in specific ghettoized labour
markets meant that the single woman and the prostitute became a part
of a continuum that categorized women according to their location in
socio-spatial registers.[52] Nurses were no exception.

[51] Jackson (2006: 106).
[52] Sangari (1993).

My respondents spoke of sexual/emotional intimacies that occurred regularly at the workspace, though it was articulated differently for different social groups. Nurses located at the top of the hierarchy spoke of intimacies as *romances* (always with a doctor or a better-off patient) that could either lead to a happy ending, marriage, or one of deception, betrayal, and harassment (always by the man). When it came to describing intimacies that women in lower social groups experienced, the dominant discourse was of promiscuity, debauchery, immorality, and prostitution. These narratives had two implications: *bhadra* (respectable) women waited for the 'right' man to choose her or was represented as a victim of patriarchy. Both deny sexual agency to the bhadramahila; in fact, this desexualization is an essential component, in marking a female body as bhadra. The chotolok woman, however, was responsible for her sexual encounters, because it was in her nature to lure, to provoke, and to satiate her carnal, animal-like sexual appetite. Thus, she was sexually active and whetted her appetite in sexual carnages at the workplace, and it was this sexualization that marked her as a chotolok woman.

The chotolok woman is one who is incapable of intellectual labour: not just lack of education, but by temperament she lacks the capability of being a nurse. Passionate violent behaviour, animalism, sexual appetite, and carnality distinctly marks her body. Not only is she the repository of dirt and filth, the source of nausea, she is also guided by animal instinct, not caring about social order or well-maintained hierarchies. Her negotiation with occupational hierarchies, her attempts to posit herself as a trained nurse, is always self-defeating as she is unable to transcend her own culture. The chotolok body is marked by a lack of culture, which she has to transcend, to be able to fit into the moral universe that marks bodies as either bhadro or *abhadro*. Soma, 40 years of age, married, General Caste and working as a registered nurse in the government hospital, insists that 'these are the women from chotolok families who give nursing a bad name. Go and see. After duty hours, she is standing in the streets soliciting customers. And people think nurses from this hospital are all prostitutes.' Women stepping out of their homes to work in the public domain have always invited social censure, as paid work threatens control over sexuality, mobility, and chastity. The nursing profession, particularly, has been plagued with allegations of immorality, which it is still unable to eradicate. Middle-class nurses in government and private hospitals blame attendants and private sisters for the ill-repute of female healthcare workers: attendants come from lowly families or *nichu paribar*; they have no education; they get into illicit relationships; and sometimes because of such low pay, they enter into sexual relationships with men both inside and outside hospitals, for money and/or gifts. Such brazen display of unbridled sexuality is what leads society to tar the whole profession with the same brush. The conflation of lack of education, sexual appetite, greed, and immorality with the lower-caste woman has enormous effect on the community of women, who are marked as chotolok. First, it justifies sexual exploitation. Secondly, it ascribes agency to women, making them responsible for their lack of culture, education, and their inability to fit into *bhadro samaj* (respectable society) that justifies their exploitation.

Those located at the bottom of the hierarchy question such ascriptions, countering their sexual practices as debauched and degenerate, to show the continuities of experience undergone by women belonging to all social groups. Sexual and emotional intimacies at workplaces are not uncommon in any profession/workplace; however, the regulation of female sexuality that is also coded by caste and class ensure that some women's bodies come under the scanner more frequently. Bodies are not just sexualized but classed as well as marked by caste. While there is ample research demonstrating that women from middle-class, upper-caste families face stricter regulations, policing, and surveillance,[53] the intimate experiences of women located in lower social groups are highlighted in arguments for sexualization of nurses. The focus on the body of the woman, particularly those labouring in stigmatized occupations is relocating the person in the corporeal, the private, and the primitive—far away from the rarefied intellectual labour of the bhadralok. The nature of the work (menial and dirty) and the nature of the worker (promiscuous, irrational, and carnal) go hand in hand. Feminists have jettisoned the idea of a passive, inert body in favour of one that is constituted by social and historical forces.[54] Sara Heinamaa argues that the body is our basic framework of meaning and truth, both the source and

---

[53] Chowdhury (2011); Desai and Krishnaraj (2004).

[54] McNay (1991).

sedimentation of significations and values.'[55] The purported lack of temperament (patience, knowledge, intelligence) to transcend menial labour, and the lack of control over the body governed by passions, to fit into the pristine, chaste, moral universe of the Hindu, Brahmin woman, renders chotolok women vulnerable, and open to exploitation.

Some women also discussed how travelling in local trains at odd hours (end/start of night shift) leads to getting clubbed with women who engage in prostitution. Sandhya, 25 years of age, Scheduled Caste, married, has been working as a private sister in the private nursing home for the last two years. Living in the district of Hooghly, she travels to work on a daily basis. She says, 'The way some of the men stare at me. The look on their face. The women whisper among themselves "era baje kaaj kore" (they do bad work). I feel ashamed. I feel sad'. Shame, as Sara Ahmed tells us, is an intense feeling. 'In shame the subject's movement back into itself is simultaneously a turning away from itself. In shame the subject may have nowhere to turn.'[56] The feeling of shame emerges when one is exposed, almost as a moment of guilt, when one has already accepted one's action/demeanour/words as that which does not fit into the norm, when one perceives one's self in the framework of lack. Shame is when one agrees to one's own humiliation. The shame and stigma of prostitution works against a subject's notion of the self; it constitutes the subject as docile, as fearful, as deprived, robbed of self-esteem and pride. How does the sense of shame, regret, sadness, and ineptitude constitute the chotolok subject? And how does the imagination of working-class culture constitute spatial registers? Nurses have hospital buses taking them to and fro to certain pick-up/drop points and do not have such odd shift hours. These institutionalized privileges are not extended to working-class attendants and private sisters. The conflation of the plebeian women with public spaces influence organizational policies. The protection that is extended to nurses is not extended to bodies marked by greed, immorality, promiscuity, and carnality.

The surveillance, policing, and regulation of sexualities are also taken on by hospital administrators. There are strict policies that forbid any form of sexual and/or romantic intimacy in the workplace,

---

[55] Heinamaa (1996).
[56] Ahmed (2004: 106).

transgression of which is perceived as going against the professional code of conduct, especially sexual 'misconduct'. It could lead to punishment, which includes suspension and termination of work contract. Women working as attendants narrate incidents of how attendants and nurses, who were suspected of having an affair, were asked to leave because such incidents continue to stigmatize 'hospital work'. While some women insist that such strict rules are necessary to ensure that the nursing profession is perceived as an honourable profession, others feel that the management has no right to interfere in women's personal lives.

Nurses, however, deny that sexual intimacies happen within their profession; such 'unprofessional' behaviour is exhibited by working-class attendants and private sisters. Interestingly, a recent newspaper article reported that a medical superintendent and a nursing staff were caught in a 'compromising position' in a hospital in the city of Asansol, in the district of Bardhaman, and were, therefore suspended. Relatives of patients and local political party leaders demonstrated in front of the hospital, alleging that healthcare was deteriorating because 'people like this … are doing the damage'.[57] The constant preoccupation with chastity of the woman is not unique to the nursing profession, but common to women entering the labour market from the early twentieth century; however, the continuous regulation of women's sexuality in nursing services could possibly be located in the nature of affective labour. Where nursing, similar to rearing children, is considered one of the inalienable qualities of the bhadramahila within the private sphere, the commodification of the labour, due to professionalization and modernization, opens up the possibility of the service no longer being intrinsically linked with the identity of the service provider, thus stripping it of its pure, selfless, altruistic nature. The constant emphasis and surveillance on the body, culture, and social location of the service provider,[58] is a move to ensure that only sexually contained, pure bhadra women enter the service and

---

[57] Creaking bed gives away doc 'dalliance', *The Telegraph*, 16 June 2011. https://www.telegraphindia.com/1110616/jsp/bengal/story_14120134.jsp (accessed in July 2011).

[58] In 1987, in Raipur (Madhya Pradesh), allegations of virginity tests being conducted on nurses joining a government hospital made news. Chhattisgarh Mahila Jagriti Sanghathana (1987).

thus bring their feminine virtues legtimized by class and caste into the market; their aim will remain altruistic and not to earn a living, thus tying it firmly to spiritual service.

* * *

The pyramidal labour market and the informal nature of the workforce is over-determined by varying but converging factors. One of the primary factors is the purportedly unskilled nature of much of the work, thus leading employer-establishments to rely on casual labour with flexible employment practices. However, health care, unlike menial factory work is a highly skilled, specialized field with heterogeneous tasks, some of which are menial hands-on care, though not necessarily unskilled. The professional trained nurse, much in demand in the global health care market, is constituted through acts of exclusion and othering, specifically in the context of India, where nursing remains a stigmatized and caste-based occupation. This chapter sought to understand the process of labour through the prisms of identity. The subject is not stable and static but comes into being through various acts of signification that is marked by class, caste, and sexualities. In a sexually segregated, stigmatized ser-vice economy with a heterogeneous workforce, the processes of identity creation are both violent and exclusionary. The relationship between the various signifiers and subject-effect enables us to understand how the category of a 'respectable worker' comes into being and how this category acquires meanings. The study of an over-determined field that produces categories, whose boundaries need to be policed in order to fix meanings, becomes essential in understanding how exploitative labour practices are legitimized and perpetuated.

7 Narratives of Resistance

Whither Politics?

The link between class and exploitation has been based on an analytic understanding of a dualistic economy, where the material well-being of one privileged group has occurred at the expense of another, determined by their location in the production processes. This understanding of exploitation and modes of oppression has been further expanded, and reformulated to understand how gender, caste, race, and sexualities have often lent themselves equally to the project of exploitation, domination, and increasing inequalities. This chapter seeks to locate domination and resistance within such intersecting inequalities. The focus is on how the working poor, the labouring class, constituted equally by gender, caste, and sexualities, articulate resistance that question oppression, including non-economic forms of domination. How do the labouring poor seek to subvert existing power relations? Central to the chapter is the proposition that not just class consciousness but identities, such as gender, caste, and sexualities, structure the range of political action that interact and overlap to challenge and resist hegemonic social structures. Transnational studies have focused on the mobilization and unionization of women working in such low-end service sectors, particularly domestic workers, considered highly invisibilized, marginalized, isolated and powerless units of labour. Some of the prominent sub-sectors of the feminized service economy, associated with women's work, such as surrogacy, domestic work, sex work, almost always marked by informality, stigma, and precarity, have witnessed some levels of unionization, organization, and engagements with law and policies. Nursing, however, is seeing a reverse trend: increasing informalization and a redefinition of nursing care that begs a reconsidering of the linkages between skill, training, and social identities.

Nursing labour markets make for an interesting case study in understanding the everyday politics of labour, given that my focus has been on a comparative analysis of women working in different ranks in different kinds of establishments, but in a similar segment within the service economy. While most studies on women workers in factories and homes have focused on the relationship between employer and employee,[1] in this chapter I examine how workers interrupt and resist exploitative practices, through everyday behaviour. I argue that hegemony, however powerful and imperative, is nevertheless incomplete—there are sites of resistances in which nurses, private sisters, and attendants take part, not just against each other and/or employer-establishment but also against patriarchal norms and the signification system that produce them as submissive workers as well as docile women. In this chapter, I examine how political subjects are constituted to try and understand how women, as agents, make choices, have critical perspectives on their own situations, and resist hegemonic ideals that seek to produce them as abject bodies. In this chapter, I trace moments of hegemonic formations as well as resistances to it—resistances inhere in the gaps, fissures, and silences within hegemonic narratives.

Narratives of Resistances: Small Acts of Living

The relation between union and women workers raises interesting questions around workplaces, political subjects, and social identities. It has traditionally been argued that women's inactivity in trade unions

---

[1] Fernandes (1997); Ong (1987); Nash and Fernandez-Kelly (1983).

emerge from their lack of class consciousness, their gendered dispositions, and their inability to look beyond the private realm. However, feminist scholars have taken painstaking care in demonstrating that worldwide, women have been equally invested in movements, unions, and associations.[2] Despite women's active participation in strikes and trade unions from the nineteenth century, in most parts of the world, trade unions have been a masculine domain. In most cases, women's participation in trade unions has been circumscribed and limited. Over and above, it is widely accepted that masculinization of the labour force worldwide was spurred, nurtured, and legitimized with the help of trade unions, leading to the notion of 'family bread winner' that successfully excluded and/or marginalized women in the labour market;[3] thus it would not be an overstatement to argue that, historically, trade unions have protected men's interest vis-à-vis women. Women have always been part of trade unions; yet, such organizations adopt the rhetoric of the labour force as a unitary whole, overlaid with an assumption of male solidarity. Thus, gender has always been marginal and peripheral to unions' demands and priorities.[4] However, the nursing labour market is such that whether it is menial, manual labourers (attendants) or highly skilled, medical workers (trained nurses), it is a workforce predominantly composed of women. Trade unions organizing workers in the hospitals are forced to take cognizance of the sheer numerical strength of women workers at the workplace, hospitals, and nursing homes. As Table 7.1 demonstrates, workers of only two segments have been able to unionize: government employed registered nurses and casually employed attendants in the private hospital.

In my research, I found that the kind of formal collective politics that these women have so far been part of, such as trade unions, have not addressed the issues of gender, caste, and sexualities that underlie the difficulties of the situation. Women are not represented in equal terms; all agendas and demands are set by men and, thus, women's experiences are excluded. I have argued elsewhere that women's disinterest in the union is not a reflection of a passive, submissive, feminine, and depoliticized subject, but one that emerges from a critical understanding

[2] Boston (1980); Martens and Mitter (1994).
[3] Janssens (1997).
[4] Fernandes (1997).

Table 7.1   Existence of trade unions in the three establishments

Category	Employer–establishment	Trade union
Registered nurses	Government hospital	Yes
	Private hospital	No
	Private nursing home	No
Unregistered nurses	Government hospital	NA
	Private hospital	No
	Private nursing home	No
Private sisters	Government hospital	No
	Private hospital	No
	Private nursing home	No
Attendants	Government hospital	No
	Private hospital	Yes
	Private nursing home	No

Source: Author's fieldwork.

of the nexus between employers and unions that work against women's interests.[5] However, I do not conflate women's lack of activities in unions with passive, feminine, inert bodies on which both capitalism and patriarchy script their exploitative practices. On the contrary, I try to understand how women, as agents, make choices, have critical perspectives on their own situations, and resist domination and subvert hegemonic ideals. The nursing labour market makes an interesting field for studying questions of hegemonies, ideologies, and everyday resistances. Given that nursing as a profession is invested heavily in feminine norms, legitimized by class and caste, the question of how women located in different ranks respond to such constructions, makes for an interesting case study in understanding resistance, that is local, context-specific, sporadic, subjective, and ad hoc. The question of agency and resistance is a tricky ground for critical thought and emancipatory politics; particularly for feminism, the question of universals has dominated much of feminist debates in the last few decades;[6] and studies on questions of agency and resistance, spurred by postmodernism, have focused on the local, the sporadic, and the unconventional.[7] Rosalind

[5] Ray (Forthcoming-c).
[6] Butler, Laclau, and Žižek (2000); Nicholson (1990).
[7] Abu-Lughod (1990); Nash (1979); Scott (1985).

O'Hanlon argues that the trap of analysing domination and resistance as a binary, bears the mark of dominant discourses, which perceive only that as resistance which is organized and large-scale. She says, 'We should look for resistance of a different kind: dispersed in fields we do not conventionally associate with the political', whether that is evasion of norms, disrespecting ruling standards of conscience, or celebrating cultural differences.[8] Thus to locate subversions, one must pay attention, as Butler urges, to those practices that constitute identities, rather than seeking a transcendental global subject. For the emergence of a new political practice, identities cannot be fixed; and secondly, politics cannot be conceived as a set of practices that respond to interests of an already 'ready-made' subject, but one that unfolds in the specific cultural context.[9]

Cultural theorists have taken 'everyday life' as an important site to understand and analyse resistance that escapes universal theories.[10] It is in the everyday life, 'the banal, the quotidian, the obvious, the common, the ordinary, the infra-ordinary, the background noise, the habitual'[11] that one locates how norms govern us and the ways we resist them. It is this everyday life that presents itself as a terrain of risk and uncertainty, of impositions of hegemonic ideals and challenges. How are norms that govern subjects adhered to and simultaneously subverted? How are everyday politics played out, and how do women as subjects resist the objectification of their lives and bodies, their construction and constitution as the 'other' to be used for the perpetuation, maintenance, and reproduction of the symbolic order? James Scott, writing on practices of resistance, argues that the subordinate classes usually cannot afford the luxury of open, organized, political activity and thus must take resort to ordinary, everyday forms of resistance—such as foot dragging, dissimulation, desertion, false compliance, pilfering, feigned ignorance, slander, arson, and sabotage to character assassination, gossiping, and the like. However, for this kind of resistance to be successful, there has to exist a shared moral universe for both the dominated and the dominant groups, which sets the limit of permissible

---

8   O'Hanlon (1985: 222).
9   Butler (1990).
10   Highmore (2002).
11   Perec (2002: 177).

behaviour.[12] Within Western metaphysics, the conception of agency was almost always predicated on a knowing subject—an already constituted rational being who chooses to act one way or the other.[13] Foucault critiques this teleological notion of agency to argue that pre-planned agendas determined by universal notions of freedom and emancipation could only lead to further domination; instead, the paramount task of critique is to closely examine institutions, practices, and norms and the way they constitute subjects.[14]

In my field research, I observed that the conflicts that women spoke of were the conflicts that occurred between different ranks of workers. The spectre of the owner/management loomed large, but most respondents narrated about power struggles between the un/registered nurse against the semi-trained private sister and the untrained attendant. The organization of the modern workforce and the dispersed nature of control and surveillance pits one section of workers against the other. Wright argues that a group of workers, mostly managers and white-collar workers who occupy 'contradictory class locations', control some aspects of production but are denied control over others: their class positions are 'contradictory', because they are neither capitalists nor manual workers, yet, they share certain common features with both groups.[15] The contradictory class location of nurses stem from their lack of control, autonomy, or decision-making power and yet they are given supervisory and administrative control over manual workers (attendants and private sisters). The differentiation and distinction between workers, who occupy different ranks as nursing staff provide an interesting entry point to understand how power, conflict, and resistances constitute subjects.

Given the failure of unions to address women and their 'petty' fights termed as feminine, irrelevant, and irrational,[16] how do they make sense of their everyday power struggles? How do women subvert, resist, and negotiate patriarchal capitalist structures that objectify them as powerless units of labour, engaged in labour that does not merit respect?

---

[12] Scott (1985).
[13] For a further discussion, see Giddens (1984).
[14] Foucault (1984).
[15] Wright (1985).
[16] Ray (Forthcoming-c).

Struggles between different categories of workers happen in different registers. One of the most obvious and visible struggle is determining work allocation, intensity, and duration that is to be performed by women of different ranks. Nursing labour, which defies easy classification, witnesses highly pitched battles amongst workers. Certain work, especially the kind which is considered degrading, becomes the focal point of struggles: for instance, bringing down dead bodies or cleaning shoes and floors. The formal division of work gets blurred as attendants, private sisters, and nurses pass around certain undesirable jobs. Neither the unions nor the management (nursing matron/ward managers) want to get involved in mundane daily issues that they term as 'petty' fights. The struggle over who will do what work is not just a struggle over allocation of tasks but a fundamental process of producing workers. In a service economy that has both components of manual and medical labour, certain tasks congeal one's identity as either a menial labourer or a medical worker, which has both material and symbolic effects.

The contest over who is to do what work and how much is central to the conflict over time and space. The registered nurse, overwhelmed by her medical-administrative-supervisory role, increasingly depends on women located in lower ranks to help her out. As the nurse sitting at her desk concentrates more and more on administrative tasks, such as writing and keeping records, she calls out instructions to attendants and private sisters to take on certain medical tasks. Similar to the struggle between the doctor and the nurse, where the shrinking of the former's medical interventions on a daily basis allows the nurse to legitimately expand her duties, subsequently carving out a diversified role for herself,[17] the attendants and private sisters, too, find themselves in a position to challenge the discourse on skills, that pegs their labour as unskilled, menial and affective. Lachmi, 42 years of age, Scheduled Caste, married, took to working as a private sister, in a private hospital after training in an unlicensed centre. Having worked for almost 15 years as a nursing aide, she says,

> Sometimes when a young nurse, who has just joined the nursing home
> is at a loss, I have to demonstrate to her some of the medical tasks. So
> we lock the door so that no one sees us, and then I tell her what to do.

[17] Iyer and Jesani (1995).

I feel important; my training is coming to some use. The nurses will not tell others, but the in-charge knows that we know a nurse's job. When there is an emergency in the ward and enough nurses are not available, the matron will ask us to take certain responsibilities, and perform certain medical tasks. (Personal interview with author)

The division of labour based on knowledge is insidiously contested when private sisters perform nursing labour. Despite having nursing training, albeit unauthorized, they are forbidden from all medical tasks. However, some of the private sisters reported that they continue doing certain nursing jobs with or without the knowledge of the management. Private sisters are a low-paid, flexible workforce that hospitals employ; however, their expenses are met by the patients. In addition, the presence of private sisters subsidizes the expenses of keeping permanent or regular contractual workers, round the year in the wards. Otherwise invisibilized, they are required in the wards when there is an emergency and then banished back to the cabins. While, on paper, a division of labour is rigidly maintained, thus justifying cultural and economic devaluation of certain workers, in practice, it is routinely breached. A category of workers is therefore created within a capitalist enterprise who acts as a reserve army of labour. Paid by patients for individual care, their unpaid labour is employed for ward work when required and subsequently relegated back to their low position in the hierarchy. While private sisters willingly agree to perform 'extra' medical work, their 'performance' contests the hierarchical binary that constitutes them as menial workers.

A modern nurse is represented as one, whose disposition is marked by affects, such as empathy and care, which is tempered or equally matched with intellectual abilities that which are scientific in nature (of course, second to the doctor). This disposition of the nurse is supposedly produced by her social position in the hierarchical ordering of society—middle-class, upper-caste feminine ideal. This doxic knowledge that women of certain dispositions are in/capable of performing certain kinds of labour, is at the heart of the power struggle between different ranks of workers. Common sense, then, clearly performs an important ideological role in relation to the maintenance of hegemony. For Stuart Hall, resistance is not necessarily circumscribed to a united working class seizing control and a complete rejection or overturning of the dominant-subordinate dyad, but a continuous negotiation and struggle to displace hegemonic ideals.[18] The use of technology and administration of medicine by lower-caste women, represented as menial-manual labourers, can become new sites of conflict as well as possibilities of articulation and assertion of Dalit and working-class identities. How resilient are these quotidian practices that stigmatize certain bodies and lives and how is this successfully challenged by the everyday politics of labour, which is spawned by contemporary capital restructuring of the nursing labour market, remains debatable. Is the constant targeting of women in lower ranks—represented as chotolok women through acts, speech, and naming—a backlash to the growing assertion of their medical knowledge as they learn on the job over the years? The overall dehumanization of women working as nurses and the continuous stigma, particularly, gives further urgency to practices that produce a differentiated workforce. The 'trained' component of nursing care is so open to contestation that social identities are deployed to deny, efface, and reject the knowledge acquired by women located at the lower ranks—the supposedly chotolok woman, who has insidiously and undeservedly wriggled into nursing services.[19]

Even attendants narrated how they were 'compelled' to perform a range of tasks—'extra work' such as cooking food, fetching water, running chores, transferring files, and undertaking personal tasks for nurses, as well emptying and replacing catheter bags, aiding in cannulation, and the like, that called for technical and specialized knowledge. On the one hand, the boundary between technical-medical and menial-manual labour gets blurred, and on the other hand, women located at the lowest ranks are exploited even further. The expanding of tasks, which includes prestigious jobs, however, does not witness a corresponding increase in status and respect. Despite doing a nurse's work, an attendant must remain in the position assigned to her in the hierarchy—she cannot sit at the nurse's table, she cannot leave the ward or rest in the changing room. A private sister should be stationed next to the patient in the cabin—she cannot be seen in the wards, thus contributing to her invisibility. This strict spatialization of hierarchy ensures that despite sharing medical-technical labour with skilled workers, there is no sense

---

[18] Hall and Jefferson (2003).

[19] I have argued this is details in Ray (Forthcoming b).

of shared entitlements. The everyday roles of different ranks of workers are challenged in an ad hoc and subjective manner, which does not compel the management to take cognizance of women's experiences and knowledge accumulated over the years. Thus there is no initiative to overhaul the pyramidal structure, which would reflect fairer labour practices. However, this failure of the pyramid also opens up opportunities for women located at the bottom of the hierarchy to challenge and resist such labour processes. This vociferous and vocal struggles that occur on a daily basis in their everyday lives contribute to the heterogeneous nature of the many acts of resistance, big and small.

Such patterns of conflicts and resistance are not just exclusive to the lower end of the pyramid; nurses and doctors engage in similar kinds of confrontation as well. Migrant nurses, who cannot speak Bangla and are often belittled by doctors, get even with the RMO by making fun of them in Hindi or in their local language. Nurses can even make a new RMO lose his/her job if they complain that s/he is not cooperating. A doctor thinks twice before insulting a nurse, because if she stops cooperating with him/her, his/her consultant status gets jeopardized. Coming in only once or twice a day to check on patients, a doctor depends on the nursing staff to report to him/her about any changes in medical condition. Sometimes, nurses play similar games of avoidance and/or non-cooperation with doctors, to register their protest against high-handedness or humiliation. Such power struggles can take place over ethnicity and community as well. Registered nurses, who have migrated from other states and work in private hospitals in the city, often face opposition from local nurses and doctors.[20] To register their protest to routine humiliation faced at the hands of senior nurses and doctors, they quit their jobs without serving notice. As one of the directors of the private hospital confided in me, 'While their work and training are good, they often have trouble with the local nurses, and suddenly batches of them will leave without serving notice. Then we get into a lot of trouble, because without GNM trained nurses, the hospital will lose registration, and it is difficult to get local GNM trained nurses to work in private organisations.'[21]

---

[20] Ray (2019).
[21] Interview on April 2012.

If not the whole batch, sometimes small groups of two or three or even a single nurse may leave without serving notice. Young women with registration, ready to work for minimum pay in the private sector, are hard to come by. Private hospitals and nursing homes are dependent on this migrant population, who come in as student interns or seeking work experience; however, to be able to retain them is difficult. Their experiences, qualifications, and the demand for trained nurses in the private sector protect them from becoming a vulnerable section in the workforce, devoid of any bargaining power. Women do resist management policies, not necessarily as a formal collective but in informal groups that are based on affective ties of friendship, camaraderie, solidarities, and even ethnicity. Maria, 21 years of age, Christian, hailing from Manipur, is working in the private hospital while she waits to migrate abroad. She says, 'Our colleagues leave as soon as they get better offers. If you need an experience letter, you give a resignation notice; otherwise we just pack our bags and leave without telling anyone. We usually apply together, so we can go to new cities together.' The commonsensical understanding of women workers, particularly young trained nurses entering the field as docile, submissive, and yielding, leads some representatives of the management to prefer female employees, particularly migrant women, as they do not unionize, enter into confrontations, or directly challenge people in power.[22] However, almost all respondents feel that they find it difficult to accept policies that directly discriminate against them. Women question, subvert, and negotiate norms of unquestioning obedience, loyalty, docility, and subservience, to find ways and means of registering their protest. These alliances are short-lived, issue-based, and contingent; however, they are effective in questioning labour processes as well as symbolic fields, that constitute different women differently.

Most of the time, direct confrontations are avoided and discussions that take place behind the back of immediate supervisors range from the unfairness of duties allocated, questioning degrees/knowledge of

[22] Discussions with members of the management and male ward managers of hospitals and nursing homes, regarding women as workers have shown a preference for female employees. In the private hospital, which employs a number of young migrant nurses, the Managing Director has also expressed that they make for good workers, as they have no connections with local people, who may incite them to protest. Interview on April 2012.

superiors, miserly nature of the management, mean and bad temperament of immediate seniors, and male predation, mostly restricted to doctors and ward boys. Given the precarity of employment, it is rare to witness direct confrontations; however, it is not uncommon to see women huddle in groups, heads together, during lunch time or night shift, when surveillance is minimal. Many a times, I was included, and sometimes I sensed the change in conversations because of my presence. The discussions touched on almost all aspects of life from violence faced at home to inflation. But more often than not, the conversations veered towards work. The person towards whom most anger is directed is usually the immediate senior. In a hospital setting, immediate supervisory positions are filled by nurses and ward managers, who also happen to be women. Therefore, most of the contests and conflicts happen between women, and not between men and women. Different class and caste locations of women workers undercut any possibilities of a collective consciousness and solidarity from developing both as women and as workers. The difference between a nurse and an attendant is not just hierarchies within a labour market but also control over a section of workers. The contradictory class location of nurses mean that they remain hostile to any collective organizing of Group D workers. Not just class and caste but also the gendered nature of the labour market itself prevents women from collaborating with other women. Judith Briles has demonstrated in her survey amongst nurses that in female-intensive services, women undermine women's authority. In health care, top-level management are mostly men (including doctors) while the staff-level is predominantly composed of women (including nurses). Conflict between a doctor and a nurse/attendant is usually rare or less open than conflicts between a trained nurse and untrained nurses or attendants. Those in power (doctors and members of the management) on the basis of their elevated status are usually excluded from becoming the targets of hostile feelings and that leaves the relatively less powerful (trained nurses, untrained nurses, and attendants) open to the frustration of women who are excluded and made invisible.[23] This means that most power struggles happen between the registered nurse and the whole gamut of unregistered nursing personnel. The structural inequalities of the labour market

---

[23] Briles (1994).

where women are isolated in low-paying enclaves produce gendered patterns of power struggles among men and among women, but rarely between them. Barnani, whom we met earlier, says, 'If we even make a small mistake, the nurses or the ward managers will shout at us. They do not tell the men anything, as they are scared of them. They harass the women.'

While most women agree that it is useless to protest or verbalize their anger and the discomfort at the injustices they face, the language that they use to describe their supervisors can get vitriolic and violent. This is in direct contrast to the subservience, respect, and compliance they show when they are in presence of the person concerned. Since disobedience to immediate supervisors within a hierarchical capitalist organization can invite retributions, most resistance is insidious. Sree, whom we met earlier, says,

> We are not in a government job. We are in a private organization, so we cannot say much. Sometimes, unnecessarily, they will pick on us and I just say sorry. Though in my heart, I know there is nothing to be sorry about, and I do not even mean it. We talk amongst each other, and discuss these things, but I try and not show my anger to the nurses. (Personal interview with author)

One can ask about the efficacy of these small, insidious acts of resistance. Scholars have argued that 'ritual resistance' is more of a process of negotiation rather than a 'solution' to class struggles. It does not provide a key to unravel structural inequalities or injustice; rather, it is a symbolic struggle that works against hegemony.[24] Given the degree and intensity of the surveillance the workers are subjected to, with security guards instructed to maintain a sharp eye on women to ensure friendships are not struck and alliances are not formed, it does point to the paranoia of the management regarding the potential of 'small groups' and their 'chattering'. In Chapter four, I detailed how spaces were organized, friendships ruptured, alliances disrupted by allocating spaces, transgressions of which invite immediate rebuke. Roma, 22 years of age, unmarried, Scheduled Caste, migrated from the district of Hooghly, and working as an attendant in the private hospital, says: 'There are three of us who

---

[24] Clarke, Hall *et al.* (2003).

come from the same district and are very close friends. When the nurses observed over the months that we are always together and so close, they immediately allocated us different wards, so that we cannot spend time in each other's company. But we still make time to meet and talk—during lunch hours, in the changing rooms, whenever we can.' Not just security guards, but even nurses are given supervisory roles to ensure that women do not convene. Given that one section of worker's interests are pitted against another, nurses partake with full gusto in this supervisory role: not so much for the interest of the employer-establishment as much as to ensure that their authority as a trained nurse remains intact.

Not just between nurses and attendants, but power struggles where women individually resist and question norms of obedience occur amongst different ranks of nurses as well. For example, in one instance, I was talking to Sanchayita (whom we met earlier), during her night shift. The sister-in-charge, who was on her daily round, took Sanchayita to task. As there was nothing else to fault, she picked on Sanchayita for not complying with nursing regulations regarding uniforms. 'Why are you not wearing your cap? Why have you not taken your earrings off? You have not wiped off your *bindi*.' This show of authority meant to reconfirm hierarchies met with immediate compliance. Sanchayita apologized, put on her cap, and wiped off her bindi. After the sister-in-charge left, she turned to me with complaints of how mean and rude the in-charge was, and how unnecessary it was to talk down to her. 'During the day, we cannot take off the cap, but at night we do. This in-charge is very bad, she does not know any work, and yet, she makes noises about other things like uniform and cap and other such particulars.' This overt compliance and simultaneous covert criticism at once institutionalizes hierarchies as well as displaces them. Sanchayita's *sotto voce* rejoinder undermined the very basis on which the in-charge's superiority in the hierarchy is determined—her supervisory function based on greater knowledge or experience. 'She does not know any work' is not a questioning of the hierarchy as much as a critique of its failures. The superior in this case compensates for her lack of superiority (according to Sanchayita) by picking on mundane issues of no great significance. While compliance and respect from immediate juniors in the hierarchy are expected and even received, those in positions of power are expected to conform to norms too—and respect from the subordinates may be undercut by transgression of such norms.

The most common response of private sisters and attendants, when they have a problem with nurses, is that 'we keep quiet and discuss it amongst ourselves'. Official complaints and open discussions do not yield results, and instead marks one out as a troublemaker. This may invite vengeance in the form of more work, undesirable work, talking down or humiliation and harassment in the wards; for nurses working in the government sector, it could even lead to a transfer to remote districts. However, answering back, complaining under the breath, and grumbling are popular and common ways of registering resistance. It also produces subjects, who challenge the pyramidal labour market that deploys gender, class, and caste to produce a discourse on skills, that is instrumental in extracting maximum labour at minimum wages. The medical hierarchy is organized in such a manner that the immediate supervisor has no authority of 'hire and fire', which allows some space, within the everyday for showing disrespect and disapproval. So, if an attendant answers back or verbalizes her disapproval, the staff sister can only report to the sister-in-charge, who in turn reports to the matron, who dismisses such forms of resistance as petty and routine. Kusum, 28 years of age, Scheduled Caste, and married, is working as an attendant in the private hospital. She says,

> Some of the sisters cannot stand it, when attendants sit down for a minute. Even if there is no work, they will make us do unnecessary extra work. So, I avoid them and do it in such a manner, that the patients do not get affected. We cannot get caught in the wrong. So I answer back; that does not affect the patient, then no one can catch me in the wrong. (Personal interview with author)

Non-cooperation is another powerful tool of resistance. While outright non-cooperation may invite retribution, it is nevertheless practiced insidiously and regularly. Mostly all work related to patient care is done with immaculate efficiency. Other tasks, especially those related to rendering services to seniors in the hierarchy, such as fetching water, pen, food, and so on, is met with resistance. Attempts to extract more work than allocated are usually met with non-cooperation rather than a formal 'no'. Sara Ahmed contends that saying a 'no' is formative, 'a subject comes from (rather than causing) a will to disobey. Disobedience is when you say no without being given a right to say no.'[25] However, replacing a direct

---

[25] Ahmed (2017).

'no' with indirect non-compliance and non-cooperation is equally effica-
cious in producing disobedient subjects, unruly workers. The refusal to
participate in one's own exploitation, the recognition of unfair labour
practices, and finding ways and means to avoid conforming to dictates
of those superior in rank, at first glance, may seem to be insignificant
acts with no long-term effects; however, these small acts, over time, chip
away at ideologies that make power structures seem incontestable, and
injustices, inevitable. It contradicts the commonsensical view of women
workers in the informal economy as passive, powerless units of labour.
There is no open insubordination, which would necessitate retribution
or urge those in power to sit up and take note of things. However, perseverant context-specific acts described above, acts that are embedded in
everyday politics of labour interrupt the smooth functioning of power
and slow it down.

Subversion, Negotiation, and Defiance: Unsettling Hegemonies, Questioning Ideologies

In this section, I examine how identities are at once constructed and
simultaneously displaced by focusing on the cultural wars that occur
between the trained nurse and the un/semi-trained nursing personnel. Hegemonic construction of certain women as chotolok and the
delegitimization of their skill, knowledge, and training give moral
justification for the exploitation of their labour, the precarity of their
employment, and the marking of their bodies as sterile of intellectual or
moral abilities. Gramsci argued that power is not just a matter of force
or domination, but rather a question of hegemony—where the power
of the dominant groups is legitimized and dependent on the consent
of the people they rule.[26] Hegemony works by means of negotiation,
incorporation, and concession, rather than by simple oppression. Thus,
hegemony is never stable; it is a process, it cannot be secured once and
for all.[27] It requires that the relation between normative ideals of those
in power and counter-hegemonic forces be constantly (re)negotiated
and (re)formulated.

[26] Gramsci, Hoare and Smith (1971).
[27] Clarke and Hall et al. (2003).

I try and understand how processes of demarcation that explicitly and visibly divide bodies as normative and deviant, the former capable of producing labour that is at once caring and equally scientific, and the latter suitable only for precarious and devalued labour, is contested. The imposition of hegemonic ideals based on intersections of gender, caste, class, and sexualities leads to struggles that question the very limits of hegemony, by those who are most excluded. Though norms produce intelligible subjects via recognition,[28] the failure to adhere to its impossible idealization provides grounds for questioning its coercive hold over subjects. While for some subjects, adherence to norms provides meaning to their lives, assists them in accumulating social and symbolic capital and lead liveable lives, for others, it delegitimizes their existence. It labels them inferior, non-normative, and deviant, leading to increasing surveillance and exploitation. Thus, conformity to gender and sexual norms and institutions of patriarchy holds out the possibility of an inclusion, a recognition that is yearned for. Examining the exploitation inherent within the labour market and its linkages with social identities provides an opportunity to tease out how inhabitation, enactment, and reproduction of norms could possibly lead to further consolidation of power; or as I will demonstrate, its internal contradiction could also lead to a displacement of existing power relations.

Given that we have moved from an understanding of a homogeneous, united working class resisting capitalist employers to an understanding of a differentiated workforce, where a section participates wholeheartedly in reproducing hegemonic norm that secure small gains for themselves at the cost of others, 'ritual resistances' becomes an important site in locating the contestation of power hierarchies. This is not to suggest that trained nurses are solely responsible and the only beneficiaries of exploitative power structures that produce precarious labour; under capitalism, who performs what labour and under what conditions is rarely a decision that is made by those who occupy contradictory class locations but rather, by employer-establishments who take advantage of social and cultural processes that open up possibilities of wringing out maximum labour for the least wage possible. This is as much true for the trained nurse as for the wide gamut of ancillary nursing staff consisting of

---

[28] Butler (2004).

un/semi-trained workers. But given that the constitution of a 'trained nurse' is dependent on certain violent exclusions, she is invested in the perpetuation, and maintenance of the devaluation and ostracism that 'untrained' workers face.

How do women located in the lower ranks negotiate, question, and challenge such norms that mark their bodies, dispositions, and selves as inferior and deviant? The workplace, thus, is a meaningful space where everyday social interactions contest hierarchies, questions ideologies, and thus contribute to the incompleteness of hegemonies. Subjectivity is not antecedent to power but produced by it. How do subjects produce themselves? When subjects play active roles in producing themselves, according to regulatory ideals, where does one locate acts of resistance? How do subjects resist and displace power's attempts to constitute them as appropriate subjects, who occupy suitable ranks in the labour market? Women workers are expected to exhibit submissiveness, compliance, and graceful femininity as an enactment of not just gender but caste and class norms that reflects not just their culture, but simultaneously constitutes them as bhadra women. Classification of some bodies as chotolok derives its legitimacy from visible evidences of primitive passion, aggression, carnality, and animality, bodies that are undisciplined and ungovernable. Atreyee, 29 years of age, General Caste, left her government posting in Assam and migrated to the city of Kolkata after marriage. She has taken employment as a registered nurse in the private hospital, while she waits for a government posting. She is dismissive of the system of employing 'unskilled' nursing aides. She says, 'These private sisters and attendants have no morals and no character. They do whatever they want. They scream their head off, they shout, and they do not listen to you.' The discipline of a modern workspace needs docile bodies, and the nursing labour market, needs feminine and restricted bodies. The failure of semi-un/trained nursing personnel to internalize such norms justifies their exploitation; as long as they remain indisciplined and ungovernable, their precarious locations remains justified. The failure of marginal bodies to fit into the hegemonic ideal is essential for the maintenance of the order.

How do such bodies resist such discourses? Agency cannot be located outside discourse, culture and power, but neither are subjects fully determined by them. The gradual and steady erosion of faith in normative ideals of the ruling order, as one moves down the ladder of stratification, stems from, first, the impossibility of maintaining and reproducing such high ideals; and secondly, the failure of even members of the elite class, for most part, to internalize, enact and reproduce norms. The ideals and norms of the cultural elite, and the working poor, are supposed to represent distinct patterns of beliefs and practices; however, it is these distinctions, that are called into question by those who are most adversely affected by it. For example, the pyramidal nature of the labour market, the understaffing of hospitals and nursing homes, the fuzzy division of labour, all call for creative ways of managing wards on an everyday basis. The perseverant (yet covert) resistance that women in the lower ranks engage in (non-cooperation, foot dragging, and non-compliance), leave some work undone, some tasks unattended to, which has to be dealt with by those in charge. The responsibility for the failure of efficient functioning of wards, falls directly on the shoulders of the trained nurse (in-charge), or the ward manager. This inadequacy of the organization of the labour market, which puts increasing, almost inhuman, pressure of performance on its supervisors and managers, results in behaviour, gestures, and mannerism that belie the image that the nurse is invested in. The image of the upwardly mobile, professional woman—graceful, rational, feminine and in control, managing home and work with equal élan. Dolon, 25 years of age, unmarried, Scheduled Caste, and working as a private sister in the government hospital, laughs when she talks of the temperament of the trained nurse:

> They think they are superior to us: their behaviour, their attitude. You should see how they scream, and rant, when they cannot get us to work, how they misbehave with patients. Some of these nurses come to work with broken arms and fractures. They get beaten by jealous husbands at home. How are they different from us? They want to be, but, they are not. (Personal interview with author)

This emphasis on the similarity of embodied experiences as workers and as women becomes a mode of negotiating norms that produce subjects. Given that there is not much divide between trained nurses and private sisters and attendants, it is these cultural distinctions that are harped on to justify the cleaved labour market as well as class hierarchy. For nurses, the struggle to maintain distance is essential to enter the ranks of the 'new middle class' marked by consumption, gender norms, and cultural and social capital; for those located at the lower ranks, however, it is these differences that need to be questioned, renegotiated, and if possible, collapsed, to make life a little more liveable and workplaces a little less violent.

The question of sexual practices, beliefs, and attitudes, for instance, was predominant in most of my conversations with both trained nurses and those under their supervision. In the previous chapter, I have, in great detail, discussed how sexualities are constitutive of caste and class: where the bhadramahila is the one lacking in sexual agency, firmly located within 'reproductive hetero-normativity', and the chotolok other bound by her sexual appetite and immoral dispositions, trapped within her immediate body. Thus, it is the body that is the cause of low-caste, working-class disposition. Patriarchal control over women's sexualities that operate at the most intimate levels of experiences is an example of power at the micro-political level, where body and sexuality become the direct locus of social control. The reproduction of sexual norms is essential to maintaining social order, which explains the extreme stigma associated with all other forms of desires that do not fit into the hetero-normative, sexual economy.[29] The abjection of certain bodies depends on the expansion, exaggeration, and overemphasis on cultural differences, between those, who fit into the ideal, and those who do not. An abject body must be kept in abeyance, and overlaps, seepages, contradictions, and creases must be ironed out. Judith Butler, citing Hegel, argues that when a group sets itself up as the universal, as representative of the general 'will', it almost always excludes certain 'individual will'. This exclusion necessitates a 'paranoid economy',[30] that is constantly haunted by the excluded, abject 'other'. I argue that sexual practices and dispositions are central to constituting normative and 'deviant' subjects and, thus, a site of contest. The promiscuous, debauched, and carnal body of the chotolok woman, is the constitutive outside that defines the sexually contained, chaste body of the bhadramahila; the latter's identity emerges by excluding or in antagonism to the former. However, this constitution

[29] Rubin (1984).
[30] Butler (2000: 14).

is saturated by paranoia. Atreyee continues to describe the private sister and the attendant:

> They go out with this man today, and they go out with another man tomorrow. For so many years, I am witnessing this: an unmarried woman will stay with another woman's husband. In the villages, this would not happen, but these women come to the city, live alone, and have a lot of money, and they feel they can do anything. They bring a bad name to the profession. (Personal interview with author)

The sexualization of certain bodies are both a reflection of moral panic as well as legitimizing cultural differences. Women's employment in modern workspaces gives them relative economic freedom, which possibly leads to assertion of some social independence. The sexualization of women working in modern factories and workspaces, and the ensuing moral panic is not a new phenomenon.[31] However, what I want to emphasize here is Atreyee's need to distance herself from the multitude of women working in different ranks with non-recognized training. Given that she is a migrant herself, and coming from a rural background, it is marriage that legitimizes her migration to the city and makes her mobility safe and chaste. This demarcation allows her to accumulate social and symbolic capital,[32] which has caste and sexuality deeply embedded in it. And, it is this accumulation of symbolic capital, that reinforces distance between antagonistic groups, where one group moves closer to hegemonic normative lives, and the other reside at the fringe. The constant attempt to impose, maintain, and reinforce this gap becomes the site of conflict. Shame, for instance, works as a deterrent, an apparatus, that produces subjects who seek to internalize norms, if it is experienced as an 'affective cost of not following the scripts of normative existence.'[33] Kalpana Viswanath argues, that the ideology of shame and honour serves as organizing principles of social relations and stratifications, 'the ideology of shame and honour has at its centre the control of women's sexuality and allowing its expression only within legitimate spaces.'[34]

---

[31] Ong (1987); Ray (forthcoming-a).
[32] Bourdieu defined symbolic capital (which includes possession of a good reputation) as an important indication of social class. Bourdieu (1984).
[33] Ahmed (2004: 107).
[34] Viswanath (1997: 316).

Shame can also have an unintended consequence—defiance. For instance, gossip is a concrete material tool, by which shaming occurs, that produces marginalized existences.' If gossip can be a tool of control for one group, it becomes an act of resistance for others, as one cannot control gossip; it has a tendency to run away; it defies ownership and circulates, seeking new subjects to latch onto. The effect that wagging tongues have on people is subjective and ad hoc; for those located at the top, it is a loss of face and honour or an erosion of symbolic capital. For those who lead 'precarious lives', a 'bad reputation' can have serious consequences—ranging from violence to loss of life; none, however, are immune to such acts of belittlement. However, in this context, gossip is less a tool of social control, and more a way of drawing clear lines of distinction between the subject and the other. This demarcation based on sexual practices is negotiated, challenged, and questioned by women, who are more affected than others. How do women respond to being represented as promiscuous, greedy women, inclined to remunerated sex? Attendants and private sisters argue that nurses and doctors have illicit relationships all the time, and yet, because of their education and money, they are exempted from such moral policing. Rohini, 23 years of age, Scheduled Caste, and unmarried, took to working as an attendant in a private nursing home when she could find no other job. She points out that though there is not much difference in sexual practices of middle-class nurses and working-class attendants, it is only the latter, who are singled out as symptomatic of the moral corruption of working women.

> Because they [nurses] are in high posts, they look down on us. They also have illicit relationships with doctors, and yet, because they are educated, they are not singled out. They will talk about our characters. Because we clean human faeces—they think we come from chotolok families, therefore we engage in such relationships. But if you scratch the surface, you will see their characters. Married women doctors and nurses have sexual relationships with other men all the time. (Personal interview with author)

What struck me as interesting in the response was the countering of the demarcation—which assigned (often) hierarchical binary traits to antagonistic groups—rather than refuting the attribution and claiming normative behavior. These attributions stem from gendered norms that are equally imposed and often self-defined. Most women latched on to how borders are constituted, social and symbolic capital are accumulated, and normative subjects are produced. Superior groups often have to resort to keeping up appearances to maintain this hegemonic role, as 'consent' of the subordinate would entail that they believe in the world as represented by those in power as natural, inevitable, and aspirational; the latter's failure live and to enact hegemonic caste, class, and gender norms, legitimizes their subordination. Any slippage by the dominant group would expose the hollowness of their claim, their stake to power, thus, the need to keep up appearances takes on such ferocious embracing of norms. The power of dominant groups can be sustained only by continuous efforts at reinforcement, maintenance, and adjustment. The questioning of the legitimacy of this group as a ruling body necessitates a displacement of their moral authority. Where a public challenge to authority, meaning a direct disobedience, is often not possible, leading to covert forms of resistance, the erosion of the dominant group's claim to power rests on the ability of subordinate groups to collapse distinctions that produce 'us' and 'them'. Given the larger context of the stigma associated with nursing, the social field is often more volatile, contradictory, and in constant flux. The investment of the middle class to promote a moral and cultural code to be accepted and internalized by the working class has always run into difficulties, with the reluctance of the latter to assimilate. This refusal being an evidence of its 'lack', which legitimizes their exploitation. On the contrary, the investment of the working class to demonstrate the continuity of experiences and lived realities between the two social groups can be seen as a counter-hegemonic move that negates the claim of the ruling bloc. The need to distance one class from another would imply that the ruling bloc would not necessarily care for a working class in its own image, but rather one that is defined negatively to it. This relation of opposition, which denies inter-dependency, becomes the site of conflict. The refusal to be the abject wills the unruly subject into being.

Understanding power as productive, rather than as repressive, leads us to a more textured understanding of how individuals are produced and how they become agents in their own 'subjectivication'. Judith Butler argues that subjects cannot come into being without social recognition, guaranteed by the norm. Thus, if power must produce subjects, norms of recognition must be imposed, which necessitates a vulnerability—the failure to live up to such norms—that then opens up possibilities of agency and resistance.[35] This would essentially mean that women are invested in the norms that discursively produce them, thus enacting strategies which produce self-regulating, 'normalized' individuals. However, within this enactment of gender norms lies the possibility of its failure, which becomes the site of agency. When attendants and private sisters respond to gossip of non-normative sexual practices and behaviour, it is not so much to deny the existence of such, as much to counter the tendency of trained nurses and even women doctors to locate themselves outside these practices, as subjects who perfectly adhere to and enact gendered norms. It is a simultaneous assent and resistance to hegemonic constructions of working-class bodies as promiscuous. While there may be a diversity of experiences, it is hard to maintain an unbridgeable gulf. Thus, gossiping interrupts the very conditions of class formation, by denying the distinctiveness of any one group's experience. Neeru, 34 years of age, married, Scheduled Caste, took to working as an attendant in the nursing home to make ends meet, says, 'Nurses have relationships with doctors. They get promotions, get taken out for vacations, good dining places. But that is not spoken about.' Trained nurses say that though women doctors have relationships with male doctors, they do not face similar disrespect. 'They are highly educated from good families; no one will talk about them like that. But women doctors also have relationships with male doctors and yet, no one says anything to them.'[36]

A theory of hegemony, which implies voluntary subordination, is based on a belief of social mobility, where those located at the bottom will rise up to the ranks of their superiors. While for trained nurses, whose aspirations to be counted among the ranks of the 'new middle class' may bear some fruit, those located at the bottom of the heap are painfully aware of the impossibility of social mobility. Women's imagination of a new social order, that reflects their lived realities and embodied experiences, fuels their resistance to hegemonic norms that produces ideal subjects. Swati, 42 years of age, married, General Caste, working as an attendant in the private nursing home, says that nurses take pleasure in discussing attendants' personal lives, sometimes even

[35] Butler (1990).

[36] An informal group discussion with nurses outside an emergency ward in a government hospital dated 5 January 2010.

making up stories, just to malign someone they do not like. However, she also admits that women working as attendants do have relationships with men, some which may not be legitimate in the eyes of society. But this, she asserts, has nothing to do with their work.

> There are attendants who have relationships with men outside the nursing home. And the nurses will sit down and discuss it. What I do outside the nursing home cannot be discussed at the workplace. There are nurses who will tell me that this or that attendant was seen with a man. So, I tell them to their face, that what an attendant does outside the nursing home is not their business. You judge our work, not our character. No one asks them (the nurses) what they are doing outside the nursing home. (Personal interview with author)

The interrogation of claims to hegemonic norms stems from a critique of the failure of power to produce ideal subjects. Asking whether those who claim to be representatives of the hegemonic bloc are true to the very ideals they disseminate is one thing; but questioning the very validity of these norms by which power is legitimized is a radical step in resisting power structures.[37] The rejection is not that of promiscuity/ remunerated sex—what is illicit and licit—but the interlinking of labour, social identity, and sexual disposition. In this act of protest, the sexual economy that flourishes outside the narrow hetero-norm is not denied or effaced. The question is no longer *what*, but rather *who* is doing it? Judith Butler argues that the theory of performativity is not very distinct from the theory of hegemony as both stress on the mechanisms by which the social world comes into being, the emergence of newer possibilities, and a reconfiguration of power equations.[38] The shift from *what* to *who* is an unintended consequence of a power struggle—a singular moment of resistance to 'reproductive hetero-normativity'.

* * *

I do not argue that women are consistently subversive agents in their everyday lives, but instead focus on a continuum of resistances that are context-specific and immediate. Scholarship on identity puts forth

[37] Scott (1990).
[38] Butler (2000: 14).

that it is defined relationally, particularly, for those located at the lower ranks of class (and in this case, caste) hierarchies. Constructing a sense of self-worth, by holding oneself to high moral standards, at the expense of others, is a way of asserting one's dignity at work.[39] It is this construction that becomes central to contests and power relations. The politics that unfold in the quotidian are important access points in understanding how subjects are constituted in specific fields—what are the various ways identity politics deploy class, caste, gender, and sexualities to intersect with the political economy that legitimizes the exploitation of certain bodies and the continuing devaluation of certain labour? I have argued that the modes of power operating in the nursing labour market that seek to discipline, control, and produce subjects who internalize hegemonic ideals of gender, class, and caste, as well as counter-hegemonic forces are to be located in the everyday; it is the quotidian that constitutes subjects—structures meaning, experiences, and affective ties. Women's agency and their resistance take on a counter-hegemonic nature, always seeking to probe the boundaries of what is permissible, the limits of the legitimate, so as to reformulate the social order in which the coercive hold of hegemonic norms over subjects, are less restrictive. Formal organized resistance does take place (wherever there are unions); however, the constant focus on unions, rallies, and other forms of headline-grabbing resistances tend to take away from the everyday insubordination that chips away at the foundational logic of power structures. I submit that the refusal to comply with power, whether in open opposition or surreptitiously in the cover of the night, wills unruly subjects into being.

[39] Lamont (2000).

Postscript

The last few years have seen some very significant changes in the nursing profession. For instance, the state of Kerala has witnessed a series of strikes that are forcing corporate hospitals to increase minimum wages of registered nurses at par with the public sector. Scholars observing the trends suggest that the 'morale economy' in which nurses are located, imply that they are encouraged to perceive themselves as feminine service providers rooted in spiritual and religious ethos rather than as workers, which comes in the way of successful collective bargaining. The entry of men into the profession has led to a spur in unionization, and subsequent strikes in the last few years.[1] In West Bengal, it was argued that the entry of men will consolidate professionalization to create an elite rank of registered nurses over-represented by men, thus masculinizing one of the few female-intensive occupations. On the contrary, there were those who argued that the entry of men will breach the association with femininity and raise the status of the profession.[2] Obviously, the West Bengal

---

[1] Biju (2013: 25–8).

[2] I am grateful to Subrato Sarkar, clinical instructor, West Bengal College of Nursing, IPGMER-SSKM, for highlighting both sides of the debate.

government's decision to continue 'protecting' nursing as a women-only profession was overturned in 2013, and for the first time, men were allowed to train and work as nurses in the public sector.

The entry of men into the profession raises new and interesting questions. Given the internal stratification within the profession, how will this turn of events influence the gendering of the occupation? Will nursing be able to resist masculinization, and be a mixed profession of both sexes? Or will it capitulate to newer trends, while drawing from older hierarchies? Will there now be an internal stratification of 'dirty' and 'prestigious' work, corresponding to a gender-based division of labour, rather than caste and class? Nursing is one of the few sectors within the service economy that has been and continues to remain fully feminized. The expansion of the sector has meant more employment for women, however, it has expanded in the informal rather than the formal end, demonstrating the linkages between female employment and informalization. In existing feminist scholarship, the denigration of women's work has been premised on the supposed disjuncture between reproductive and productive labour, home and factory, use and exchange value, where the first part of the pairing has been associated with the feminine and the second with the masculine. These binaries have followed from the attempts to understand the impact of industrial capitalism. Though historically such binaries never held, early factory labour saw in many parts of the world the participation of women and children in large numbers, and in South Asia, we see the participation of men in commodified reproductive labour, such as domestic work. One could say that the Fordist period in developed capitalism saw some aspects of the binary best in operation. This was followed immediately in the Post-Fordist era by increasing fuzziness in the division between use value and exchange value, home and market, reproductive and productive labour. Over the past century, we have seen different kinds of reproductive labour brought into the market, leading to its commodification, and nursing is one major example of this process. The processes of formalization have been more difficult in nursing, perhaps because of its feminine character. The registration of nurses was put in place in 1930s, but it took many decades to place nursing on a relatively organized basis. In the early years of formalization, race played an important role; thus, earlier processes of informalization were along racial lines. In more recent times, however, caste, class, and access to training/education have played critical roles in the differentiation within the profession. Consequently, the increase in the number of workers in nursing has been disproportionately at the informal end of the market, which has employed women with purportedly no or minimum skills, at less than minimum wages. The entry of men in large numbers into the profession will possibly change the internal gender composition, with more women employed in precarious conditions to perform menial-corporeal-affective labour required for healing; while relatively less number of men will now take on the medical-administrative-supervisory roles. The pyramidal structure of the labour market will not only be further institutionalized but also deeply gendered, like the rest of the informal economy, with clear links between precarity and feminization.

The story of women working as nurses, private sisters, and attendants in the hospitals and nursing homes in Kolkata, is the story of women who work in the marginalized sub-sectors of the health service industry. However, the story is as much about struggles, defiance, and resistances, as it about stigma, abjection, and precarity. To understand both domination/subordination and submission/resistance is to delve into discourses and ideologies of gender, sexualities, caste, and class as well as an analysis of the increasing fragmentation of markets and labour processes. The nursing sector, thus, presents itself as a critical territory to study how a differentiated workforce is maintained, legitimized, and reproduced. The co-existence of registered nurses, formally employed as professional workers within a knowledge-driven global economy, along with unregistered nursing aides, raises new and interesting questions about gender, caste, and class formations. What are the politics that arise from such a differentiated workforce? I argue that women in different ranks participate and perpetuate politics of differentiation, distinction, and distancing to prevent any homogenization of the workforce. These politics are essential for the cleaving of the workforce, into two distinct parts, which prevents any unitary conceptualization of the category 'woman' and of the 'worker'. I have argued that the quotidian relation of subordination, domination, humiliation, as well as practices of resistance are informed by such discursively produced identities. The falling back to social identities and cultural practices by a certain section of workers has been central to politics of distinction and distancing. Identities are not fixed and static, and subjects come into being through politics embedded in the quotidian. Despite the fact that modern workplaces and discriminatory social identities co-exist in uneasy terms, the working class is projected as a cohesive whole. This is in direct contradiction to the politics of caste, community, gender, and sexualities that constitutes a differentiated workforce. The various contestations around identities are essential to the organization of the modern labour market. I examine how subjects are produced by these contestations, their complicity as well as their antagonism towards norms, cultures, and discourses that seek to discipline them. Women seem to embrace as well as reject, appropriate as well as question, submit as well as disrupt norms that produce them. Identities are not necessarily complete and subjects stable. Thus, social norms that articulate intelligible subjects are open to revisions, contestations, and subversions. As Butler argues, the normative conceptual framework that produces subjects, is grounded in the politics of recognition, thus limiting acts of transgression that displaces hegemonic subjects.[3] Our ability to think, act, and feel are thus conditioned by social norms. However, the relationship of the subject with the norm is never unilateral and static, but constantly negotiated. Thus, the link between norms and recognition is a critical territory in understanding agency and resistance. In this book, I argue that women's resistance to being reduced to a subordinate group, incapable of intellectual labour, morality, and reason—the framework that deploys social identities to legitimize exploitation—is challenged on a daily basis. The seeds of this challenge lie in the very high idealization of hegemonic norms, whose interpellation of the subject, is never fully complete. Thus, the very volatility of the subject, and the instability of identities, provide grounds for effecting change. The quotidian that informs everyday practices, actions, social intercourses, behaviour, gestures, affect, and solidarities, more often than not, compromises identity claims.

[3] Butler (2004).

Appendix

Social Economic Profile of Respondents[1]

Table A.1 Distribution of 100 respondents according to marital status (in percentage)

Marital status	Registered nurses	Unregistered nurses	Private sisters	Attendants	Total
Married	10.6	12.7	8.5	19.1	51
Unmarried	13.8	7.4	9.5	7.4	38.2
Deserted/divorced	0	0	1	4.2	5.3
Widowed	0	1	2.1	2.1	5.3

[1] All tables are based on author's fieldwork.

Table A.2   Distribution of 100 respondents according to levels of education (in percentage)

Formal education	Registered nurses	Unregistered nurses	Private sisters	Attendants	Total
Less than class X	0	0	3.1	25.5	28.6
Class X	0	6.3	12.7	3.1	22.1
Class XII	20.2	10.6	5.3	3.1	39.2
Graduation with honours	4.2	0	0	0	4.2
Graduation with pass	0	4.2	0	1	5.2

Table A.3   Distribution of 100 respondents according to their perception of sons as a better investment (in percentage)

A male child is a better investment	Registered nurses	Unregistered nurses	Private sisters	Attendants	Total
Yes	22.3	21.2	21.2	29.7	94.4
No	2.1	0	0	3.1	5.2

Table A.4   Distribution of 100 respondents according to perceptions of expectations being met in this profession (in percentage)

Expectations	Registered nurses	Unregistered nurses	Private sisters	Attendants	Total
Not matched	5.3	17	21.2	27.6	71.2
Matched	9.5	1	0	1	11.7
Did not have any expectations	1	3.1	0	4.2	8.5
Do not know	8.5	0	0	0	8.5

Table A.5   Distribution of 100 respondents according to desire for further nursing training (in percentage)

Further training	Registered nurses	Unregistered nurses	Private sisters	Attendants	Total
Will take	4.2	0	1	0	5.2
Not possible	7.3	16.9	14.8	30.8	62.7
No such aspiration	12.7	4.2	5.3	2.1	24.4

Table A.6 Distribution of 100 respondents according to aspirations for their sons (in percentage)

Aspirations for son	Registered nurses	Unregistered nurses	Private sisters	Attendants	Total
Doctor	1	0	0	0	1
Other profession	4.2	3.1	6.3	19.1	32.9
Not applicable	19.1	18	14.8	13.8	65.9

Table A.7 Distribution of 100 respondents according to aspirations for their daughters (in percentage)

Aspirations for daughter	Registered nurses	Unregistered nurses	Private sisters	Attendants	Total
Nurse	0	0	0	0	0
Doctor	1	0	0	0	1
Other profession	3.1	8.5	1	5.3	18
Marriage	0	0	2.1	15.9	18
Not applicable	20.2	12.7	18	11.7	62.7

Table A.8 Distribution of 100 respondents according to acceptance of marriage by both families (in percentage)

Acceptance of marriage	Registered nurses	Unregistered nurses	Private sisters	Attendants	Total
Conflict	6.3	4.2	3.1	6.3	20.2
Consent	4.2	9.5	8.5	19.1	41.4
Not applicable	13.8	7.4	9.5	7.4	38.2

Table A.9 Distribution of 100 respondents according to perceptions on whether working as nursing staff facilitates a better match in marriage (in percentage)

Easier finding a groom	Registered nurses	Unregistered nurses	Private sisters	Attendants	Total
Yes	13.8	7.4	4.2	1	26.5
No	4.2	11.7	14.8	17	47.8
Cannot say	6.3	2.1	2	14.2	25.5

Table A.10   Distribution of 100 respondents according to caste (in percentage)

Caste	Registered nurses	Unregistered nurses	Private sisters	Attendants	Total
Scheduled Caste	1	6.3	14.6	22	43.9
Scheduled Tribe	4.5	0	0	0	4.5
General Caste	17.7	12.7	6.6	8.7	45.7
Did not disclose/ not applicable	1	2	0	2.1	5.1

Table A.11   Distribution of 100 respondents according to queries on stigmatization of the profession (in percentage)

Stigma to your profession	Registered nurses	Unregistered nurses	Private sisters	Attendants	Total
Yes	21.2	20.2	21.2	32.9	95.7
No	0	0	0	0	0
Yes, but it is changing	3.1	1	0	0	4.2

Table A.12   Distribution of 100 respondents according to aspiration for giving up employment if there is an improvement in family's finances (in percentage)

Would you give up current jobs if the situation is better at home?	Registered nurses	Unregistered nurses	Private sisters	Attendants	Total
Yes	6.3	13.8	21.2	32.9	74.4
No	17	5.3	0	0	22.3
Maybe	1	2.1	0	0	3.1

Table A.13   Distribution of 100 respondents according to age group (in percentage)

Age	Registered nurses	Unregistered nurses	Private sisters	Attendants	Total
18–25	9.6	9.6	7.5	4.3	31
25–30	4.3	5.3	3.2	9.6	22.4
30–45	7.5	5.3	9.6	17.3	39.7
45–60	2.1	1	1	1	5.1
60 and above	1	0	0	0	1

Table A.14 Distribution of 100 respondents according to religion (in percentage)

Religion	Registered nurses	Unregistered nurses	Private sisters	Attendants	Total
Hindu	15.9	20.2	21.2	30.8	88.2
Muslim	0	1	0	0	1
Christian	8.5	0	0	2.1	10.6

Table A.15 Distribution of 100 respondents according to regional variations (in percentage)

Regional variations	Registered nurses	Unregistered nurses	Private sisters	Attendants	Total
Kolkata	9.5	12.7	11.7	21.2	55.3
Districts of West Bengal	2.1	8.5	9.5	10.6	30.8
Outside West Bengal	12.7	0	0	1	13.8

Table A.16 Distribution of 100 respondents according to reasons cited for choosing nursing (in percentage)

Reasons to enter the profession	Registered nurses	Unregistered nurses	Private sisters	Attendants	Total
Easily available jobs	15.7	13.8	4.1	32.9	66.5
Easily available training	0	7.1	15.9	0	23
Selfless service/ attracted to the uniform	2.1	0	0	0	2.1
Family choice	5.3	1	1	0	7.3
Other	1	0	0	0	1

Table A.17   Distribution of 100 respondents according to source of funding for nursing education (in percentage)

Source of funding	Registered nurses	Unregistered nurses	Private sisters	Attendants	Total
Free training with a bond (unlicensed center)	0	21.2	21.2	1	43.6
Family/church/loan	12.3	0	0	0	12.3
Government course	11.7	0	0	0	11.7
No training	0	0	0	31.9	31.9

Table A.18   Distribution of 100 respondents according to ambitions/ aspirations in professional life (in percentage)

Future ambitions	Registered nurses	Unregistered nurses	Private sisters	Attendants	Total
Promotion/ better job offer	18	9.5	14.8	14.8	57.4
Leave profession	2.1	7.4	6.3	10.6	26.5
No ambition	4.1	4.1	0	7.4	15.8

Table A.19   Distribution of 100 respondents according to reasons cited for choosing waged work (in percentage)

Reasons for choosing waged work	Registered nurses	Unregistered nurses	Private sisters	Attendants	Total
Independence	10.6	2.1	3.1	1	17
To support family	12.7	19.1	18	31.9	81.9
To earn for paying dowry	1	0	0	0	1

Bibliography

Film

Ray, Satyajit, dir. 1970. *Pratidwandi*. Calcutta.

Archives: Calcutta, West Bengal State Archives, Government of Bengal Files

West Bengal State Archives (WBSA). 1914. *Proceedings B 63, File No. IR/33, Minutes of the Half Yearly Meeting of General Committee, Calcutta Hospital Nursing Institution, dated 27 February 1913*. West Bengal: Finance Department, Medical Branch.

———. 1922a. *Proceedings A 12–19, File N-7(1), Training and Registration for Nurses and Midwives in Bengal, February*. West Bengal: Local Self Government Department, Medical Branch.

———. 1922b. *Proceedings A, 19, File No 2-R, August*. West Bengal: Local Self Government Department, Medical Branch.

———. 1922c. *Medical Branch, Proceedings B 52–53, File No. N/3, December*. West Bengal: Miscellaneous Department.

Newspaper Clippings

Telegraph, The. 2011. 'Creaking Bed Gives Away Doc "Dalliance".' 16 June. Accessed July 2011. https://www.telegraphindia.com/1110616/jsp/bengal/story_14120134.jsp.

Hindustan Times. 2013. 'West Bengal Govt to Start Training Programmes for Male Nurses.' 8 October. Accessed 19 September 2017. http://www.hindustantimes.com/kolkata/west-bengal-govt-to-start-training-programmes-for-male-nurses/story-IL3VAtZblpS7EQtPuVcPhM.html.

Reports

Government of India, Ministry of Labour and Employment. 1961. *Careers in Nursing and Allied Health Occupations.* Occupational Field Review No. 2. New Delhi: Samrat Press.

Indian Health Survey and Development Committee. 1946. *Report of the Health Survey and Development Committee.* Vol. I. Delhi: Manager of Publications.

Matsuno, Ayaka. 2009. *Nurse Migration: The Asian Perspective.* Technical note. ILO/EU Asian Programme on the Governance of Labour Migration. Accessed June 2017. http://www.ilo.org/asia/publications/WCMS_160629/lang--en/index.htm.

Ministry of Health and Family Welfare. 1988. *National Convention of Nurses.* New Delhi: National Institute of Family and Health Welfare.

Statistics Division, Ministry of Health and Family Welfare. 2011. *Family Welfare Statistics in India.* New Delhi: Ministry of Health and Family Welfare, Government of India.

The Association of Nursing Superintendents in India. 1905. *Report of the Nursing Conference held in Lucknow, January 1905.* Cawnpur: Christ Church Mission Press.

———. 1908. *Report of the Nursing Conference held in Lucknow: January 1908.* Cawnpur: Christ Church Mission Press.

The Countess of Dufferin's Fund. 1888. *A Record of Three Year's work of the National Association for Supplying Female Medical Aid to the Women of India, August 1885–1888.* Calcutta: Thacker Spink and Co.

———. 1925. *Forty First Annual Report of the National Association for Supplying Female Medical Aid to the Women of India.* Calcutta: Superintendent Government Printing India.

———. 1926. *Forty Second Annual Report of the National Association for Supplying Female Medical Aid to the Women of India.* Calcutta: Bengal Secretariat Press.

———. 1935. *Fifty First Annual Report of the National Association for Supplying Female Medical Aid to the Women of India.* Calcutta: Superintendent Government Printing India.

———. 1936. *Fifty Second Annual Report of the National Association for Supplying Female Medical Aid to the Women of India.* Calcutta: Superintendent Government Printing India.

Victoria Memorial Scholarship Fund. 1918. *Improvement of the Conditions of Childbirth in India: Including a Special Report on the Work of the Victoria Memorial Scholarships Fund during the past Fifteen Years and Papers written by Medical Women and Qualified Midwives.* Calcutta: Superintendent Government Printing India.

World Health Organization. 1957. *Seminar on Categories and Functions of Nursing Personnel.* New Delhi: WHO Regional Office for South East Asia.

———. 1958. *Report on WHO Conference on Auxiliary Nursing, 3–15 November 1958.* New Delhi: WHO Regional office for South East Asia.

Internet Sources

Ahmed, Sara. 2017. 'No.' Accessed 8 July 2017. https://feministkilljoys.com/2017/06/30/no/.

'The Nightingale Pledge.' n.d. Accessed 10 July 2017. http://www.truthaboutnursing.org/press/pioneers/nightingale_pledge.html.

Trained Nurses' Association of India. n.d. 'Policy and Position Statements.' Accessed 10 July 2017. http://www.tnaionline.org/policy.htm.

Thesis

Guha, Supriya. 1996. 'A History of Medicalisation of Childbirth in the late Nineteenth and Early Twentieth Century.' PhD thesis, Calcutta University.

Hardeman, Katherine. 1946. 'The Trends in the Aims of The Trained Nurses Association of India, 1926–1946.' MSc thesis, Western Reserve University.

Lal, Maneesha. 1996. 'Women, Medicine and Colonialism in British India, 1869–1925.' PhD thesis, University of Pennsylvania.

Madhavi, Upot Poovadan. 1968. 'A Study of Mutual Professional Role Expectation of Physicians and Nurses in the Public Health Team in India.' PhD thesis, University of Boston.

Paul, Chandrika. 1997. 'Uneasy Alliances: The Work of Bengal and British Women Medical Professionals in Bengal, 1870–1935.' PhD thesis, University of Cincinnati.

Books and Articles

Abu-Lughod, Lila. 1990. 'The Romance of Resistance: Tracing Transformation of Power through Bedouin Women.' *American Ethnologist* 17 (1): 41–55.

Ahmed, Sara. 2004. *The Cultural Politics of Emotion*. Chicago: Routledge.

Althusser, Louis. 1969. *For Marx*. New York: Vintage Books.

———. 1971. *Lenin and Philosophy and Other Essays*. Translated by Ben Brewster. London: Allen Lane.

Arendt, Hannah. 1958. *The Human Condition*. Chicago: University of Chicago Press.

Arles, Siga. 2008. 'Medical Missions—A Mega Contribution of Christian Missionaries.' In *Preach and Heal: A History of the Missionaries in India*, edited by Sandeep Sinha. Kolkata: Readers Service, pp. 420–47.

Arnold, David. 1993. *Colonizing the Body: State Medicine and Epidemic Diseases in Nineteenth-century India*. Berkeley: University of California.

Bala, Poonam. 1991. *Imperialism and Medicine in Bengal: A Socio-Historical Perspective*. New Delhi: SAGE Publications.

Balfour, Margaret Ida, and Ruth Young. 1929. *The Work of Medical Women in India*. London: Oxford University Press.

Balmurli, Natrajan. 2009. 'Place and Pathology in Caste.' *Economic and Political Weekly* 44 (51): 79–82.

Banerjee, Nirmala. 1989. 'Women in Colonial Bengal: Modernization and Marginalization.' In *Recasting Women: Essays in Colonial History*, edited by Kumkum Sangari and Sudesh Vaid. New Delhi: Kali for Women, pp. 237–98.

Banerjee, Nirmala, ed. 1991a. *Indian Women in a Changing Industrial Scenario*. New Delhi: SAGE Publications.

———. 1991b. 'The More it Changes the More it Remains the Same.' In *Indian Women in a Changing Industrial Scenario*, edited by Nirmala Banerjee. Newsbury Park/London/New Delhi. Indo-Dutch Studies on Development Alternatives -5: SAGE Publications, pp. 237–98.

———. 1999. 'Analyzing Women's Work under Patriarchy.' In *From Myths to Markets: Essays on Gender*, edited by Kumkum Sangari and Uma Chakravarti. New Delhi: Indian Institute of Advanced Study, Manohar Publishers, pp. 321–37.

———. 2002. 'Between the Devil and the Deep Sea: Shrinking options for Women in Contemporary India.' In *The Violence of Development: The Politics of Identity, Gender and Social Inequalities in India*, edited by Karin Kapadia. New Delhi: Kali for Women, pp. 43–68.

Banerjee, Swapna M. 2004. *Men, Women and Domestics: Articulating Middle-Class Identity in Colonial Bengal*. New Delhi: Oxford University Press.

Bannerjee, Himani. 2001. *Invention of Subjects: Studies in Hegemony, Patriarchy and Colonialism*. New Delhi: Tulika Books.

Bardhan, Pranab. 1984. *The Political Economy of Development in India*. New Delhi: Oxford University Press.

Barker, Drucilla K. 2005. 'Beyond Women and Economics: Rereading "Women's Work".' *Signs* 30 (4): 2189–209.

Barrett, Michele. 1980. *Women's Oppression Today: Problems in Marxist Feminist Analysis*. London: Verso.

Baru, Rama. 1998. *Private Health Care in India: Social Characteristics and Trends*. New Delhi: SAGE Publications.

———. 2001. 'Health Sector Reforms and Structural Adjustment: A State-Level Analysis.' In *Public Health and the Poverty of Reforms: The South Asian Predicaments*, edited by Imrana Qadeer, Kasturi Sen, and K.R. Nayar. New Delhi: SAGE Publications, pp. 211–34.

———. 2004. 'Privatization of Health Care: Conditions of Workers in Private Hospitals.' In *Globalization*, edited by Malini Bhattacharya. New Delhi: Tulika Books.

Bashford, Alison. 2004. 'Medicine, Gender and Empire.' In *Gender and Empire: The Oxford History of the British Empire, Companion Series*, edited by Levine Philippa. New York: Oxford University Press.

Basu, Ananya. 2016. *Informalisation of Work: A Regional Overview*. New Delhi: Public Services International, South Asia.

Beauchamp, Tom L. and James F. Childress. 1994. *Principles of Biomedical Ethics*. New York: Oxford University Press.

Beneria, Lourdes. 1992. 'The Mexican Debt Crisis: Restructuring the Economy and the Household.' In *Unequal Burden: Economic Crises, Persistent Poverty, and Women's Work*, edited by Lourdes Beneria and Shelly Feldman. Colorado: Westview Press, pp. 83–104.

———. 2008. 'The Crisis of Care, International Migration, and Public Policy.' *Feminist Economics* 14 (3): 1–21.

Beneria, Lourdes, and Shelly Feldman, eds. 1992. *Unequal Burden: Economic Crises, Persistent Poverty, and Women's Work*. Colorado: Westview Press.

Berman, Peter, and Rajeev Ahuja. 2008. 'Government Health Spending in India.' *Economic and Political Weekly* 43 (26/27): 209–16.

Bernard, Andreas. 2014. *Lifted: A Cultural History of the Elevator*. New York and London: New York University Press.

Beteille, Andre. 1993. 'The Family and the Reproduction of Inequality.' In *Family, Kinship and Marriage in India*, edited by Patricia Uberoi. Delhi: Oxford University Press.

Biju, B.L. 2013. 'Angels are Turning Red: Nurses' Strikes in Kerala.' *Economic and Political Weekly* 48 (52): 25–8.

Bhattacharya, Sabyasachi. 2002. 'Introduction: An Approach to Education and Inequality.' In *Education and the Disprivileged: Nineteenth and Twentieth*

Century India, edited by Sabyasachi Bhattacharya. New Delhi: Orient Blackswan, pp. 1–32.

Bleakley, Ethel. 1940. *Meet the Indian Nurse*. London: Zenith Press.

Borthwick, Meredith. 1984. *The Changing Role of Women in Bengal, 1849–1905*. New Jersey: Princeton University Press.

Boston, Sarah. 1980. *Women Workers and the Trade Union Movements*. London: Davis-Poynter.

Bourdieu, Pierre. 1969. 'Intellectual Field and Creative Project.' *Social Science Information* 8 (2): 89–119.

———. 1976. 'Marriage Strategies as Strategies of Social Reproduction.' In *Family and Society: Selections from the Annales: Economies, Societies, Civilizations*, edited by Robert Forster, O. Ranum, Elbory Forster, Patricia M. Ranum. Baltimore: Johns Hopkins University Press.

———. 1984. *Distinction: A Social Critique of the Judgement of Taste*. Cambridge, MA: Harvard University Press.

———. 1990. *In other Words: Essays towards a Reflexive Sociology*. Stanford: Stanford University Press.

Braverman, Harry. 1974. *Labor and Monopoly Capital: The Degradation of Work in Twentieth Century*. New York: Monthly Review Press.

Brennan, David M. 2006. 'Defending the Indefensible? Culture's Role in Productive/Unproductive Dichotomy.' *Feminist Economics* 12 (3): 403–25.

Brenner, Johanna. 2000. *Women and the Politics of Class*. New York: Monthly Review Press.

Brian, Abel-Smith. 1961. *A History of the Nursing Profession*. London: William Heinemann Ltd.

Briles, Judith. 1994. *The Briles Report on Women in Health Care: Changing Conflict to Collaboration in a Toxic Workplace*. San Francisco: Jossey-Bose Publishers.

Buchan, James. 2007. 'International Recruitment of Nurses: Policy and Practices in the United Kingdom.' *Health Services Research* 42 (3): 1321–35.

Burton, Antoinette M. 1992. 'The White Woman's Burden: British Feminists and "The Indian Woman", 1865–1915'. In *Western Women and Imperialism: Complicity and Resistance*, edited by Nupur Chaudhuri and Margaret Strobel. Bloomington: Indiana University Press, pp. 137–57.

———. 1996. 'Contesting the Zenana: The Mission to Make "Lady Doctors for India", 1874–1885'. *Journal of British Studies* 35 (3): 368–97.

Butler, Judith. 1990. *Gender Trouble: Feminism and the Subversion of Identity*. New York and London: Routledge.

———. 1997a. *Excitable Speech: A Politics of the Performative*. New York: Routledge.

———. 1997b. 'Merely Cultural.' *Social Text* 52/53 (3–4): 265–77.

———. 2000. 'Restaging the Universal: Hegemony and the Limits of Formalism.' In *Contingency, Hegemony, Universality*, edited by Judith Butler, Ernesto Laclau, and Slavoj Žižek. London: Verso.

———. 2004. *Undoing Gender*. New York: Routledge.

Butler, Judith, Ernesto Laclau, and Slavoj Žižek. 2000. *Contingency, Hegemony, Universality*. London: Verso.

Caplan, Pat. 2008. 'Crossing the Veg/Non-Veg Divide: Commensality and Sociality among the Middle Classes in Madras/Chennai.' *South Asia: Journal of South Asian Studies* 31 (1): 118–42.

Carpenter, Mick. 1993. 'The Subordination of Nurses in Health Care: Towards as Social Division Approach.' In *Gender, Work and Medicine: Women and the Medical Division of Labour*, edited by Elianne Riska and Katarina Wegar. London: SAGE Publications, pp. 95–130.

Chakraborty, Dipesh. 1989. *Rethinking Working-Class History: Bengal, 1890– 1940*. Princeton: Princeton University Press.

———. 1993. 'The Difference-Deferral of a Colonial Modernity: Public Debates on Domesticity in Bengal.' *History Workshop Journal* 36 (1): 1–34.

Chakravarti, Uma. 1993. 'Conceptualising Brahminical Patriarchy in Early India: Gender, Caste, Class and State.' *Economic and Political Weekly* 28 (14): 579–85.

———. 2006. *Gendering Caste: Through a Feminist Lens*. Calcutta: Stree.

Chakravarty, Deepita, and Ishita Chakravarty. 2016. *Women, Labour and the Economy in India: From Migrant Menservants to Uprooted Girl Children Maids*. London and New York: Routledge.

Chanter, Tina. 2006. *Gender: Key Concepts in Philosophy*. London: Continuum.

Chandavarkar, Rajnarayan. 1994. *The Origins of Industrial Capitalism in India: Business Strategies and the Working Classes in Bombay, 1900–1940*. Cambridge: Cambridge University Press.

Chatterjee, Partha. 1989. 'The Nationalist Resolution of the Women's Question.' In *Recasting Women: Essays in Colonial History*, edited by Kumkum Sangari and Sudesh Vaid. New Delhi: Kali for Women, pp. 233–53.

———. 1993. *The Nation and Its Fragments: Colonial and Postcolonial Histories*. Princeton, NJ: Princeton University Press.

Chattopadhyay, Molly. 1993. *Occupational Socialization: A Study of Hospital Nurses*. Calcutta: Sarat Book House.

Chen, Martha, Joann Vanek, and James Heintz. 2006. 'Informality, Gender and Poverty; A Global Picture.' *Economic and Political Weekly* 41 (21): 2131–9.

Chhattisgarh Mahila Jagriti Sanghathana. 1987. *Virginity Test on Nurses? A Report on an Investigation*. Raipur: C. M. J. Sanghathana.

Chin, Christine B.N. 1998. *In Service and Servitude: Foreign Female Domestic Workers and The Malaysian "Modernity" Project*. New York and Chichester: Columbia University Press.

Chowdhury, Dhruba Narayan, ed. 1997. *Nirad Chandra Chowdhury: Nirbachito Probandha*. Kolkata: Ananda Publishers.

Chowdhury, Prem. 2007. *Contentious Marriages, Eloping Couples: Gender, Caste, and Patriarchy in Northern India*. New Delhi: Oxford University Press

———. 2011. *Political Economy of Production and Reproduction: Caste, Custom, and Community in North India*. New Delhi: Oxford University Press.

Clark, Alice. 1919. *The Working Life of Women in the Seventeenth Century*. London: Routledge.

Clarke, John, Stuart Hall, Tony Jefferson, and Brian Roberts. 1976 (2003). 'Subcultures, Cultures and Class: A Theoretical Overview.' In *Resistance Through Rituals: Youth Subcultures in Post-war Britain*, edited by Stuart Hall and T. Jefferson. London: Routledge, pp. 9–79.

Cock, Jacklyn. 1989. *Maids and Madams: Domestic Workers under Apartheid*. London: The Women's Press.

Collins, Patricia Hill. 1986. 'Learning from the Outsider Within: The Sociological Significance of Black Feminist Thought.' *Social Problems* 33 (6): S14–S32.

———. 1990. *Black Feminist Thought: Knowledge, Consciousness and the Politics of Empowerment*. Boston: Unwin Hyman.

Crapanzano, Vincent. 1986 (2011). 'Hermes' Dilemma: The Masking of Subversion in Ethnographic Description.' In *Writing Culture: The Poetics and Politics of Ethnography*, edited by James Clifford and George Marcus. Berkeley: University of California Press, pp. 51–76.

Cresswell, Tim. 1996. *In Place/Out of Place: Geography, Ideology and Transgression*. Minneapolis: Minnesota University Press.

Dagmar, Engels. 1996. *Beyond Purdah? Women in Bengal 1890–1930*. Delhi: Oxford University Press.

Dali, Caroline. 1888. *The Life of Dr. Anandibai Joshi: A Kinswoman of Pundita Ramabai*. Boston: Roberts Brothers.

Damodaran, Sumangala and Krishna Menon. 2007. *Migrant Women and Wage Employment: Exploring Issues of Work and Identity among Health Care Professionals*. Noida: V.V. Giri National Labour Institute, NL Research Studies (073).

Davis, Angela Y. 1981. *Women, Race, & Class*. New York: Random House.

de Beauvoir, Simone. (1949) 2011. *The Second Sex*. Translated by Constance Borde and Sheila Malovany-Chevallier. London: Vintage.

Deliège, Robert. 2010. 'Introduction: Is there still Untouchability in India?' In *From Stigma to Assertion: Untouchability, Identity and Politics in Early and*

Modern India, edited by Mikael Aktor and Robert Deliège. Copenhagen: Museum Tusculanum Press, pp. 13–30.

Delphy, Christine. 1984. *Close to Home: A Materialist Analysis of Women's Oppression*. Translated and edited by Diana Leonard. Amherst, MA: University of Massachusetts Press.

Desai, Neera, and Maithrei Krishnaraj. 2004. 'An Overview of the Status of Women in India.' In *Class, Caste and Gender*, edited by Manoranjan Mohanty. New Delhi: SAGE Publications, pp. 296–319.

Deshpande, Ashwini. 2007. 'Overlapping Identities under Liberalization: Gender and Caste in India.' *Economic Development and Cultural Change* 55 (4): 735–60.

Deshpande, Satish. 2003. *Contemporary India. A Sociological View*. New Delhi: Penguin Books.

Devi, Mahasweta. 1979. 'Stanadayini.' In *Stanadaini O Onnanno Golpo*. Calcutta: Nath Brothers.

De Vault, Marjorie. 1999. *Liberating Method: Feminism and Social Research*. Philadelphia: Temple University Press.

Dolan, Josephine. 1973. *Nursing in Society: A Historical Perspective*. Philadelphia: W.B. Saunders Co.

Donald, James. 1992. 'Metropolis: The City as Text.' In *Social and Cultural Forms of Modernity*, edited by Robert Bocock and Kenneth Thompson. Cambridge: Polity Press, pp. 418–61.

Douglas, Mary. (1966) 2002. *Purity and Danger: An Analysis of Concepts of Pollution and Taboo*. United Kingdom: Routledge.

Dube, Leela. 1997. *Women and Kinship: Comparative Perspectives on Gender in South and South-East Asia*. Tokyo: The United Nations University Press.

Duffy, Mignon. 2011. *Making Care Count: A Century of Gender, Race and Paid Care Work*. New Brunswick, New Jersey and London: Rutgers University Press.

Duggal, Ravi. 2005. 'Historical Review of Health Policy Making.' In *Review of Health Care in India*, edited by Leena V. Gangolli, Ravi Duggal, and Abhay Shukla. Mumbai: CEHAT, pp. 21–40.

Dutta, G.P., and Ravi Narayan. 2004. *Perspective in Health: Human Power Development in India- Medical, Nursing and Paramedical India*. New Delhi: Independent Commission on Development and Health in India.

Eisenstein, Zillah (ed.) 1979. *Capitalist Patriarchy and the Case for Socialist Feminism*. New York: Monthly Review Press.

Ehrenreich, Barbara, and Arlie Russell Hochschild, eds. 2002. *Global Woman: Nannies, Maids and Sex Workers in the New Economy*. New York: Holt Paperback.

Ehrenreich, Barbara and Deirdre English. (1973) 2010. *Witches, Midwives and Nurses: A History of Women Healers*. New York: Feminist Press.

Elson, Diane, and Ruth Pearson. 1981. '"Nimble Fingers Make Cheap Workers": An Analysis of Women's Employment in Third World Export Manufacturing.' *Feminist Review* 7 (1): 87–107.

England, Paula and Nancy Folbre. 1999. 'The Cost of Caring.' *Annals of the American Academy of Political and Social Science* 561 (1): 39–51.

Eswara, Suryamani. 1989. *The Organization and The Semi-Professional: A Sociological Study of Nurses*. New Delhi: Jainson Publications.

Ferguson, Ann. 1979.'Women as a New Revolutionary Class in the US.' In *Between Labour and Capital*, edited by Pat Walker. Boston: South End, pp. 279–309.

Fernandes, Leela. 1997. *Producing Workers: The Politics of Gender, Class and Culture in the Calcutta Jute Mills*. New Delhi: Vistaar Publications.

———. 2000. 'Restructuring the New Middle Class in Liberalizing India.' *Comparative Studies of South Asia, Africa and the Middle East* 20 (1): 88–104.

———. 2006. *India's New Middle Class: Democratic Politics in an Era of Economic Reform*. Minneapolis: Minnesota University Press.

Fernandes, Leela, and Patrick Heller. 2006. 'Hegemonic Aspirations: New Middle Class Politics and India's Democracy in Comparative Perspective.' *Critical Asian Studies* 38 (4): 495–522.

Fitzgerald, Rosemary. 2006. '"Making and Moulding the Nursing of the Indian Empire": Re-casting Nurses in Colonial India.' In *Rhetoric and Reality: Gender and the Colonial Experience in South Asia*, edited by Siobhan Lambert-Hurley and Avril Powell. New Delhi: Oxford University Press, pp. 185–222.

Folbre, Nancy. 2006. '"Nursebots to the Rescue?" Immigration, Automation, and Care.' *Globalizations* 3 (3): 349–60.

Forbes, Geraldine. 1994.'Medical Careers and Health Care for Indian Women: Patterns of Control.' *Women's History Review* 3 (4): 515–30.

———. 2005. *Women in Colonial India, Essays on Politics, Medicines and Historiography*. New Delhi: Chronicle Books.

Forbes, Geraldine, and Tapan Raychaudhuri, eds. 2000. *The Memoirs of Haimabati Sen: From Child Widow to Lady Doctor*. New Delhi: Roli Books.

Foss, Karen A., and Sonja K. Foss. 1994.'Personal Experience as Evidence in Feminist Scholarship.' *Western Journal of Communication* 58 (1): 39–43.

Foster, E.A. 1911. 'The Untrained Midwife in India.' *The American Journal of Nursing* 12 (1): 34–5.

Foucault, Michel. 1972. *The Archaeology of Knowledge*. Translated by Alan Sheridan. New York: Pantheon Books.

———. (1978) 1990. *The History of Sexuality: An Introduction*. vol. 1. Translated by Robert Hurley. New York: Vintage Books.

———. (1986) 1990. *The Care of the Self: The History of Sexuality*. 3 vols. Translated by Robert Hurley. London: Penguin Books.

———. 1984. 'What is Enlightenment?' In *The Foucault Reader*, edited by Paul Rabinow. New York: Pantheon Books, pp. 32–51.

———. 1994 (2001). 'The Subject and Power.' In *Power: Essential Works of Foucault: Vol. 3*, edited by James D. Faubion. London: The Penguin Press pp. 326–348.

———. (1977) 1991. *Discipline and Punish: The Birth of the Prison*. England: Penguin Books.

———. 1997. 'Lecture 11.' In *Society Must be Defended: Lectures at the College de France, 1975–76*, edited by Mauro Bertani and Alessandro Fontana. Translated by David Macey. New York: Picador, pp. 239–64.

———. (1999) 2003. *Abnormal: Lectures at the Collège de France, 1974–1975*, edited by Valerio Marchetti and Antonella Salomoni. Translated by Graham Burchell. London and New York: Verso Books.

———. (1978) 2007. 'The Incorporation of Hospital in Modern Technology.' In *Space, Knowledge and Power: Foucault and Geography*, edited by Jeremy W. Crampton and Stuart Elden. Translated by Edgar Knowlton Jr.,. William J. King, and Stuart Elden. Hampshire: Ashgate.

Friedan, Betty. 1963. *The Feminine Mystique*. New York: Norton.

Froystad, K. 2003. 'Master–Servant Relations and the Domestic Reproduction of Caste in Northern India.' *Ethnos* 68 (1): 73–94.

Gangolli, Leena V., Ravi Duggal, and Abhay Shukla. 2005. *Review of Health Care in India*. Mumbai: CEHAT.

Gamarnikow, Eva. 1991. 'Nurse or Women: Gender and Professionalism in Reformed Nursing; 1860–1923.' In *Anthropology and Nursing*, edited by Pat Hol and Jenny Littlewood. New York: Routledge, pp. 110–29.

Gatens, Moira. 1996. *Imaginary Bodies: Ethics, Power, and Corporeality*. London: Routledge.

George, Sheba. 2000. '"Dirty Nurses" and "Men who Play": Gender and Class in Transnational Migration.' In *Global Ethnography: Forces, Connections and Imaginations in a Post Modern World*, edited by Michael Burawoy et al. Berkeley: University of California Press, pp. 144–74.

Ghosh, Jayati. 1994. 'Gender Concerns in Macro-Economic Policy.' *Economic and Political Weekly* 29 (18): WS2–WS4.

———. 2009. *Never done and Poorly Paid: Women's Work in Globalizing India*. New Delhi: Women Unlimited.

Giddens, Anthony. 1984. *The Constitution of Society: Outline of a Theory of Structuration*. Berkeley: University of California Press.

Gilligan, Carol. 1982. '*In a Different Voice: Psychological Theory and Women's Development.'* Cambridge, MA: Harvard University Press.

Glaser, William A. 1966. 'Nursing Leadership and Policy: Some Cross National Comparisons.' In *The Nursing Profession. Five Sociological Essays*, edited by Davis Fed. New York: John Wiley & Sons, pp. 8–11.

Glenn, Evelyn Nakano. 1992. 'From Servitude to Service Work: Historical Continuities in the Racial Division of Paid Reproductive Labor.' *Signs: Journal of Women in Culture and Society* 18 (1): 1–43.

Goffman, Erving. 1963. *Stigma: Notes on the Management of Spoiled Identities.* New Jersey: Prentice-Hall: Englewood Cliffs.

Grosz, Elizabeth. 1994. *Volatile Bodies: Toward a Corporeal Feminism.* Bloomington: Indiana University Press.

Guha, Ranajit. 1987. 'Chandra's Death.' In *Subaltern Studies*, edited by Ranajit Guha. Vol. 5. Delhi: Oxford University Press, pp. 135–65.

Guha, Supriya. 1998. 'From Dais to Doctors: The Medicalisation of Childbirth in Colonial India.' In *Understanding Women's Health Issues: A Reader*, edited by L. Lingam. New Delhi: Kali for Women, pp. 145–62.

———. 2006. '"The Best Swadeshi": Reproductive Health in Bengal, 1840–1940.' In *Reproductive Health in India: History, Politics, Controversies*, edited by Sarah Hodges. Hyderabad: Orient Longman, pp. 139–66.

Gupta, Charu. 2016. *The Gender of Caste: Representing Dalits in Print.* Seattle: University of Washington Press.

Guru, Gopal. 2009. 'Rejection of Rejection: Foregrounding Self Respect.' In *Humiliation: Claims and Context*, edited by Gopal Guru. New Delhi: Oxford University Press, pp. 209–55.

———. 2015. 'Labouring Intellectuals: The Conceptual World of Dalit Women.' In *Interrogating Women's leadership and Empowerment*, edited by Omita Goyal. New Delhi: SAGE Publications, pp. 55–68.

Guru, Gopal, and Sundar Sarukkai, eds. 2012. *The Cracked Mirror: An Indian Debate on Experience and Theory.* New Delhi: Oxford University Press.

Hall, Stuart. 1958. 'A Sense of Classlessness.' *Universities and New Left Review* 1 (5): 26–32.

———. (1996) 2005. 'New Ethnicities.' In *Stuart Hall: Critical Dialogues in Cultural Studies*, edited by D. Morley and K. Chen. London: Routledge, pp. 442–51.

Hall, Stuart, and Jefferson T., eds. (1976) 2003. *Resistance Through Rituals*, London: Hutchinson.

Harding, Sandra, ed. 2004. *The Feminist Standpoint Theory Reader.* New York and London: Routledge.

Hardt, Michael. 1999. 'Affective Labour.' *Boundary 2* 26 (2): pp. 89–100.

Hardt, Michael, and Antonio Negri. 2000. *Empire.* Cambridge: Harvard University Press.

———. 2004. *Multitude: War and Democracy in the Age of Empire.* New York: Penguin.

Fraad, Harriet, Stephen Resnick, and Richard Wolff. 1994. *Bringing It All Back Home: Class, Gender and Power in the Modern Household.* London: Pluto Press.

Harriss-White, Barbara, and Valentina Prosperi. 2014. 'The Micro Political Economy of Gains by Unorganised Workers in India.' *Economic and Political Weekly* 29 (9): 39–43.

Harriss-White, Barbara, and Nandini Gooptu. 2001. 'Mapping India's World of Unorganized Labour.' *Socialist Register* 37: 89–118.

Harstock, Nancy. 2004. 'The Feminist Standpoint: Developing the Ground for a Specifically Feminist Historical Materialism.' In *The Feminist Standpoint Theory Reader*, edited by Sandra Harding. New York and London: Routledge, pp. 35–54.

Hazarika, Indrajit. 2013. 'Health Workforce in India: Assessment of Availability, Production and Distribution.' *WHO South-East Asia Journal of Public Health* 2 (2), 106–112.

Healey, Madelaine. 2008. '"Seeds That May Have Been Planted May Take Root": International Aid Nurses and Projects of Professionalism in Postindependence India, 1947–65.' *Nursing History Review* 16 (1): 58–90.

———. 2010. '"Regarded, Paid and Housed as Menials": Nursing in Colonial India, 1900–1948.' *South Asian History and Culture* 2 (1): 55–75.

———. 2013. *Indian Sisters: A History of Nursing and the State, 1907–2007*. New Delhi and London: Routledge.

Heinamaa, Sara. 1996. 'Woman—Nature, Product Style? Rethinking the Feminist Foundations of Science.' In *Feminism, Science and the Philosophy of Science*, edited by Lynn Hankinson Nelson and Jack Nelson. Dordrecht/Boston/London: Kluwer Academic Publishers, pp. 289–308.

———. 2003. *Towards a Phenomenology of Sexual Difference: Husserl, Merleau-Ponty, Beauvoir*. Lanham, MD: Rowman & Littlefield.

Hekman, Susan. 1997. 'Truth and Method: Feminist Standpoint Theory Revisited.' *Signs* 22 (2): 341–365.

Hesse-Biber, Sharlene Nagy, P. Leavy, and M.L. Yaiser. 2004. 'Feminist Approaches to Research as a Process.' In *Feminist Perspectives on Social Research*, edited by Sharlene Nagy Hesse-Biber and Michelle L. Yaiser. New York: Oxford University Press, pp. 3–26.

Highmore, Ben. 2002. 'Introduction: Questioning Everyday Life.' In *The Everyday Life Reader*, edited by Ben Highmore, 1–34. London: Routledge.

Gramsci, Antonio, 1971. *Selections from the Prison Notebooks of Antonio Gramsci*. Edited and Translated by Hoare, Quentin, and Geoffrey Nowell Smith. London: Lawrence & Wishart.

Hochschild, Arlie Russell. 1983. *The Managed Heart: Commercialization of Human Feeling*. Berkeley: University of California Press.

———. 2000. 'Global Care Chains and Emotional Surplus Value.' In *On the Edge: Living With Global Capitalism*, edited by Will Hutton and Anthony Giddens. London: Jonathan Cape, pp. 130–46.

hooks, bell. 1984. *Feminist Theory from Margin to Center*. Boston, MA: South End Press.

———. 1990. *Yearning: Race, Gender and Cultural Politics*. Boston, MA: South End Press.

———. 2000. *Feminism is for Everybody: Passionate Politics*. Cambridge, MA: South End Press.

World Health Organization. 2010. 'Wanted: 2.4 Million Nurses, and that's just in India.' *Bulletin of the World Health Organization* 88: 321–400.

Irigaray, Luce. 1991. 'Love Between Us.' In *Who Comes after the Subject?* edited by Eduardo Cadava, Peter Connor, and Jean-Luc Nancy. New York and London: Routledge, pp. 167–77.

Iyer, Aditi, and Amar Jesani. 1995. *Women in Health Care: Auxiliary Nurse Midwives*. Mumbai: The Foundation for Research In Community Health.

Jackson, Stevi. 2006. 'Gender, Sexuality and Heterosexuality: The Complexity (and limits) of Heteronormativity.' *Feminist Theory* 7 (1): 105–21.

Jain, Devaki, and Nirmala Banerjee, eds. 1985. *Tyranny of the Household: Investigative Essays on Women's Work*. Delhi: Shakti Books.

Jameson, Fredric. 1991. *Postmodernism, and the Late Logic of Capitalism*. London: Verso.

Janssens, Angelique. 1997. 'The Rise and Decline of the Male Breadwinner Family? An Overview of the Debate.' *International Review of Social History* 42 Supplement, 1–23.

Jecker, Nancy S., and Donnie J. Self. 1991. 'Separating Care and Cure: An Analysis of Historical and Contemporary Images of Nursing and Medicine.' *The Journal of Medicine and Philosophy* 16 (3): pp. 285–306.

Jeffery, Roger. 1988. *Politics of Health in India*. Berkeley: University California Press.

John, Mary E. 1996. 'Gender and Development in India, 1970s–1990s: Some Reflections on the Constitutive Role of Contexts.' *Economic and Political Weekly* 31 (47): 3071–7.

———. 2013. 'The Problem of Women's Labour: Some Autobiographical Perspectives.' *Indian Journal of Gender Studies* 20 (2): pp. 177–212.

John, Mary E., and Janaki Nair, eds. 1998. *A Question of Silence. The Sexual Economies of Modern India*. London and New York: Zed Books.

Kabeer, Naila. 1994. *Reversed Realities: Gender Hierarchies in Development Thought*. New Delhi: Kali for Women.

Kannan, K.P. 2014. *Interrogating Inclusive Growth: Poverty and Inequality in India*. New York, London and New Delhi: Routledge.

Kapadia, Karin, ed. 2002. *The Violence of Development: The Politics of Identity, Gender and Social Inequalities in India*, London: Zed Books.

Kelman, Janet Harvey. 1923. *Labour in India: A Study of the Conditions of Indian Women in Modern Industry*. London: Central Council Publications.

Khadria, Binod. 2007. 'International Nurse Recruitment in India.' *Health Service Research* 42 (3): 1429–36.

Khanna, Suwersh K. 1991. *The History of Nursing in India from 1947–1989.* USA: Nursing Honour Society of India.

Knowles, Elizabeth, ed. 2005. *The Oxford Dictionary of Phrase and Fable.* 2nd ed. Oxford: Oxford University Press.

Kotiswaran, Prabha. 2011. *Dangerous Sex, Invisible Labour: Sex Work and the Law in India.* New Delhi: Oxford University Press.

Kristeva, Julia. 1982. *Powers of Horror: An Essay on Abjection.* Translated by Leon S. Roudiez. New York: Columbia University Press.

Lal, Maneesha. 2006. 'Purdah as Pathology: Gender and the Circulation of Medical Knowledge in Late Colonial India.' In *Reproductive Health in India: History, Politics, Controversies,* edited by Sarah Hodges. Hyderabad: Orient Longman, pp. 85–114.

Lamont, Michele. 2000. *The Dignity of Working Men: Morality and the Boundaries of Race, Class and Immigration.* New York: Russell Sage Foundation and Harvard University Press.

Lazarus, Hilda. 1945. 'Our Nursing Services'. Tract no. 5. Aundh: The All India Women's Conference.

Lebbacqz, Karen. 1985. *Professional Ethics: Power and Paradox.* Nashville: Abington Press.

Lefebvre, Bertrand. 2009. '"Bringing World-class Health Care to India": The Rise of Corporate Hospitals.' In *Indian Health Landscapes under Globalization,* edited by Alain Vaguet. Manohar: Centre de Sciences, pp. 83–99.

Lefebvre, Henri. 1991 (1974). *The Production of Space.* Translated by Donald Nicholson-Smith. Oxford: Basil Blackwell.

Leslie, Julia, and Dominik Wujastyk. 1991. 'The Doctor's Assistant: Nursing in Ancient Indian Medical Text.' In *Anthropology and Nursing,* edited by Pat Holden and Jenny Littlewood. New York: Routledge, pp. 25–30.

Li, P.S. 2000. 'Earning Disparities between Immigrants and Native- born Canadians.' *Canadian Review of Sociology/Revue canadienne de sociologie* 37 (3): 289–311.

Lindberg, Anna. 2005. *Modernization and Effeminization in India: Kerala Cashew Workers since 1930.* Denmark: Nordic Institute of Asian Studies.

Link, Bruce G., and Jo C. Phelan. 2001. 'Conceptualizing Stigma.' *Annual Review of Sociology* 27 (3): 363–85.

Llyod, Genevieve. (1984) 1994. *The Man of Reason: 'Male' and 'Female' in Western Philosophy.* London: Routledge.

Lowe, John. (1886) 1903. *Medical Missions: Their Place and Power.* New York and Chicago: F.H. Revell Company.

Mainardi, Pat. 1970. *The Politics of Housework.* New York: Redstockings.

Malhotra, Anshu. 2006. 'Of *dais* and Midwives: "Middle Class" Interventions in the Management of Women's Reproductive Health in Colonial Punjab.' In *Reproductive Health in India: History, Politics, Controversies*, edited by S. Hodges. Hyderabad: Orient Longman, pp. 199–226.

Malik, Bela. 1999. 'Untouchability and Dalit Women's Oppression.' *Economic and Political Weekly* 34 (6): 323–4.

Mani, Lata. 1998. *Contentious Traditions: The Debate on Sati in Colonial India.* Berkeley: University of California Press.

Martens, Margaret H., and Swasti Mitter. 1994. *Women in Trade Unions: Organizing the Unorganized.* Geneva: International Labour Office.

Massey, Doreen. 1994. *Space, Place, and Gender.* Minneapolis: University of Minnesota Press.

Mazumdar, Indrani, and N. Neetha. 2011. 'Gender Dimensions: Employment Trends in India, 1993–94 to 2009–10.' *Economic and Political Weekly* 46 (43): 118–26.

Mazumdar, Indrani. 2007. *Women Workers and Globalization: Emergent Contradictions in India.* Kolkata: Stree.

McLaren, Margaret A. 2002. *Feminism, Foucault and Embodied Subjectivity.* Albany: State University of New York Press.

McNay, Lois. 1991. 'The Foucauldian Body and the Exclusion of Experience.' *Hypatia* 6 (3): 125–39.

Medical College. 1935. *Centenary Volume: Calcutta Medical College.* Calcutta: Centenary Volume Sub-Committee.

Meek, Robert. 1956. *Studies in the Labor Theory of Value.* New York and London: Monthly Review Press.

Menon, Nivedita. 2012. *Seeing Like a Feminist.* New Delhi: Zubaan Books.

Mitra, U. 1960. 'Nursing Team.' *Nursing Journal of India*, 70–1.

Mukhopadhyay, Amiya Jibon. 1943. *Nurse O Nursing.* Kolkata: Dasgupta and Company.

Mukhopadhyay, Subodh Kumar. 1998. *Bangali Maddhyabitta O Tar Manaslok.* Calcutta: Progressive Publishers.

Nahar, Miratun, ed. 2001. *Rokeya Rachana Samgraha.* Kolkata: Bishwakosh Parishad.

Nair, Janaki. 1990. 'Uncovering the Zenana: Visions of Indian Womanhood in Englishwomen's Writings, 1813–1940.' *Journal of Women's History* 2 (1): 8–34.

———. 1998. *Miners and Millhands: Work, Culture and Politics in Princely Mysore.* New Delhi: SAGE Publications.

Nair, Sreelekha. 2012. *Moving with the Times: Gender, Status and Migration of Nurses in India.* New Delhi: Routledge.

Nair, Sreelekha, and Madelaine Healey. 2006. *A Profession on the Margins: Status Issues in Indian Nursing.* Occasional Paper, New Delhi: Centre for Women's Development Studies.

Nair, Sreelekha, and Marie Percot. 2007. *Transcending Boundaries: Indian Nurses in Internal and International Migration.* Occasional Paper, New Delhi: Center for Women's Development Studies.

Nair, Sreelekha, and S. Irudaya Rajan. 2017. 'Nursing Education in India Changing Facets and Emerging Trends.' *Economic and Political Weekly* 52 (24): 38–42.

Nash, June. 1979. *We Eat the Mines and the Mines Eat Us: Dependency and Exploitation in Bolivian Tin Times.* New York: Columbia University Press.

Nash, June, and María Patricia Fernández-Kelly (eds). 1983. *Women, Men and the International Division of Labour.* Albany: State University of New York Press.

Nelson, H.L. 1992. 'Against Caring.' *Journal of Clinical Ethics* 3 (1): 8–15.

Nestel, Sheryl. 1998. '(Ad)ministering Angels: Colonial Nursing and the Extension of the Empire.' *Journal of Medical Humanities* 19 (4): 257–77.

Nicholson, Linda. 1990. 'Introduction.' In *Feminism/Postmodernism*, edited by Linda Nicholson. New York: Routledge.

———. 1994. 'Interpreting Gender.' *Signs* 20 (1): 79–105.

Niranjana, Seemanthini. 2001. *Gender and Space: Femininity, Sexualization and the Female Body*, New Delhi: SAGE Publications.

Nivedita, Sister. 1967. *The Complete Works of Sister Nivedita*, Volume 1–5. Calcutta: Ramakrishna Sarada Mission, Sister Nivedita Girls' School. Distributed by Ananda Publishers.

Noordyk, Wilhelmina. 1921. 'Nursing in India.' *The American Journal of Nursing.* 21 (5): 296–9.

Oakley, Anne. 1993. *Essays on Women, Medicine and Health.* Edinburgh: Edinburgh University Press.

O'Hanlon, Rosalind. 1985. *Caste, Conflict and Hierarchy: Mahatma Jotirao Phule and Low Caste Protest in Nineteenth-Century Western India.* Cambridge University Press.

Omvedt, Gail. 1994. *Dalits and the Democratic Revolution: Dr. Ambedkar and the Dalit Movement in Colonial India.* New Delhi: SAGE Publications.

Ong, Aihwa. 1987. *Spirits of Resistance and Capitalist Discipline: Factory Women in Malaysia.* New York: State University of New York Press.

Oommen, T. 1978. *Doctors and Nurses: A Study in Occupational Role Structures.* New Delhi: Macmillan Company of India.

Pande, Amrita. 2009. 'Not an "Angel", not a 'Whore': Surrogates as "Dirty" Workers in India.' *Indian Journal of Gender Studies* 16 (2): 141–73.

Papanek, Hanna. 1979. "Family Status Production: The "Work" and "Non-Work" of Women.' *Signs* 4 (4): 775–81.

Parrenas, Rhacel Salazar. 2000. 'Migrant Filipina Domestic Workers and the International Division of Reproductive Labor.' *Gender and Society* 14 (4): 560–80.

Pateman, Carole. 1988. *The Sexual Contract*, Stanford: Stanford University Press.

Patrick, M. 2001. 'Unorganized Women in Urban Settings: Opportunities and Challenges.' In *Informal Sector in India: Perspectives and Policies*, edited by Amitabh Kundu and A.N. Sharma. New Delhi: IHD-IAMR.

Pence, Terry and Janice Cantrall. 1990. *Ethics in Nursing: An Anthology*. New York: National League of Nursing.

Percot, Marie. 2006. 'Indian Nurses in the Gulf: Two Generations of Female Migration.' *South Asia Research* 26 (1): 41–62.

Perec, George. 2002.'Approaches to What [1973].' In *The Everyday Life Reader*, edited by Ben Highmore. London: Routledge, pp. 176–8.

Phadke, Shilpa, Sameera Khan, and Shilpa Ranade. 2011. *Why Loiter?: Women and Risk on Mumbai Streets*. New Delhi: Penguin Books.

Philips, Anne. 1992.'Universal Pretensions in Political Thought.' In *Destabilizing Theory: Contemporary Feminist Debates*, edited by Michelle Barrett and Anne Philips. Cambridge: Polity Press.

Plumwood, Val. 1993. *Feminism and Mastery of Nature*. London and New York: Routledge.

Power, Nina. 2009. *One-Dimensional Woman*. Washington: Zero Books.

Prasad, Srirupa. 2015. 'Sanitizing the Domestic: Hygiene and Gender in Late Colonial Bengal.' *Journal of Women's History* 27 (3): 132–53.

Qadeer Imrana. 1999. 'The World Bank Development Report 1993; The Brave New World of Primary Health Care.' In *Disinvesting in Health: The World Bank's Prescription for Health*, edited by Mohan Rao. New Delhi: SAGE Publications.

Qayum, Seemin, and Raka Ray. 2003. 'Grappling with Modernity: India's Respectable Classes and the Culture of Domestic Servitude.' *Ethnography* 4 (4): 520–55.

Raghavachari, Ranjana. 1990. *Conflicts and Adjustments: Indian Nurses in an Urban Milieu*. Delhi: Academic Foundation.

Raj, Pruthi. 2006. *Medical Tourism in India*. New Delhi: Arise Publishers.

Rajan, Rajeshwari S. 1993. *Real and Imagined Women: Gender, Culture and Postcolonialism*. London and New York: Routledge.

Raju, Saraswati. 2011.'Introduction.' In *Gendered Geographies: Space and Place in South Asia*, edited by Saraswati Raju. New Delhi: Oxford University Press, pp. 1–28.

Ranade, Shilpa. 2007.'The Way She Moves: Mapping the Everyday Production of Gender-Space.' *Economic and Political Weekly* 42 (17): 1519–26.

Ramusack, Barbara N. 1992. 'Cultural Missionaries, Maternal Imperialists, Feminist Allies; British Women Activists in India, 1865–1945.' In *Western Women and Imperialism: Complicity and Resistance*, edited by Nupur

Chaudhuri and Margaret Strobel. Bloomington: Indiana University Press, pp. 119–36.

———. 2006. 'Authority and Ambivalence: Medical Women and Birth Control in India.' In *Reproductive Health in India: History, Politics, Controversies*, edited by Sarah Hodges. Hyderabad: Orient Longman, pp. 51–84.

Rao, Anupama. 2011. *The Caste Question: Dalits and Politics of Modern India*. Ranikhet: Permanent Black.

Rao, Anupama, Chayanika Shah, Mary E. John, Rinchin, and Rohini Hensman. 2005. 'Symposium: Marriage, Family and Community: A Feminist Dialogue.' *Economic and Political Weekly* 40 (08): 709–22.

Rao, B. Shiva. 1939. *The Industrial Worker in India*. London: George Allen and Unwin Ltd.

Rao, Krishna D., Aarushi Bhatnagar, and Peter Berman. 2012. 'So Many, Yet Few: Human Resources for Health in India.' *Human Resources for Health* 10 (19). Accessed March 2014. https://human-resources-health.biomedcentral.com/track/pdf/10.1186/1478-4491-10-19.

Ray, Panchali. 2016a. 'Care (un)skilled: Fragmented Markets and Nursing Labour, Contemporary Kolkata.' In *Land, Labour and Livelihoods: Indian Women's Perspectives*, edited by Bina Fernandez, Meena Gopal, and Orlanda Ruthven. Palgrave: Macmillan, pp. 239–60.

———. 2016b. "Is this Even Work?' Nursing Care and Stigmatised Labour.' *Economic and Political Weekly* 47 (2): 60–9.

Ray, Panchali. 2019. 'Nursing Labour, Employment Regimes, and Affective Spaces: Experiencing Migration in the City of Kolkata' in S. Irudaya Rajan and N. Neetha (eds). *Migration, Gender and Care Economy*. 47–68. London and New York: Routledge.

———. Forthcoming (a). 'Caring or Whoring? Nurses and the Politics of Representation, Colonial to Contemporary Calcutta.' In Anuradha Roy and Melitta Waligora (Eds) *Kolkata in Space, Time and Imagination: Rethinking of Heritage*. New Delhi: Primus Books.

———. Forthcoming (b). 'The Everyday Politics of Labour: Power and Subjectivities at Work in the Contemporary Nursing Profession.' *South Asia Research*.

———. Forthcoming (c). 'Women in/and Trade Unions: Consciousness, Agency and (Im)possibilities of Alliances, Nurses and Attendants in Kolkata.' *Contemporary South Asia*.

Ray, Raka, and Seemin Qayum. 2009. *Cultures of Servitude: Modernity, Domesticity, and Class in India*. Stanford, CA: Stanford University Press.

Ray, Sharmita. 2014. 'Women Doctor's Masterful Manoeuverings: Colonial Bengal, Late Nineteenth and Early Twentieth Centuries.' *Social Scientist* 42 (3/4): 59–76.

Razavi, Shahra. 2007. *The Political and Social Economy of Care in a Development Context: Contextual Issues, Research Questions, and Policy Options*. Gender and Development Paper Number 3. Geneva: United Nations Research Institute for Social Development.

Rege, Sharmila. 1998. 'Dalit Women talk Differently: A Critique of "Difference" and Towards a Dalit Feminist Standpoint Position.' *Economic and Political Weekly* 33 (44): 39–46.

———. 2002. 'Conceptualizing Popular Culture "Lawani" and "Powada" Maharashtra.' *Economic and Political Weekly* 37 (11): 1038–47.

Rich, Adrienne. 1980. 'Compulsory Heterosexuality and Lesbian Existence.' *Signs* 5 (4): 631–60.

Rinchin. 2005. 'Querying Marriage and Family.' *Economic and Political Weekly* 40 (8): 718–21.

Robinson, Andrew. 1989. *Satyajit Ray: The Inner Eye*. Berkeley: University of California Press.

Rubin, Gayle. 1975. 'The Traffic in Women: Notes on the "Political Economy" of Sex.' In *Toward an Anthropology of Women*, edited by Rayna Reiter. New York: Monthly Review Press, pp. 157–210.

———. 1984. 'Thinking Sex: Notes for a Radical Theory of the Politics of Sexuality.' In *Pleasure and Danger*, edited by Carole Vance. Boston, London, Melbourne, and Henley: Routledge & Kegan Paul, pp. 267–321.

Sangari, Kumkum. 1993. 'The "Amenities of Domestic Life": Questions on Labour.' *Social Scientist* 21 (9/11): 3–46.

Sarkar, Sumit. 1992. 'Kaliyuga, Chakri and Bhakti: Ramakrishna and His Times.' *Economic and Political Weekly* 27 (29): pp. 1543–66.

Sarkar, Tanika. 2001. *Hindu Wife, Hindu Nation: Community, Religion, and Cultural Nationalism*. New Delhi: Permanent Black.

Sarukkai, Sundar. 2012. 'Phenomenology of Untouchability.' In *The Cracked Mirror: An Indian Debate on Experience and Theory*, edited by Gopal Guru and Sundar Sarukkai. New Delhi: Oxford University Press.

Scott, James. 1985. *Weapons of the Weak: Everyday Forms of Peasant Resistance*. New Haven: Yale University Press.

———. 1990. *Domination and the Arts of Resistance: Hidden Transcripts*. New Haven: Yale University Press.

Scott, Joan W. 1992. 'Experience.' In *Feminists Theorize the Political*, edited by Judith Butler and Joan W. Scott. London: Routledge, pp. 22–40.

Sehrawat, Samiksha. 2005. 'The Foundation of Lady Hardinge Medical College and Hospital for Women at Delhi: Issues in Women's Medical Education and Imperial Governance.' In *Exploring Gender Equations: Colonial and Post Colonial India*, edited by Shakti Kak and Biswamoy Pati. New Delhi: Nehru Memorial Museum and Library, pp. 117–46.

Sen, Indrani. 2009. 'Colonial Domesticities, Contentious Interactions: Ayahs, Wet-Nurses and Memsahibs in Colonial India.' *Indian Journal of Gender Studies* 16 (3): 299–328.

Sen, Samita. 1999. *Women and Labour in Colonial India: The Bengal Jute Industry*. Cambridge: Cambridge University Press.

———. 2008. 'Gender and Class: Women in Indian Industry, 1800–1990.' *Modern Asian Studies* 42 (1): 75–116.

Shah, Chayanika. 2005. 'The Roads that E/Merged: Feminist Activism and Queer Understanding.' In *Because I have a Voice: Queer Politics in India*, edited by Gautam Bhan and Arvind Narrain. New Delhi: Yoda Press, pp. 143–154.

Silver, Beverly. 2003. *Forces of Labor: Workers' Movements and Globalization Since 1870*. Cambridge: Cambridge University Press.

Singh, Maina Chawla. 2005. 'Gender, Medicine and Empire: Early Initiatives in Institution-Building and Professionalisation (1890s–1940s).' In *Exploring Gender Equations: Colonial and Post Colonial India*, edited by Shakti Kak and Biswamoy Pati. New Delhi: Nehru Memorial Museum and Library, pp. 93–115.

Smith, Pam. 1992. *The Emotional Labour of Nursing*. Hampshire: Macmillan Education Ltd.

Smith, Pam, and Maureen Mackintosh. 2007. 'Profession, Market and Class: Nurse Migration and Remaking of Division and Disadvantage.' *Journal of Clinical Nursing* 16 (12): 2213–20.

Soja, Edward W. 1980. 'The Socio-Spatial Dialectic.' *Annals of the Association of American Geographers* 70 (2): 207–25.

———. 1989. *Postmodern Geographies: The Reassertion of Space in Critical Social Theory*. London: Verso.

Somjee, Geeta. 1991. 'Social Changes in the Nursing Profession in India.' In *Anthropology and Nursing*, edited by Pat Holden and Jenny Littlewood. New York: Routledge, pp. 31–55.

Spivak, Gayatri Chakravorty. 1994. 'Introduction.' In *Bringing It All Back Home: Class, Gender and Power in the Modern Household*, edited by Harriet Fraad, Stephen Resnick, and Richard Wolff. London Pluto Press, pp. ix–xvi.

———. 1997. '"Breast Giver": For Author, Teacher, Subaltern, Historian.' In *Breast Stories*, edited by Mahasweta Devi. Translated and introduced by Gayatri Spivak. Calcutta: Seagull Books, pp. 75–133.

Standing, Guy. 1989. 'Global Feminization through Flexible Labor.' *World Development* 17 (7): 1077–95.

———. 2011. *The Precariat: The New Dangerous Class*. London: Bloomsbury Academic.

State Bureau of Health Intelligence. 2017. *Health on the March 2015–2016*. Kolkata: Directorate of Health Services, Government of West Bengal. www.wbhealth.gov.in. Accessed June 2017.

Stewart, Isabel M., and Anne L. Austin. (1920) 1962. *A History of Nursing; From Ancient to Modern Times*. Fifth Edition. New York: G.P. Putnam's Sons.

Stimson, Julia C. 1936. 'The Nurse's Uniform.' *The American Journal of Nursing* 36 (4): 367–72.

Stoler, Ann Laura. 2002. 'Colonial Archives and the Arts of Governance.' *Archival Science* 2 (1–2): 87–109.

Talpade, Chandra Mohanty. 1991. 'Introduction.' In *Cartographies of Struggle: Third World Women and the Politics of Feminism*, edited by C.T. Mohanty, A. Russo, and L. Torres. Bloomington: Indiana University Press, pp. 1–50.

Tharu, Susie, and Tejaswini Niranjana. 1994. 'Problems for a Contemporary Theory of Gender.' *Social Scientist* 22 (3/4): 93–117.

The Trained Nurses Association of India. 2001. *History and Trends in Nursing in India*. New Delhi: The Trained Nurses Association of India.

Thomas, Philomina. 2006. 'The International Migration of Indian Nurses.' *International Nursing Review* 53 (4): 277–83.

Thompson, E.P. (1963) 1966. *The Making of the English Working Class*. New York: Vintage Books.

Thorstein, Veblen. (1899) 1934. *The Theory of the Leisure Class: An Economic Study of Institutions*. New York: The Modern Library.

Tinker, Irene, ed. 1990. *Persistent Inequalities: Women and World Development*. New York: Oxford University Press.

Tooley, Sarah. 1906. *History of Nursing in the British Empire*. London: S.H. Bousfield and Co.

Tripathi, Amalesh. 1994. *Italir Renaissances Bangalir Sanskriti*. Calcutta: Ananda Publishers.

Tronto, Joan C. 1987. 'Beyond Gender Differences to a Theory of Care.' *Signs* 12 (4): 644–63.

Unni, Jeemol. 2001. 'Gender and Informality in Labour Market in South Asia.' *Economic and Political Weekly* 36 (26): 2360–77.

V., Geetha. 2009. 'Bereft of Being: The Humiliations of Untouchability.' In *Humiliation: Claims and Context*, edited by Gopal Guru. New Delhi: Oxford University Press, pp. 95–107.

Vallee, Gerard, ed. 2006. *Florence Nightingale on Health in India*. In the *Collected Works of Florence Nightingale*. Volume 9, edited by Lynn McDonald. Waterloo: Wilfrid Laurier University Press.

Van Hollen, Cecilia. 2003. *Birth on the Threshold: Childbirth and Modernity in South India*. Berkeley and Los Angeles: University of California Press.

Viswanath, Kalpana. 1997. 'Shame and Control: Sexuality and Power in Feminist Discourse in India.' In *Embodiment: Essays on Gender and Identity*, edited by Meenakshi Thapan. Delhi: Oxford University Press, pp. 313–28.

Visweswaran, Kamala. 1994. *Fictions of Feminist Ethnography*. Minneapolis: Minnesota University Press.

Vivekananda, Swami. 1971. *The Complete Works of Swami Vivekananda*. Calcutta: Advaita Ashrama. Distributed by Vedanta Press.

Wacquant, Loic. 2008. *Urban Outcasts: A Comparative Sociology of Advanced Marginality*. Cambridge: Polity Press.

Walby, Sylvia. 1990. *Theorizing Patriarchy*. Oxford, UK: B. Blackwell.

Weeks, Kathi. 2007. 'Life Within and Against Work: Affective Labor, Feminist Critique, and Post-Fordist Politics.' *Ephemera: Theory & Politics in Organization* 7 (1): 233–49.

Wilkinson, Alice. 1958. *A Brief History of Nursing in India and Pakistan*. Delhi: Trained Nurses Association of India.

Wilson, Emma. 1974. *Gone with the Raj*. Norfolk: Geo R. Reeve Ltd.

Wittig, Monique. 1992. *The Straight Mind and Other Essays*. New York: Harvester Wheatsheaf.

Witz, Anne. 1990. 'Patriarchy and Professions: The Gendered Politics of Occupational Closure.' *Sociology* 24 (4): 675–90.

———. 1992. *Professions and Patriarchy*. London and New York: Routledge.

Wright, E.O. 1985. *Classes*. London: Verso Books.

Yeats, Nicola. 2009. 'Production for Export: The Role of the State in the Development and Operation of Global Care Chains.' *Population, Space and Place* 15 (2): 175–87.

Young, Kate, ed. 1989. *Serving Two Masters. Third World Women in Development*. Ahmedabad: Allied Publishers Ltd.

Young, Kate, C. Wolkowitz, and R. McCullagh, eds. 1981. *Of Marriage and the Market: Women's Subordination in International Perspective*. London: CSE Books.

Zierbert, G. 1957. 'The Upright Nurse.' *The Nursing Journal of India*. XLVIII (3): 1017–19.

Index

About the Author

Panchali Ray is an independent researcher based in New Delhi, India. Her areas of interest include labour, livelihood, migration, sexualities, and collective politics. Her forthcoming publications include the edited volume *Women Speak Nation: Gender, Culture, and Politics.*